Pope S Complete Set of Encyclicals
by
Pope St Pius X

St Athanasius Press
Copyright © 2016

ISBN-13: 978-1533093981

ISBN-10: 1533093989

A Compilation of all of
Pope St Pius X's Encyclicals

St Athanasius Press
2016

Specializing in Reprinting Catholic Classics!

CONTENTS

E SUPREMI
ENCYCLICAL OF POPE PIUS X
ON THE RESTORATION OF ALL THINGS
IN CHRIST

TO THE PATRIARCHS, PRIMATES,
ARCHBISHOPS, BISHOPS, AND OTHER ORDINARIES
IN PEACE AND COMMUNION WITH THE APOSTOLIC
SEE

Venerable Brethren,
Health and the Apostolic Benediction.

In addressing you for the first time from the Chair of the supreme apostolate to which We have, by the inscrutable disposition of God, been elevated, it is not necessary to remind you with what tears and warm instance We exerted Ourselves to ward off this formidable burden of the Pontificate. Unequal in merit though We be with St. Anselm, it seems to us that We may with truth make Our own the words in which he lamented when he was constrained against his will and in spite of his struggles to receive the honor of the episcopate. For to show with what dispositions of mind and will We subjected Ourselves to the most serious charge of feeding the flock of Christ, We can well adduce those same proofs of grief which he invokes in his own behalf. "My tears are witnesses," he wrote, "and the sounds and moaning issuing from the anguish of my heart, such as I never remember before to have come from me for any sorrow, before that day on which there seemed to fall upon me that great misfortune of the archbishop of Canterbury. And those who fixed their gaze on my face that day could not fail to see it . . . I, in color more like a dead than a living man, was pale for amazement and alarm. Hitherto I have resisted as far as I could, speaking the truth, my election or rather the violence done me. But now I am constrained to confess, whether I will or no, that the judgments of God oppose greater and greater resistance to my efforts, so that I see no way of escaping them. Wherefore vanquished as I am by the violence not so much of men as of God, against which there is no providing, I realize that nothing is left for me, after having prayed as much as I could and striven that this chalice should if possible pass from me without my drinking it, but to set aside my feeling and my will and resign myself entirely to the design and the will of God."

2. In truth reasons both numerous and most weighty were not lacking to justify this resistance of Ours. For, beside the fact that We deemed Ourselves altogether unworthy through Our littleness of the honor of the Pontificate; who would not have been disturbed at seeing himself designated to succeed him who, ruling the Church with supreme wisdom for nearly twenty six years, showed himself adorned with such sublimity of mind, such luster of every virtue, as to attract to himself the admiration even of adversaries, and to leave his memory stamped in glorious achievements?

3. Then again, to omit other motives, We were terrified beyond all else by the disastrous state of human society today. For who can fail to see that society is at the present time, more than in any past age, suffering from a terrible and deep rooted malady which, developing every day and eating into its inmost being, is dragging it to destruction? You understand, Venerable Brethren, what this disease is - apostasy from God, than which in truth nothing is more allied with ruin, according to the word of the Prophet: "For behold they that go far from Thee shall perish" (Ps. lxxii., 17). We saw therefore that, in virtue of the ministry of the Pontificate,

which was to be entrusted to Us, We must hasten to find a remedy for this great evil, considering as addressed to Us that Divine command: "Lo, I have set thee this day over the nations and over kingdoms, to root up, and to pull down, and to waste, and to destroy, and to build, and to plant" (Jerem. i., 10). But, cognizant of Our weakness, We recoiled in terror from a task as urgent as it is arduous.

4. Since, however, it has been pleasing to the Divine Will to raise Our lowliness to such sublimity of power, We take courage in Him who strengthens Us; and setting Ourselves to work, relying on the power of God, We proclaim that We have no other program in the Supreme Pontificate but that "of restoring all things in Christ" (Ephes. i., 10), so that "Christ may be all and in all" (Coloss. iii, 2). Some will certainly be found who, measuring Divine things by human standards will seek to discover secret aims of Ours, distorting them to an earthly scope and to partisan designs. To eliminate all vain delusions for such, We say to them with emphasis that We do not wish to be, and with the Divine assistance never shall be aught before human society but the Minister of God, of whose authority We are the depositary. The interests of God shall be Our interest, and for these We are resolved to spend all Our strength and Our very life. Hence, should anyone ask Us for a symbol as the expression of Our will, We will give this and no other: "To renew all things in Christ." In undertaking this glorious task, We are greatly quickened by the certainty that We shall have all of you, Venerable Brethren, as generous cooperators. Did We doubt it We should have to regard you, unjustly, as either unconscious or heedless of that sacrilegious war which is now, almost everywhere, stirred up and fomented against God. For in truth, "The nations have raged and the peoples imagined vain things" (Ps.ii., 1.) against their Creator, so

frequent is the cry of the enemies of God: "Depart from us" (Job. xxi., 14). And as might be expected we find extinguished among the majority of men all respect for the Eternal God, and no regard paid in the manifestations of public and private life to the Supreme Will - nay, every effort and every artifice is used to destroy utterly the memory and the knowledge of God.

5. When all this is considered there is good reason to fear lest this great perversity may be as it were a foretaste, and perhaps the beginning of those evils which are reserved for the last days; and that there may be already in the world the "Son of Perdition" of whom the Apostle speaks (II. Thess. ii., 3). Such, in truth, is the audacity and the wrath employed everywhere in persecuting religion, in combating the dogmas of the faith, in brazen effort to uproot and destroy all relations between man and the Divinity! While, on the other hand, and this according to the same apostle is the distinguishing mark of Antichrist, man has with infinite temerity put himself in the place of God, raising himself above all that is called God; in such wise that although he cannot utterly extinguish in himself all knowledge of God, he has held in contempt God's majesty and, as it were, made of the universe a temple wherein he himself is to be adored. "He sitteth in the temple of God, showing himself as if he were God" (II. Thess. ii., 2).

6. Verily no one of sound mind can doubt the issue of this contest between man and the Most High. Man, abusing his liberty, can violate the right and the majesty of the Creator of the Universe; but the victory will ever be with God - nay, defeat is at hand at the moment when man, under the delusion of his triumph, rises up with most audacity. Of this we are assured in the holy books by God Himself. Unmindful,

as it were, of His strength and greatness, He "overlooks the sins of men" (Wisd. xi., 24), but swiftly, after these apparent retreats, "awaked like a mighty man that hath been surfeited with wine" (Ps. lxxvii., 65), "He shall break the heads of his enemies" (Ps. lxxvii., 22), that all may know "that God is the king of all the earth" (Ib. lxvi, 8), "that the Gentiles may know themselves to be men"(Ib. ix., 20).

7. All this, Venerable Brethren, We believe and expect with unshakable faith. But this does not prevent us also, according to the measure given to each, from exerting ourselves to hasten the work of God - and not merely by praying assiduously: "Arise, O Lord, let not man be strengthened" (Ib. ix., 19), but, more important still, by affirming both by word and deed and in the light of day, God's supreme dominion over man and all things, so that His right to command and His authority may be fully realized and respected. This is imposed upon us not only as a natural duty, but by our common interest. For, Venerable Brethren, who can avoid being appalled and afflicted when he beholds, in the midst of a progress in civilization which is justly extolled, the greater part of mankind fighting among themselves so savagely as to make it seem as though strife were universal? The desire for peace is certainly harbored in every breast, and there is no one who does not ardently invoke it. But to want peace without God is an absurdity, seeing that where God is absent thence too justice flies, and when justice is taken away it is vain to cherish the hope of peace. "Peace is the work of justice" (Is. xxii., 17). There are many, We are well aware, who, in their yearning for peace, that is for the tranquility of order, band themselves into societies and parties, which they style parties of order. Hope and labor lost. For there is but one party of order capable of restoring peace in the midst of all this turmoil, and that is the party of God. It is this party,

therefore, that we must advance, and to it attract as many as possible, if we are really urged by the love of peace.

8. But, Venerable Brethren, we shall never, however much we exert ourselves, succeed in calling men back to the majesty and empire of God, except by means of Jesus Christ. "No one," the Apostle admonishes us, "can lay other foundation than that which has been laid, which is Jesus Christ." (I. Cor.,iii., II.) It is Christ alone "whom the Father sanctified and sent into this world" (Is. x., 36), "the splendor of the Father and the image of His substance" (Hebr.i., 3), true God and true man: without whom nobody can know God with the knowledge for salvation, "neither doth anyone know the Father but the Son, and he to whom it shall please the Son to reveal Him." (Matth. xi., 27.) Hence it follows that to restore all things in Christ and to lead men back to submission to God is one and the same aim. To this, then, it behooves Us to devote Our care - to lead back mankind under the dominion of Christ; this done, We shall have brought it back to God. When We say to God We do not mean to that inert being heedless of all things human which the dream of materialists has imagined, but to the true and living God, one in nature, triple in person, Creator of the world, most wise Ordainer of all things, Lawgiver most just, who punishes the wicked and has reward in store for virtue.

9. Now the way to reach Christ is not hard to find: it is the Church. Rightly does Chrysostom inculcate: "The Church is thy hope, the Church is thy salvation, the Church is thy refuge." (Hom. de capto Euthropio, n. 6.) It was for this that Christ founded it, gaining it at the price of His blood, and made it the depositary of His doctrine and His laws, bestowing upon it at the same time an inexhaustible treasury of graces for the sanctification and salvation of men. You see,

then, Venerable Brethren, the duty that has been imposed alike upon Us and upon you of bringing back to the discipline of the Church human society, now estranged from the wisdom of Christ; the Church will then subject it to Christ, and Christ to God. If We, through the goodness of God Himself, bring this task to a happy issue, We shall be rejoiced to see evil giving place to good, and hear, for our gladness, " a loud voice from heaven saying: Now is come salvation, and strength, and the kingdom of our God and the power of his Christ." (Apoc. xii., 10.) But if our desire to obtain this is to be fulfilled, we must use every means and exert all our energy to bring about the utter disappearance of the enormous and detestable wickedness, so characteristic of our time - the substitution of man for God; this done, it remains to restore to their ancient place of honor the most holy laws and counsels of the gospel; to proclaim aloud the truths taught by the Church, and her teachings on the sanctity of marriage, on the education and discipline of youth, on the possession and use of property, the duties that men owe to those who rule the State; and lastly to restore equilibrium between the different classes of society according to Christian precept and custom. This is what We, in submitting Ourselves to the manifestations of the Divine will, purpose to aim at during Our Pontificate, and We will use all our industry to attain it. It is for you, Venerable Brethren, to second Our efforts by your holiness, knowledge and experience and above all by your zeal for the glory of God, with no other aim than that Christ may be formed in all.

10. As to the means to be employed in attaining this great end, it seems superfluous to name them, for they are obvious of themselves. Let your first care be to form Christ in those who are destined from the duty of their vocation to form Him in others. We speak of the priests, Venerable Brethren.

For all who bear the seal of the priesthood must know that they have the same mission to the people in the midst of whom they live as that which Paul proclaimed that he received in these tender words: "My little children, of whom I am in labor again until Christ be formed in you" (Gal. iv., 19). But how will they be able to perform this duty if they be not first clothed with Christ themselves? and so clothed with Christ as to be able to say with the Apostle: "I live, yet not I, but Christ lives in me" (Ibid. ii., 20). "For me to live is Christ" (Phlipp. i., 21). Hence although all are included in the exhortation "to advance towards the perfect man, in the measure of the age of the fullness of Christ" (Ephes. iv., 3), it is addressed before all others to those who exercise the sacerdotal ministry; thus these are called another Christ, not merely by the communication of power but by reason of the imitation of His works, and they should therefore bear stamped upon themselves the image of Christ.

11. This being so, Venerable Brethren, of what nature and magnitude is the care that must be taken by you in forming the clergy to holiness! All other tasks must yield to this one. Wherefore the chief part of your diligence will be directed to governing and ordering your seminaries aright so that they may flourish equally in the soundness of their teaching and in the spotlessness of their morals. Regard your seminary as the delight of your hearts, and neglect on its behalf none of those provisions which the Council of Trent has with admirable forethought prescribed. And when the time comes for promoting the youthful candidates to holy orders, ah! do not forget what Paul wrote to Timothy: "Impose not hands lightly upon any man" (I. Tim. v., 22), bearing carefully in mind that as a general rule the faithful will be such as are those whom you call to the priesthood. Do not then pay heed to private interests of any kind, but have at heart only God and

the Church and the eternal welfare of souls so that, as the Apostle admonishes, "you may not be partakers of the sins of others" (Ibid.). Then again be not lacking in solicitude for young priests who have just left the seminary. From the bottom of Our heart, We urge you to bring them often close to your breast, which should burn with celestial fire - kindle them, inflame them, so that they may aspire solely after God and the salvation of souls. Rest assured, Venerable Brethren, that We on Our side will use the greatest diligence to prevent the members of the clergy from being drawn to the snares of a certain new and fallacious science, which savoureth not of Christ, but with masked and cunning arguments strives to open the door to the errors of rationalism and semi-rationalism; against which the Apostle warned Timothy to be on his guard, when he wrote: "Keep that which is committed to thy trust, avoiding the profane novelties of words, and oppositions of knowledge falsely so called which some promising have erred concerning the faith" (I. Tim. vi., 20 s.). This does not prevent Us from esteeming worthy of praise those young priests who dedicated themselves to useful studies in every branch of learning the better to prepare themselves to defend the truth and to refute the calumnies of the enemies of the faith. Yet We cannot conceal, nay, We proclaim in the most open manner possible that Our preference is, and ever will be, for those who, while cultivating ecclesiastical and literary erudition, dedicate themselves more closely to the welfare of souls through the exercise of those ministries proper to a priest jealous of the divine glory. "It is a great grief and a continual sorrow to our heart" (Rom. ix., 2) to find Jeremiah's lamentation applicable to our times: "The little ones asked for bread, and there was none to break it to them" (Lam. iv., 4). For there are not lacking among the clergy those who adapt themselves according to their bent to works of more apparent than real solidity - but not so numerous perhaps are those who, after the example of Christ, take to themselves the words of the Prophet: "The Spirit of the Lord hath anointed me, hath sent me to evangelize the poor, to heal the contrite of heart, to announce freedom to the captive, and sight to the blind" (Luke iv., 18-19).

12. Yet who can fail to see, Venerable Brethren, that while men are led by reason and liberty, the principal way to restore the empire of God in their souls is religious instruction? How many there are who mimic Christ and abhor the Church and the Gospel more through ignorance than through badness of mind, of whom it may well be said: "They blaspheme whatever things they know not" (Jude ii., 10). This is found to be the case not only among the people at large and among the lowest classes, who are thus easily led astray, but even among the more cultivated and among those endowed moreover with uncommon education. The result is for a great many the loss of the faith. For it is not true that the progress of knowledge extinguishes the faith; rather is it ignorance, and the more ignorance prevails the greater is the havoc wrought by incredulity. And this is why Christ commanded the Apostles: "Going forth teach all nations" (Matth. xxvii., 19).

13. But in order that the desired fruit may be derived from this apostolate and this zeal for teaching, and that Christ may be formed in all, be it remembered, Venerable Brethren, that no means is more efficacious than charity. "For the Lord is not in the earthquake" (III Kings xix., II) - it is vain to hope to attract souls to God by a bitter zeal. On the contrary, harm is done more often than good by taunting men harshly with their faults, and reproving their vices with asperity. True the Apostle exhorted Timothy: "Accuse, beseech, rebuke," but he took care to add: "with all patience" (II. Tim.iv., 2). Jesus

has certainly left us examples of this. "Come to me," we find Him saying, "come to me all ye that labor and are burdened and I will refresh you" (Matth. xi., 28). And by those that labor and are burdened he meant only those who are slaves of sin and error. What gentleness was that shown by the Divine Master! What tenderness, what compassion towards all kinds of misery! Isaias has marvelously described His heart in the words: "I will set my spirit upon him; he shall not contend, nor cry out; the bruised reed he will not break, he will not extinguish the smoking flax" (Is. xlii., I, s.). This charity, "patient and kind" (I. Cor. xiii., 4.), will extend itself also to those who are hostile to us and persecute us. "We are reviled," thus did St. Paul protest, "and we bless; we are persecuted and we suffer it; we are blasphemed and we entreat" (I. Cor., iv., 12, s.). They perhaps seem to be worse than they really are. Their associations with others, prejudice, the counsel, advice and example of others, and finally an ill-advised shame have dragged them to the side of the impious; but their wills are not so depraved as they themselves would seek to make people believe. Who will prevent us from hoping that the flame of Christian charity may dispel the darkness from their minds and bring to them light and the peace of God? It may be that the fruit of our labors may be slow in coming, but charity wearies not with waiting, knowing that God prepares His rewards not for the results of toil but for the good will shown in it.

14. It is true, Venerable Brethren, that in this arduous task of the restoration of the human race in Christ neither you nor your clergy should exclude all assistance. We know that God recommended everyone to have a care for his neighbor (Eccli. xvii., 12). For it is not priests alone, but all the faithful without exception, who must concern themselves with the interests of God and souls - not, of course, according to

their own views, but always under the direction and orders of the bishops; for to no one in the Church except you is it given to preside over, to teach, to "govern the Church of God which the Holy Ghost has placed you to rule" (Actsxx., 28). Our predecessors have long since approved and blessed those Catholics who have banded together in societies of various kinds, but always religious in their aim. We, too, have no hesitation in awarding Our praise to this great idea, and We earnestly desire to see it propagated and flourish in town and country. But We wish that all such associations aim first and chiefly at the constant maintenance of Christian life, among those who belong to them. For truly it is of little avail to discuss questions with nice subtlety, or to discourse eloquently of rights and duties, when all this is unconnected with practice. The times we live in demand action - but action which consists entirely in observing with fidelity and zeal the divine laws and the precepts of the Church, in the frank and open profession of religion, in the exercise of every kind of charitable works, without regard to self-interest or worldly advantage. Such luminous examples given by the great army of soldiers of Christ will be of much greater avail in moving and drawing men than words and sublime dissertations; and it will easily come about that when human respect has been driven out, and prejudices and doubting laid aside, large numbers will be won to Christ, becoming in their turn promoters of His knowledge and love which are the road to true and solid happiness. Oh! when in every city and village the law of the Lord is faithfully observed, when respect is shown for sacred things, when the Sacraments are frequented, and the ordinances of Christian life fulfilled, there will certainly be no more need for us to labor further to see all things restored in Christ. Nor is it for the attainment of eternal welfare alone that this will be of service - it will also contribute largely to temporal welfare and the advantage of human society. For when these conditions have been secured, the upper and wealthy classes will learn to be just and charitable to the lowly, and these will be able to bear with tranquility and patience the trials of a very hard lot; the citizens will obey not lust but law, reverence and love will be deemed a duty towards those that govern, "whose power comes only from God" (Rom. xiii., I). And then? Then, at last, it will be clear to all that the Church, such as it was instituted by Christ, must enjoy full and entire liberty and independence from all foreign dominion; and We, in demanding that same liberty, are defending not only the sacred rights of religion, but are also consulting the common weal and the safety of nations. For it continues to be true that "piety is useful for all things" (I. Tim. iv., 8) - when this is strong and flourishing "the people will" truly "sit in the fullness of peace" (Is. xxxii., 18).

15. May God, "who is rich in mercy" (Ephes.ii., 4), benignly speed this restoration of the human race in Jesus Christ for "it is not of him that willeth, or of him that runneth, but of God that showeth mercy" (Rom. ix., 16). And let us, Venerable Brethren, "in the spirit of humility" (Dan. iii., 39), with continuous and urgent prayer ask this of Him through the merits of Jesus Christ. Let us turn, too, to the most powerful intercession of the Divine Mother - to obtain which We, addressing to you this Letter of Ours on the day appointed especially for commemorating the Holy Rosary, ordain and confirm all Our Predecessor's prescriptions with regard to the dedication of the present month to the august Virgin, by the public recitation of the Rosary in all churches; with the further exhortation that as intercessors with God appeal be also made to the most pure Spouse of Mary, the Patron of the Catholic Church, and the holy Princes of the Apostles, Peter and Paul.

16. And that all this may be realized in fulfillment of Our ardent desire, and that everything may be prosperous with you, We invoke upon you the most bountiful gifts of divine grace. And now in testimony of that most tender charity wherewith We embrace you and all the faithful whom Divine Providence has entrusted to Us, We impart with all affection in the Lord, the Apostolic Blessing to you, Venerable Brethren, to the clergy and to your people.

Given at Rome at St. Peter's, on the 4th day of October, 1903, in the first year of Our Pontificate.
PIUS X

AD DIEM ILLUM LAETISSIMUM
ENCYCLICAL OF POPE PIUS X
ON THE IMMACULATE CONCEPTION

TO THE PATRIARCHS, PRIMATES, ARCHBISHOPS, BISHOPS, AND OTHER ORDINARIES IN PEACE AND COMMUNION WITH THE APOSTOLIC SEE

Venerable Brethren,
Health and the Apostolic Blessing.

An interval of a few months will again bring round that most happy day on which, fifty years ago, Our Predecessor Pius IX., Pontiff of holy memory, surrounded by a noble crown of Cardinals and Bishops, pronounced and promulgated with the authority of the infallible magisterium as a truth revealed by God that the Most Blessed Virgin Mary in the first instant of her conception was free from all stain of original sin. All the world knows the feelings with which the faithful of all the nations of the earth received this proclamation and the manifestations of public satisfaction and joy which greeted it, for truly there has not been in the memory of man any more universal or more harmonious expression of sentiment shown towards the august Mother of God or the Vicar of Jesus Christ.

2. And, Venerable Brethren, why should we not hope to-day after the lapse of half a century, when we renew the memory of the Immaculate Virgin, that an echo of that holy joy will be awakened in our minds, and that those magnificent scenes of a distant day, of faith and of love towards the august Mother of God, will be repeated? Of all this We are, indeed, rendered ardently desirous by the devotion, united with supreme gratitude for benefits received, which We have

18

always cherished towards the Blessed Virgin; and We have a sure pledge of the fulfillment of Our desires in the fervor of all Catholics, ready and willing as they are to multiply their testimonies of love and reverence for the great Mother of God. But We must not omit to say that this desire of Ours is especially stimulated by a sort of secret instinct which leads Us to regard as not far distant the fulfillment of those great hopes to which, certainly not rashly, the solemn promulgation of the dogma of the Immaculate Conception opened the minds of Pius, Our predecessor, and of all the Bishops of the universe.

3. Many, it is true, lament the fact that until now these hopes have been unfulfilled, and are prone to repeat the words of Jeremias: "We looked for peace and no good came; for a time of healing, and beheld fear" (Jer. viii., 15). But all such will be certainly rebuked as "men of little faith," who make no effort to penetrate the works of God or to estimate them in the light of truth. For who can number the secret gifts of grace which God has bestowed upon His Church through the intercession of the Blessed Virgin throughout this period? And even overlooking these gifts, what is to be said of the Vatican Council so opportunely convoked; or of the dogma of Papal Infallibility so suitably proclaimed to meet the errors that were about to arise; or, finally, of that new and unprecedented fervor with which the faithful of all classes and of every nation have long been flocking to venerate in person the Vicar of Christ? Surely the Providence of God has shown itself admirable in Our two predecessors, Pius and Leo, who ruled the Church in most turbulent times with such great holiness through a length of Pontificate conceded to no other before them. Then, again, no sooner had Pius IX, proclaimed as a dogma of Catholic faith the exemption of Mary from the original stain, than the Virgin herself began

in Lourdes those wonderful manifestations, followed by the vast and magnificent movements which have produced those two temples dedicated to the Immaculate Mother, where the prodigies which still continue to take place through her intercession furnish splendid arguments against the incredulity of our days.

4. Witnesses, then, as we are of all these great benefits which God has granted through the benign influence of the Virgin in those fifty years now about to be completed, why should we not believe that our salvation is nearer than we thought; all the more since we know from experience that, in the dispensation of Divine Providence, when evils reach their limit, deliverance is not far distant. "Her time is near at hand, and her days shall not be prolonged. For the Lord will have mercy on Jacob and will choose one out of Israel" (Isaias xiv., 1). Wherefore the hope we cherish is not a vain one that we, too, may before long repeat: "The Lord hath broken the staff of the wicked, the rod of the rulers. The whole earth is quiet and still, it is glad and hath rejoiced" (Ibid. 5, 7).

5. But the first and chief reason, Venerable Brethren, why the fiftieth anniversary of the proclamation of the dogma of the Immaculate Conception should excite a singular fervour in the souls of Christians lies for us in that restoration of all things in Christ which we have already set forth in Our first Encyclical letter. For can anyone fail to see that there is no surer or more direct road than by Mary for uniting all mankind in Christ and obtaining through Him the perfect adoption of sons, that we may be holy and immaculate in the sight of God? For if to Mary it was truly said: "Blessed art thou who hast believed because in thee shall be fulfilled the things that have been told thee by the Lord" (Luke i., 45); or in other words, that she would conceive and bring forth the

Son of God and if she did receive in her breast Him who is by nature Truth itself in order that "He, generated in a new order and with a new nativity, though invisible in Himself, might become visible in our flesh" (St. Leo the Great, Ser. 2, De Nativ. Dom.): the Son of God made man, being the "author and consummator of our faith"; it surely follows that His Mother most holy should be recognized as participating in the divine mysteries and as being in a manner the guardian of them, and that upon her as upon a foundation, the noblest after Christ, rises the edifice of the faith of all centuries.

6. How think otherwise? Could not God have given us, in another way than through the Virgin the Redeemer of the human race and the Founder of the Faith? But, since Divine Providence has been pleased that we should have the Man-God through Mary, who conceived Him by the Holy Ghost and bore Him in her breast, it only remains for us to receive Christ from the hands of Mary. Hence whenever the Scriptures speak prophetically of the grace which was to appear among us, the Redeemer of mankind is almost invariably presented to us as united with His mother. The Lamb that is to rule the world will be sent - but He will be sent from the rock of the desert; the flower will blossom, but it will blossom from the root of Jesse. Adam, the father of mankind, looked to Mary crushing the serpent's head, and he dried the tears that the malediction had brought into his eyes. Noë thought of her when shut up in the ark of safety, and Abraham when prevented from the slaying of his son; Jacob at the sight of the ladder on which angels ascended and descended; Moses amazed at the sight of the bush which burned but was not consumed; David escorting the arc of God with dancing and psalmody; Elias as he looked at the little cloud that rose out of the sea. In fine, after Christ, we

find in Mary the end of the law and the fulfillment of the figures and oracles.

7. And that through the Virgin, and through her more than through any other means, we have offered us a way of reaching the knowledge of Jesus Christ, cannot be doubted when it is remembered that with her alone of all others Jesus was for thirty years united, as a son is usually united with a mother, in the closest ties of intimacy and domestic life. Who could better than His Mother have an open knowledge of the admirable mysteries of the birth and childhood of Christ, and above all of the mystery of the Incarnation, which is the beginning and the foundation of faith? Mary not only preserved and meditated on the events of Bethlehem and the facts which took place in Jerusalem in the Temple of the Lord, but sharing as she did the thoughts and the secret wishes of Christ she may be said to have lived the very life of her Son. Hence nobody ever knew Christ so profoundly as she did, and nobody can ever be more competent as a guide and teacher of the knowledge of Christ.

8. Hence it follows, as We have already pointed out, that the Virgin is more powerful than all others as a means for uniting mankind with Christ. Hence too since, according to Christ Himself, "Now this is eternal life: That they may know thee the only truly God, and Jesus Christ whom thou hast sent" (John xvii., 3), and since it is through Mary that we attain to the knowledge of Christ, through Mary also we most easily obtain that life of which Christ is the source and origin.

9. And if we set ourselves to consider how many and powerful are the causes by which this most holy Mother is filled with zeal to bestow on us these precious gifts, oh, how our

hopes will be expanded!

10. For is not Mary the Mother of Christ? Then she is our Mother also. And we must in truth hold that Christ, the Word made Flesh, is also the Savior of mankind. He had a physical body like that of any other man: and again as Savior of the human family, he had a spiritual and mystical body, the society, namely, of those who believe in Christ. "We are many, but one sole body in Christ" (Rom. xii., 5). Now the Blessed Virgin did not conceive the Eternal Son of God merely in order that He might be made man taking His human nature from her, but also in order that by means of the nature assumed from her He might be the Redeemer of men. For which reason the Angel said to the Shepherds: "To-day there is born to you a Savior who is Christ the Lord" (Luke ii., 11). Wherefore in the same holy bosom of his most chaste Mother Christ took to Himself flesh, and united to Himself the spiritual body formed by those who were to believe in Him. Hence Mary, carrying the Savior within her, may be said to have also carried all those whose life was contained in the life of the Savior. Therefore all we who are united to Christ, and as the Apostle says are members of His body, of His flesh, and of His bones (Ephes. v., 30), have issued from the womb of Mary like a body united to its head. Hence, though in a spiritual and mystical fashion, we are all children of Mary, and she is Mother of us all. Mother, spiritually indeed, but truly Mother of the members of Christ, who are we (S. Aug. L. de S. Virginitate, c. 6).

11. If then the most Blessed Virgin is the Mother at once of God and men, who can doubt that she will work with all diligence to procure that Christ, Head of the Body of the Church (Coloss. i., 18), may transfuse His gifts into us, His members, and above all that of knowing Him and living through

Him (I John iv., 9)?

12. Moreover it was not only the prerogative of the Most Holy Mother to have furnished the material of His flesh to the Only Son of God, Who was to be born with human members (S. Bede Ven. L. Iv. in Luc. xl.), of which material should be prepared the Victim for the salvation of men; but hers was also the office of tending and nourishing that Victim, and at the appointed time presenting Him for the sacrifice. Hence that uninterrupted community of life and labors of the Son and the Mother, so that of both might have been uttered the words of the Psalmist "My life is consumed in sorrow and my years in groans" (Ps xxx., 11). When the supreme hour of the Son came, beside the Cross of Jesus there stood Mary His Mother, not merely occupied in contemplating the cruel spectacle, but rejoicing that her Only Son was offered for the salvation of mankind, and so entirely participating in His Passion, that if it had been possible she would have gladly borne all the torments that her Son bore (S. Bonav. 1. Sent d. 48, ad Litt. dub. 4). And from this community of will and suffering between Christ and Mary she merited to become most worthily the Reparatrix of the lost world (Eadmeri Mon. De Excellentia Virg. Mariae, c. 9) and Dispensatrix of all the gifts that Our Savior purchased for us by His Death and by His Blood.

13. It cannot, of course, be denied that the dispensation of these treasures is the particular and peculiar right of Jesus Christ, for they are the exclusive fruit of His Death, who by His nature is the mediator between God and man. Nevertheless, by this companionship in sorrow and suffering already mentioned between the Mother and the Son, it has been allowed to the august Virgin to be the most powerful mediatrix and advocate of the whole world with her Divine Son (Pius

IX. Ineffabilis). The source, then, is Jesus Christ "of whose fullness we have all received" (John i., 16), "from whom the whole body, being compacted and fitly joined together by what every joint supplieth, according to the operation in the measure of every part, maketh increase of the body unto the edifying of itself in charity" (Ephesians iv., 16). But Mary, as St. Bernard justly remarks, is the channel (Serm. de temp on the Nativ. B. V. De Aquaeductu n. 4); or, if you will, the connecting portion the function of which is to join the body to the head and to transmit to the body the influences and volitions of the head - We mean the neck. Yes, says St. Bernardine of Sienna, "she is the neck of Our Head, by which He communicates to His mystical body all spiritual gifts" (Quadrag. de Evangel. aetern.Serm. x., a. 3, c. iii.).

14. We are then, it will be seen, very far from attributing to the Mother of God a productive power of grace - a power which belongs to God alone. Yet, since Mary carries it over all in holiness and union with Jesus Christ, and has been associated by Jesus Christ in the work of redemption, she merits for us de congruo, in the language of theologians, what Jesus Christ merits for us de condigno, and she is the supreme Minister of the distribution of graces. Jesus "sitteth on the right hand of the majesty on high" (Hebrews i. b.). Mary sitteth at the right hand of her Son - a refuge so secure and a help so trusty against all dangers that we have nothing to fear or to despair of under her guidance, her patronage, her protection. (Pius IX. in Bull Ineffabilis).

15. These principles laid down, and to return to our design, who will not see that we have with good reason claimed for Mary that - as the constant companion of Jesus from the house at Nazareth to the height of Calvary, as beyond all others initiated to the secrets of his Heart, and as the dis-

tributor, by right of her Motherhood, of the treasures of His merits, - she is, for all these reasons, a most sure and efficacious assistance to us for arriving at the knowledge and love of Jesus Christ. Those, alas! furnish us by their conduct with a peremptory proof of it, who seduced by the wiles of the demon or deceived by false doctrines think they can do without the help of the Virgin. Hapless are they who neglect Mary under pretext of the honor to be paid to Jesus Christ! As if the Child could be found elsewhere than with the Mother!

16. Under these circumstances, Venerable Brethren, it is this end which all the solemnities that are everywhere being prepared in honor of the holy and Immaculate Conception of Mary should have in view. No homage is more agreeable to her, none is sweeter to her than that we should know and really love Jesus Christ. Let then crowds fill the churches - let solemn feasts be celebrated and public rejoicings be made: these are things eminently suited for enlivening our faith. But unless heart and will be added, they will all be empty forms, mere appearances of piety. At such a spectacle, the Virgin, borrowing the words of Jesus Christ, would address us with the just reproach: "This people honoureth me with their lips, but their heart is far from me" (Matth. xv., 8).

17. For to be right and good, worship of the Mother of God ought to spring from the heart; acts of the body have here neither utility nor value if the acts of the soul have no part in them. Now these latter can only have one object, which is that we should fully carry out what the divine Son of Mary commands. For if true love alone has the power to unite the wills of men, it is of the first necessity that we should have one will with Mary to serve Jesus our Lord. What this most prudent Virgin said to the servants at the marriage feast of

Cana she addresses also to us: "Whatsoever he shall say to you, do ye" (John ii., 5). Now here is the word of Jesus Christ: "If you would enter into life, keep the commandments" (Matt. xix., 17). Let them each one fully convince himself of this, that if his piety towards the Blessed Virgin does not hinder him from sinning, or does not move his will to amend an evil life, it is a piety deceptive and lying, wanting as it is in proper effect and its natural fruit.

18. If anyone desires a confirmation of this it may easily be found in the dogma of the Immaculate Conception of Mary. For leaving aside tradition which, as well as Scripture, is a source of truth, how has this persuasion of the Immaculate Conception of the Virgin appeared so conformed to the Catholic mind and feeling that it has been held as being one, and as it were inborn in the soul of the faithful? "We shrink from saying," is the answer of Dionysius of Chartreux, "of this woman who was to crush the head of the serpent that had been crushed by him and that Mother of God that she had ever been a daughter of the Evil One" (Sent. d. 3, q. 1). No, to the Christian intelligence the idea is unthinkable that the flesh of Christ, holy, stainless, innocent, was formed in the womb of Mary of a flesh which had ever, if only for the briefest moment, contracted any stain. And why so, but because an infinite opposition separates God from sin? There certainly we have the origin of the conviction common to all Christians that Jesus Christ before, clothed in human nature, He cleansed us from our sins in His blood, accorded Mary the grace and special privilege of being preserved and exempted, from the first moment of her conception, from all stain of original sin.

19. If then God has such a horror of sin as to have willed to keep free the future Mother of His Son not only from stains

which are voluntarily contracted but, by a special favor and in prevision of the merits of Jesus Christ, from that other stain of which the sad sign is transmitted to all us sons of Adam by a sort of hapless heritage: who can doubt that it is a duty for everyone who seeks by his homage to gain the heart of Mary to correct his vicious and depraved habits and to subdue the passions which incite him to evil?

20. Whoever moreover wishes, and no one ought not so to wish, that his devotion should be worthy of her and perfect, should go further and strive might and main to imitate her example. It is a divine law that those only attain everlasting happiness who have by such faithful following reproduced in themselves the form of the patience and sanctity of Jesus Christ: "for whom He foreknew, He also predestined to be made conformable to the image of His Son; that He might be the first-born amongst many brethren" (Romans viii., 29). But such generally is our infirmity that we are easily discouraged by the greatness of such an example: by the providence of God, however, another example is proposed to us, which is both as near to Christ as human nature allows, and more nearly accords with the weakness of our nature. And this is no other than the Mother of God. "Such was Mary," very pertinently points out St. Ambrose, "that her life is an example for all." And, therefore, he rightly concludes: "Have then before your eyes, as an image, the virginity and life of Mary from whom as from a mirror shines forth the brightness of chastity and the form of virtue" (De Virginib. L. ii., c. ii.)

21. Now if it becomes children not to omit the imitation of any of the virtues of this most Blessed Mother, we yet wish that the faithful apply themselves by preference to the principal virtues which are, as it were, the nerves and joints

of the Christian life - we mean faith, hope, and charity to-wards God and our neighbor. Of these virtues the life of Mary bears in all its phases the brilliant character; but they attained their highest degree of splendor at the time when she stood by her dying Son. Jesus is nailed to the cross, and the malediction is hurled against Him that "He made Him-self the Son of God" (John xix., 7). But she unceasingly recognized and adored the divinity in Him. She bore His dead body to the tomb, but never for a moment doubted that He would rise again. Then the love of God with which she burned made her a partaker in the sufferings of Christ and the associate in His passion; with him moreover, as if forget-ful of her own sorrow, she prayed for the pardon of the ex-ecutioners although they in their hate cried out: "His blood be upon us and upon our children" (Matth. xxvii., 25).

22. But lest it be thought that We have lost sight of Our subject, which is the Immaculate Conception, what great and effectual succour will be found in it for the preservation and right development of those same virtues. What truly is the point of departure of the enemies of religion for the sowing of the great and serious errors by which the faith of so many is shaken? They begin by denying that man has fallen by sin and been cast down from his former position. Hence they regard as mere fables original sin and the evils that were its consequence. Humanity vitiated in its source vitiated in its turn the whole race of man; and thus was evil introduced amongst men and the necessity for a Redeemer involved. All this rejected it is easy to understand that no place is left for Christ, for the Church, for grace or for anything that is above and beyond nature; in one word the whole edifice of faith is shaken from top to bottom. But let people believe and con-fess that the Virgin Mary has been from the first moment of her conception preserved from all stain; and it is straightway

necessary that they should admit both original sin and the rehabilitation of the human race by Jesus Christ, the Gospel, and the Church and the law of suffering. By virtue of this Rationalism and Materialism is torn up by the roots and destroyed, and there remains to Christian wisdom the glory of having to guard and protect the truth. It is moreover a vice common to the enemies of the faith of our time especially that they repudiate and proclaim the necessity of repudiating all respect and obedience for the authority of the Church, and even of any human power, in the idea that it will thus be more easy to make an end of faith. Here we have the origin of Anarchism, than which nothing is more pernicious and pestilent to the order of things whether natural or supernatural. Now this plague, which is equally fatal to society at large and to Christianity, finds its ruin in the dogma of the Immaculate Conception by the obligation which it imposes of recognizing in the Church a power before which not only has the will to bow, but the intelligence to subject itself. It is from a subjection of the reason of this sort that Christian people sing thus the praise of the Mother of God: "Thou art all fair, O Mary, and the stain of original sin is not in thee." (Mass of Immac. Concep.) And thus once again is justified what the Church attributes to this august Virgin that she has exterminated all heresies in the world.

23. And if, as the Apostle declares, faith is nothing else than the substance of things to be hoped for" (Hebr. xi. 1) everyone will easily allow that our faith is confirmed and our hope aroused and strengthened by the Immaculate Conception of the Virgin. The Virgin was kept the more free from all stain of original sin because she was to be the Mother of Christ; and she was the Mother of Christ that the hope of everlasting happiness might be born again in our souls.

30

24. Leaving aside charity towards God, who can contemplate the Immaculate Virgin without feeling moved to fulfill that precept which Christ called peculiarly His own, namely that of loving one another as He loved us? "A great sign," thus the Apostle St. John describes a vision divinely sent him, appears in the heavens: "A woman clothed with the sun, and with the moon under her feet and a crown of twelve stars upon her head" (Apoc. xii., 1). Everyone knows that this woman signified the Virgin Mary, the stainless one who brought forth our Head. The Apostle continues: "And, being with child, she cried travailing in birth, and was in pain to be delivered" (Apoc. xii., 2). John therefore saw the Most Holy Mother of God already in eternal happiness, yet travailing in a mysterious childbirth. What birth was it? Surely it was the birth of us who, still in exile, are yet to be generated to the perfect charity of God, and to eternal happiness. And the birth pains show the love and desire with which the Virgin from heaven above watches over us, and strives with unwearying prayer to bring about the fulfillment of the number of the elect.

25. This same charity we desire that all should earnestly endeavor to attain, taking special occasion from the extraordinary feasts in honour of the Immaculate Conception of the Blessed Virgin. Oh how bitterly and fiercely is Jesus Christ now being persecuted, and the most holy religion which he founded! And how grave is the peril that threatens many of being drawn away by the errors that are afoot on all sides, to the abandonment of the faith! "Then let him who thinks he stands take heed lest he fall" (I Cor. x., 12). And let all, with humble prayer and entreaty, implore of God, through the intercession of Mary that those who have abandoned the truth may repent. We know, indeed, from experience that such prayer, born of charity and relying on the Virgin, has

never been vain. True, even in the future the strife against the Church will never cease, "for there must be also heresies, that they also who are reproved may be made manifest among you" (I Cor. xi., 19). But neither will the Virgin ever cease to succor us in our trials, however grave they be, and to carry on the fight fought by her since her conception, so that every day we may repeat: "To-day the head of the serpent of old was crushed by her" (Office Immac. Con., 11. Vespers, Magnif.).

26. And that heavenly graces may help Us more abundantly than usual during this year in which We pay her fuller honour, to attain the imitation of the Virgin, and that thus We may more easily secure Our object of restoring all things in Christ, We have determined, after the example of Our Predecessors at the beginning of their Pontificates, to grant to the Catholic world an extraordinary indulgence in the form of a Jubilee.

27. Wherefore, confiding in the mercy of Almighty God and in the authority of the Blessed Apostles Peter and Paul, by virtue of that power of binding and loosing which, unworthy though We are, the Lord has given Us, We do concede and impart the most plenary indulgence of all their sins to the faithful, all and several of both sexes, dwelling in this Our beloved City, or coming into it, who from the first Sunday in Lent, that is from the 21st of February, to the second day of June, the solemnity of the Most Sacred Body of Christ, inclusively, shall three times visit one of the four Patriarchal basilicas, and there for some time pray God for the liberty and exaltation of the Catholic Church and this Apostolic See, for the extirpation of heresies and the conversion of all who are in error, for the concord of Christian Princes and the peace and unity of all the faithful, and according to Our

intention; and who, within the said period, shall fast once, using only meager fare, excepting the days not included in the Lenten Indult; and, after confessing their sins, shall receive the most holy Sacrament of the Eucharist; and to all others, wherever they be, dwelling outside this city, who, within the time above mentioned or during a space of three months, even not continuous, to be definitely appointed by the ordinaries according to the convenience of the faithful, but before the eighth day of December, shall three times visit the cathedral church, if there be one, or, if not, the parish church; or, in the absence of this, the principal church; and shall devoutly fulfill the other works abovementioned. And We do at the same time permit that this indulgence, which is to be gained only once, may be applied in suffrage for the souls which have passed from this life united in charity with God.

28. We do, moreover, concede that travelers by land or sea may gain the same indulgence immediately they return to their homes provided they perform the works already noted.

29. To confessors approved by their respective ordinaries We grant faculties for commuting the above works enjoined by Us for other works of piety, and this concession shall be applicable not only to regulars of both sexes but to all others who cannot perform the works prescribed, and We do grant faculties also to dispense from Communion children who have not yet been admitted to it.

30. Moreover to the faithful, all and several, the laity and the clergy both secular and regular of all orders and institutes, even those calling for special mention, We do grant permission and power, for this sole object, to select any priest regular or secular, among those actually approved (which faculty

may also be used by nuns, novices and other women living in the cloister, provided the confessor they select be one approved for nuns) by whom, when they have confessed to him within the prescribed time with the intention of gaining the present jubilee and of fulfilling all the other works requisite for gaining it, they may on this sole occasion and only in the forum of conscience be absolved from all excommunication, suspension and every other ecclesiastical sentence and censure pronounced or inflicted for any cause by the law or by a judge, including those reserved to the ordinary and to Us or to the Apostolic See, even in cases reserved in a special manner to anybody whomsoever and to Us and to the Apostolic See; and they may also be absolved from all sin or excess, even those reserved to the ordinaries themselves and to Us and to the Apostolic See, on condition however that a salutary penance be enjoined together with the other prescriptions of the law, and in the case of heresy after the abjuration and retraction of error as is enjoined by the law; and the said priests may further commute to other pious and salutary works all vows even those taken under oath and reserved to the Apostolic See (except those of chastity, of religion, and of obligations which have been accepted by a third person); and with the said penitents, even regulars, in sacred orders such confessions may dispense from all secret irregularities contracted solely by violation of censures affecting the exercise of said orders and promotion to higher orders.

31. But We do not intend by the present Letters to dispense from any irregularities whatsoever, or from crime or defect, public or private, contracted in any manner through notoriety or other incapacity or inability; nor do We intend to derogate from the Constitution with its accompanying declaration, published by Benedict XIV, of happy memory, which begins with the words Sacramentum poenitentiae; nor is it

Our intention that these present Letters may, or can, in any way avail those who, by Us and the Apostolic See, or by any ecclesiastical judge, have been by name excommunicated, suspended, interdicted or declared under other sentences or censures, or who have been publicly denounced, unless they do within the allotted time satisfy, or, when necessary, come to an arrangement with the parties concerned.

32. To all this We are pleased to add that We do concede and will that all retain during this time of Jubilee the privilege of gaining all other indulgences, not excepting plenary indulgences, which have been granted by Our Predecessors or by Ourself.

33. We close these letters, Venerable Brethren, by manifesting anew the great hope We earnestly cherish that through this extraordinary gift of Jubilee granted by Us under the auspices of the Immaculate Virgin, large numbers of those who are unhappily separated from Jesus Christ may return to Him, and that love of virtue and fervor of devotion may flourish anew among the Christian people. Fifty years ago, when Pius IX, proclaimed as an article of faith the Immaculate Conception of the most Blessed Mother of Christ, it seemed, as we have already said, as if an incredible wealth of grace were poured out upon the earth; and with the increase of confidence in the Virgin Mother of God, the old religious spirit of the people was everywhere greatly augmented. Is it forbidden us to hope for still greater things for the future? True, we are passing through disastrous times, when we may well make our own the lamentation of the Prophet: "There is no truth and no mercy and no knowledge of God on the earth. Blasphemy and Lying and homicide and theft and adultery have inundated it" (Os. iv.,1-2). Yet in the midst of this deluge of evil, the Virgin Most Clement rises before

our eyes like a rainbow, as the arbiter of peace between God and man: "I will set my bow in the clouds and it shall be the sign of a covenant between me and between the earth" (Gen. ix.,13). Let the storm rage and sky darken - not for that shall we be dismayed. "And the bow shall be in the clouds, and I shall see it and shall remember the everlasting covenant" (Ibid.16). "And there shall no more be waters of a flood to destroy all flesh" (Ibid.15.). Oh yes, if we trust as we should in Mary, now especially when we are about to celebrate, with more than usual fervor, her Immaculate Conception, we shall recognize in her that Virgin most powerful "who with virginal foot did crush the head of the serpent" (Off. Immac. Conc.).

34. In pledge of these graces, Venerable Brethren, We impart the Apostolic Benediction lovingly in the Lord to you and to your people.

Given at Rome in St. Peter's on the second day of February, 1904, in the first year of Our Pontificate.
PIUS X

IUCUNDA SANE
ENCYCLICAL OF POPE PIUS X
ON POPE GREGORY THE GREAT

TO OUR VENERABLE BRETHREN, THE PATRIARCHS,
PRIMATES, ARCHBISHOPS, BISHOPS, AND OTHER
ORDINARIES IN PEACE AND COMMUNION WITH
THE APOSTOLIC SEE

Venerable Brethren, Health and the Apostolic Benediction.

1. Joyful indeed comes the remembrance, Venerable Brethren, of that great and incomparable man, the Pontiff Gregory, first of the name, whose centenary solemnity, at the close of the thirteenth century since his death, we are about to celebrate. By that God who killeth and maketh alive, who humbleth and exalteth, it was ordained, not, We think, without a special providence, that amid the almost innumerable cares of Our Apostolic ministry, amid all the anxieties which the government of the Universal Church imposes upon Us, amid our pressing solicitude to satisfy as best We may your claims, Venerable Brethren, who have been called to a share in Our Apostolate, and those of all the faithful entrusted to Our care, Our gaze at the beginning of Our Pontificate should be turned at once towards that most holy and illustrious Predecessor of Ours, the honor of the Church and its glory. For Our heart is filled with great confidence in his most powerful intercession with God, and strengthened by the memory of the sublime maxims he inculcated in his lofty office and of the virtues devoutly practiced by him. And since by the force of the former and the fruitfulness of the latter he has left on God's Church a mark so vast, so deep, so lasting, that his contemporaries and posterity have justly given him the name of Great, and today, after all these

centuries, the eulogy of his epitaph is still verified: "He lives eternal in every place by his innumerable good works" (Apud Joann. Diac., Vita Greg. iv. 68) it will surely be given, with the help of Divine grace, to all followers of his wonderful example, to fulfill the duties of their own offices, as far as human weakness permits.

2. There is but little need to repeat here what public documents have made known to all. When Gregory assumed the Supreme Pontificate the disorder in public affairs had reached its climax; the ancient civilization had all but disappeared and barbarism was spreading throughout the dominions of the crumbling Roman Empire. Italy, abandoned by the Emperors of Byzantium, had been left a prey of the still unsettled Lombards who roamed up and down the whole country laying waste everywhere with fire and sword and bringing desolation and death in their train. This very city, threatened from without by its enemies, tried from within by the scourges of pestilence, floods and famine, was reduced to such a miserable plight that it had become a problem how to keep the breath of life in the citizens and in the immense multitudes who flocked hither for refuge. Here were to be found men and women of all conditions, bishops and priests carrying the sacred vessels they had saved from plunder, monks and innocent spouses of Christ who had sought safety in flight from the swords of the enemy or from the brutal insults of abandoned men. Gregory himself calls the Church of Rome: "An old ship woefully shattered; for the waters are entering on all sides, and the joints, buffeted by the daily stress of the storm, are growing rotten and herald shipwreck" (Registrum i., 4 ad Joannem episcop. Constantino.). But the pilot raised up by God had a strong hand, and when placed at the helm succeeding not only in making the port in despite of the raging seas, but in saving the vessel from future

storms.

3. Truly wonderful is the work he was able to effect during his reign of little more than thirteen years. He was the restorer of Christian life in its entirety, stimulating the devotion of the faithful, the observance of the monks, the discipline of the clergy, the pastoral solicitude of the bishops. Most prudent father of the family of Christ that he was (Joann. Diac., Vita Greg. ii. 51), he preserved and increased the patrimony of the Church, and liberally succored the impoverished people, Christian society, and individual churches, according to the necessities of each. Becoming truly God's Consul (Epitaph), he pushed his fruitful activity far beyond the walls of Rome, and entirely for the advantage of civilized society. He opposed energetically the unjust claims of the Byzantine Emperors; he checked the audacity and curbed the shameless avarice of the exarchs and the imperial administrators, and stood up in public as the defender of social justice. He tamed the ferocity of the Lombards, and did not hesitate to meet Agulfus at the gates of Rome in order to prevail upon him to raise the siege of the city, just as the Pontiff Leo the Great did in the case of Attila; nor did he desist in his prayers, in his gentle persuasion, in his skillful negotiation, until he saw that dreaded people settle down and adopt a more regular government; until he knew that they were won to the Catholic faith, mainly through the influence of the pious Queen Theodolinda, his daughter in Christ. Hence Gregory may justly be called the savior and liberator of Italy - his own land, as he tenderly calls her.

4. Through his incessant pastoral care the embers of heresy in Italy and Africa die out, ecclesiastical life in the Gauls is reorganized, the Visigoths of the Spains are welded together in the conversion which has already been begun among

them, and the renowned English nation, which, "situated in a corner of the world, while it had hitherto remained obstinate in the worship of wood and stone" (Reg. viii. 29, 30, ad Eulog. Episcop. Alexandr.), now also receives the true faith of Christ. Gregory's heart overflowed with joy at the news of this precious conquest, for his is the heart of a father embracing his most beloved son, and in attributing all the merit of it to Jesus the Redeemer, "for whose love," as he himself writes, "we are seeking our unknown brethren in Britain, and through whose grace we find unknown ones we were seeking" (Reg. xi. 36 (28), ad Augustin. Anglorum Episcopum). And so grateful to the Holy Pontiff was the English nation that they called him always: our Master, our Doctor, our Apostle, our Pope, our Gregory, and considered itself as the seal of his apostolate. In fine, so salutary and so efficacious was his action that the memory of the works wrought by him became deeply impressed on the minds of posterity, especially during the Middle Ages, which breathed, so to say, the atmosphere infused by him, fed on his words, conformed its life and manners according to the example inculcated by him, with the result that Christian social civilization was happily introduced into the world in opposition to the Roman civilization of the preceding centuries, which now passed away forever.

5. This is the change of the right hand of the Most High! And well may it be said that in the mind of Gregory the hand of God alone was operative in these great events. What he wrote to the most holy monk Augustine about this same conversion of the English may be equally applied to all the rest of his apostolic action: "Whose work is this but His who said: My Father worketh till now, and I work? (John v. 17). To show the world that He wished to convert it, not by the wisdom of men, but by His own power, He chose unlet-

tered men to be preachers to the world; and the same He has now done, vouchsafing to accomplish through weak men great things among the nation of the Angles" (Reg. xi. 36 (28)). We, indeed, may discern much that the holy Pontiff's profound humility hid from his own sight: his knowledge of affairs, his talent for bringing his undertakings to a successful issue, the wonderful prudence shown in all his provisions, his assiduous vigilance, his persevering solicitude. But it is, nevertheless, true that he never put himself forward as one invested with the might and power of the great ones of the earth, for instead of using the exalted prestige of the Pontifical dignity, he preferred to call himself the Servant of the Servants of God, a title which he was the first to adopt. It was not merely by profane science or the "persuasive words of human wisdom (I Cor. ii. 4) that he traced out his career, or by the devices of civil politics, or by systems of social renovation, skillfully studied, prepared and put in execution; nor yet, and this is very striking, by setting before himself a vast program of apostolic action to be gradually realized; for we know that, on the contrary, his mind was full of the idea of the approaching end of the world which was to have left him but little time for great exploits. Very delicate and fragile of body though he was, and constantly afflicted by infirmities which several times brought him to the point of death, he yet possessed an incredible energy of soul which was forever receiving fresh vigor from his lively faith in the infallible words of Christ, and in His Divine promises. Then again, he counted with unlimited confidence on the supernatural force given by God to the Church for the successful accomplishment of her divine mission in the world. The constant aim of his life, as shown in all his words and works, was, therefore, this: to preserve in himself, and to stimulate in others this same lively faith and confidence, doing all the good possible at the moment in expectation of the Divine

41

judgment.

6. And this produced in him the fixed resolve to adopt for the salvation of all the abundant wealth of supernatural means given by God to His Church, such as the infallible teaching of revealed truth, and the preaching of the same teaching in the whole world, and the sacraments which have the power of infusing or increasing the life of the soul, and the grace of prayer in the name of Christ which assures heavenly protection.

7. These memories, Venerable Brethren, are a source of unspeakable comfort to Us. When We glance around from the walls of the Vatican We find that like Gregory, and perhaps with even more reason than he, We have grounds for fear, with so many storms gathering on every side, with so many hostile forces massed and advancing against Us, and at the same time so utterly deprived are We of all human aid to ward off the former and to help us to meet the shock of the latter. But when We consider the place on which Our feet rest and on which this Pontifical See is rooted, We feel Ourself perfectly safe on the rock of Holy Church. "For who does not know," wrote St. Gregory to the Patriarch Eulogius of Alexandria, "that Holy Church stands on the solidity of the Prince of the Apostles, who got his name from his firmness, for he was called Peter from the word rock? (Registr. vii. 37 (40)). Supernatural force has never during the flight of ages been found wanting in the Church, nor have Christ's promises failed; these remain today just as they were when they brought consolation to Gregory's heart nay, they are endowed with even greater force for Us after having stood the test of centuries and so many changes of circumstances and events.

8. Kingdoms and empires have passed away; peoples once renowned for their history and civilization have disappeared; time and again the nations, as though overwhelmed by the weight of years, have fallen asunder; while the Church, indefectible in her essence, united by ties indissoluble with her heavenly Spouse, is here today radiant with eternal youth, strong with the same primitive vigor with which she came from the Heart of Christ dead upon the Cross. Men powerful in the world have risen up against her. They have disappeared, and she remains. Philosophical systems without number, of every form and every kind, rose up against her, arrogantly vaunting themselves her masters, as though they had at last destroyed the doctrine of the Church, refuted the dogmas of her faith, proved the absurdity of her teachings. But those systems, one after another, have passed into books of history, forgotten, bankrupt; while from the Rock of Peter the light of truth shines forth as brilliantly as on the day when Jesus first kindled it on His appearance in the world, and fed it with His Divine words: "Heaven and earth shall pass, but my words shall not pass" (Matth. xxiv. 35).

9. We, strengthened by this faith, firmly established on this rock, realizing to the full all the heavy duties that the Primacy imposes on Us - but also all the vigor that comes to Us from the Divine Will - calmly wait until all the voices be scattered to the winds that now shout around Us proclaiming that the Church has gone beyond her time, that her doctrines are passed away for ever, that the day is at hand when she will be condemned either to accept the tenets of a godless science and civilization or to disappear from human society. Yet at the same time We cannot but remind all, great and small, as Pope St. Gregory did, of the absolute necessity of having recourse to this Church in order to have eternal salvation, to follow the right road of reason, to feed on the truth,

to obtain peace and even happiness in this life.

10. Wherefore, to use the words of the Holy Pontiff, "Turn your steps towards this unshaken rock upon which Our Savior founded the Universal Church, so that the path of him who is sincere of heart may not be lost in devious windings" (Reg. viii. 24, ad Sabin. episcop.). It is only the charity of the Church and union with her which "unite what is divided, restore order where there is confusion, temper inequalities, fill up imperfections" (Registr. v. 58 (53) ad Virgil. episcop.). It is to be firmly held "that nobody can rightly govern in earthly things, unless he knows how to treat divine things, and that the peace of States depends upon the universal peace of the Church" (Registr. v. 37 (20) ad Mauric. Aug.). Hence the absolute necessity of a perfect harmony between the two powers, ecclesiastical and civil, each being by the will of God called to sustain the other. For, "power over all men was given from heaven that those who aspire to do well may be aided, that the path to heaven may be made broader, and that earthly sovereignty may be handmaid to heavenly sovereignty" (Registr. iii. 61(65) ad Mauric. Aug.).

11. From these principles was derived that unconquerable firmness shown by Gregory, which We, with the help of God, will study to imitate, resolved to defend at all costs the rights and prerogatives of which the Roman Pontificate is the guardian and the defender before God and man. But it was the same Gregory who wrote to the patriarchs of Alexandria and Antioch: When the rights of the Church are in question, "we must show, even by our death that we do not, through love of some private interest of our own want anything contrary to the common weal" (Registr. v. 41). And to the Emperor Maurice: "He who through vainglory raises his neck against God Almighty and against the statutes of

the Fathers, shall not bend my neck to him, not even with the cutting of swords, as I trust in the same God Almighty" (Registr. v. 37). And to the Deacon Sabinian: "I am ready to die rather than permit that the Church degenerate in my days. And you know well my ways, that I am longsuffering; but when I decide not to bear any longer, I face danger with a joyful soul" (Registr. v. 6 (iv. 47)).

12. Such were the fundamental maxims which the Pontiff Gregory constantly proclaimed, and men listened to him. And thus, with Princes and peoples docile to his words, the world regained true salvation, and put itself on the path of a civilization which was noble and fruitful in blessings in proportion as it was founded on the incontrovertible dictates of reason and moral discipline, and derived its force from truth divinely revealed and from the maxims of the Gospel.

13. But in those days the people, albeit rude, ignorant, and still destitute of all civilization, were eager for life, and this no one could give except Christ, through the Church, who "came that they may have life and have it more abundantly" (John x. 10). And truly they had life and had it abundantly, precisely because as no other life but the supernatural life of souls could come from the Church, this includes in itself and gives additional vigor to all the energies of life, even in the natural order. "If the root be holy so are the branches," said St. Paul to the Gentiles, "and thou being a wild olive art ingrafted in them, and art made partaker of the root and of the fatness of the olive tree (Rom. xi. 16, 17).

14. Today, on the contrary, although the world enjoys a light so full of Christian civilization and in this respect cannot for a moment be compared with the times of Gregory, yet it seems as though it were tired of that life, which has been and

still is the chief and often the sole fount of so many bless-ings - and not merely past but present blessings. And not only does this useless branch cut itself off from the trunk, as happened in other times when heresies and schisms arose, but it first lays the ax to the root of the tree, which is the Church, and strives to dry up its vital sap that its ruin may be the surer and that it may never blossom again.

15. In this error, which is the chief one of our time and the source whence all the others spring, lies the origin of so much loss of eternal salvation among men, and of all the ruins affecting religion which we continue to lament, and of the many others which we still fear will happen if the evil be not remedied. For all supernatural order is denied, and, as a consequence, the divine intervention in the order of creation and in the government of the world and in the possibility of miracles; and when all these are taken away the foundations of the Christian religion are necessarily shaken. Men even go so far as to impugn the arguments for the existence of God, denying with unparalleled audacity and against the first principles of reason the invincible force of the proof which from the effects ascends to their cause, that is God, and to the notion of His infinite attributes. "For the invisible things of him, from the creation of the world, are clearly seen, be-ing understood by the things that are made: his eternal power also and divinity" (Rom. i. 20). The way is thus opened to other most grievous errors, equally repugnant to right reason and pernicious to good morals.

16. The gratuitous negation of the supernatural principles, proper to knowledge falsely so called, has actually become the postulate of a historical criticism equally false. Every-thing that relates in any way to the supernatural order, either as belonging to it, constituting it, presupposing it, or merely

finding its explanation in it, is erased without further investigation from the pages of history. Such are the Divinity of Jesus Christ, His Incarnation through the operation of the Holy Ghost, His Resurrection by His own power, and in general all the dogmas of our faith. Science once placed on this false road, there is no law of criticism to hold it back; and it cancels at its own caprice from the holy books everything that does not suit it or that it believes to be opposed to the pre-established theses it wishes to demonstrate. For take away the supernatural order and the story of the origin of the Church must be built on quite another foundation, and hence the innovators handle as they list the monuments of history, forcing them to say what they wish them to say, and not what the authors of those monuments meant.

17. Many are captivated by the great show of erudition which is held out before them, and by the apparently convincing force of the proofs adduced, so that they either lose the faith or feel that it is greatly shaken in them. There are many too, firm in the faith, who accuse critical science of being destructive, while in itself it is innocent and a sure element of investigation when rightly applied. Both the former and the latter fail to see that they start from a false hypothesis, that is to say, from science falsely so called, which logically forces them to conclusions equally false. For given a false philosophical principle everything deduced from it is vitiated. But these errors will never be effectively refuted, unless by bringing about a change of front, that is to say, unless those in error be forced to leave the field of criticism in which they consider themselves firmly entrenched for the legitimate field of philosophy through the abandonment of which they have fallen into their errors.

18. Meanwhile, however, it is painful to have to apply to

men not lacking in acumen and application the rebuke addressed by St. Paul to those who fail to rise from earthly things to the things that are invisible: "They became vain in their thoughts and their foolish heart was darkened; for professing themselves to be wise they became fools" (Rom. i. 21, 22). And surely foolish is the only name for him who consumes all his intellectual forces in building upon sand.

19. Not less deplorable are the injuries which accrue from this negation to the moral life of individuals and of civil society. Take away the principle that there is anything divine outside this visible world, and you take away all check upon unbridled passions even of the lowest and most shameful kind, and the minds that become slaves to them riot in disorders of every species. "God gave them up to the desires of their heart, unto uncleanness, to dishonor their own bodies among themselves" (Rom. i. 24). You are well aware, Venerable Brethren, how truly the plague of depravity triumphs on all sides, and how the civil authority wherever it fails to have recourse to the means of help offered by the supernatural order, finds itself quite unequal to the task of checking it. Nay, authority will never be able to heal other evils as long as it forgets or denies that all power comes from God. The only check a government can command in this case is that of force; but force cannot be constantly employed, nor is it always available yet the people continue to be undermined as by a secret disease, they become discontented with everything, they proclaim the right to act as they please, they stir up rebellions, they provoke revolutions, often of extreme violence, in the State; they overthrow all rights human and divine. Take away God, and all respect for civil laws, all regard for even the most necessary institutions disappears; justice is scouted; the very liberty that belongs to the law of nature is trodden underfoot; and men go so far as to destroy

the very structure of the family, which is the first and firmest foundation of the social structure. The result is that in these days hostile to Christ, it has become more difficult to apply the powerful remedies which the Redeemer has put into the hands of the Church in order to keep the peoples within the lines of duty.

20. Yet there is no salvation for the world but in Christ: "For there is no other name under heaven given to men whereby we may be saved" (Acts iv. 12). To Christ then we must return. At His feet we must prostrate ourselves to hear from His divine mouth the words of eternal life, for He alone can show us the way of regeneration, He alone teach us the truth, He alone restore life to us. It is He who has said: "I am the way, the truth, and the life" (John xiv. 16). Men have once more attempted to work here below without Him, they have begun to build up the edifice after rejecting the corner stone, as the Apostle Peter rebuked the executioners of Jesus for doing. And lo! The pile that has been raised again crumbles and falls upon the heads of the builders, crushing them. But Jesus remains forever the corner stone of human society, and again the truth becomes apparent that without Him there is no salvation: "This is the stone which has been rejected by you, the builders, and which has become the head of the corner, neither is there salvation in any other" (Acts iv. 11, 12).

21. From all this you will easily see, Venerable Brethren, the absolute necessity imposed upon every one of us to receive with all the energy of our souls and with all the means at our disposal, this supernatural life in every branch of society - in the poor working man who earns his morsel of bread by the sweat of his brow, from morning to night, and in the great ones of the earth who preside over the destiny of nations. We must, above all else, have recourse to prayer, both public and

private, to implore the mercies of the Lord and His powerful assistance. "Lord, save us - we perish" (Matthew viii. 25), we must repeat like the Apostles when buffeted by the storm.

22. But this is not enough. Gregory rebukes the bishop who, through love of spiritual solitude and prayer, fails to go out into the battlefield to combat strenuously for the cause of the Lord: "The name of bishop, which he bears, is an empty one." And rightly so, for men's intellects are to be enlightened by continual preaching of the truth, and errors are to be efficaciously refuted by the principles of true and solid philosophy and theology, and by all the means provided by the genuine progress of historical investigation. It is still more necessary to inculcate properly on the minds of all the moral maxims taught by Jesus Christ, so that everybody may learn to conquer himself, to curb the passions of the mind, to stifle pride, to live in obedience to authority, to love justice, to show charity towards all, to temper with Christian love the bitterness of social inequalities, to detach the heart from the goods of the world, to live contented with the state in which Providence has placed us, while striving to better it by the fulfillment of our duties, to thirst after the future life in the hope of eternal reward. But, above all, is it necessary that these principles be instilled and made to penetrate into the heart, so that true and solid piety may strike root there, and all, both as men and as Christians, may recognize by their acts, as well as by their words, the duties of their state and have recourse with filial confidence to the Church and her ministers to obtain from them pardon for their sins, to receive the strengthening grace of the Sacraments, and to regulate their lives according to the laws of Christianity.

23. With these chief duties of the spiritual ministry it is necessary to unite the charity of Christ, and when this moves us

there will be nobody in affliction who will not be consoled by us, no tears that will not be dried by our hands, no need that will not be relieved by us. To the exercise of this charity let us dedicate ourselves wholly; let all our own affairs give way before it, let our personal interests and convenience be set aside for it, making ourselves "all things to all men" (I Cor. ix. 22), to gain all men to the Lord, giving up our very life itself, after the example of Christ: "The good shepherd gives his life for his sheep (John x. 11).

24. These precious admonitions abound in the pages which the Pontiff St. Gregory has left written, and they are expressed with far greater force in the manifold examples of his admirable life.

25. Now since all this springs necessarily both from the nature of the principles of Christian revelation, and from the intrinsic properties which Our Apostolate should have, you see clearly, Venerable Brethren, how mistaken are those who think they are doing service to the Church, and producing fruit for the salvation of souls, when by a kind of prudence of the flesh they show themselves liberal in concessions to science falsely so called, under the fatal illusion that they are thus able more easily to win over those in error, but really with the continual danger of being themselves lost. The truth is one, and it cannot be halved; it lasts forever, and is not subject to the vicissitudes of the times. "Jesus Christ, today and yesterday, and the same forever" (Hebr. xiii. 8).

26. And so too are all they seriously mistaken who, occupying themselves with the welfare of the people, and especially upholding the cause of the lower classes, seek to promote above all else the material well-being of the body and of life, but are utterly silent about their spiritual welfare and

the very serious duties which their profession as Christians enjoins upon them. They are not ashamed to conceal sometimes, as though with a veil, certain fundamental maxims of the Gospel, for fear lest otherwise the people refuse to hear and follow them. It will certainly be the part of prudence to proceed gradually in laying down the truth, when one has to do with men completely strangers to us and completely separated from God. "Before using the steel, let the wounds be felt with a light hand," as Gregory said (Registr. v. 44 (18) ad Joannem episcop.). But even this carefulness would sink to mere prudence of the flesh, were it proposed as the rule of constant and everyday action - all the more since such a method would seem not to hold in due account that Divine Grace which sustains the sacerdotal ministry and which is given not only to those who exercise this ministry, but to all the faithful of Christ in order that our words and our action may find an entrance into their heart. Gregory did not at all understand this prudence, either in the preaching of the Gospel, or in the many wonderful works undertaken by him to relieve misery. He did constantly what the Apostles had done, for they, when they went out for the first time into the world to bring into it the name of Christ, repeated the saying: "We preach Christ crucified, a scandal for the Jews, a folly for the Gentiles" (I Cor. i. 23). If ever there was a time in which human prudence seemed to offer the only expedient for obtaining something in a world altogether unprepared to receive doctrines so new, so repugnant to human passions, so opposed to the civilization, then at its most flourishing period, of the Greeks and the Romans, that time was certainly the epoch of the preaching of the faith. But the Apostles disdained such prudence, because they understood well the precept of God: "It pleased God by the foolishness of our preaching to save them that believe (I Cor. i. 21). And as it ever was, so it is today, this foolishness "to them that are saved, that is, to us, is the power of God" (I Cor. i. 18). The scandal of the Crucified will ever furnish us in the future, as it has done in the past, with the most potent of all weapons; now as of yore in that sign we shall find victory.

27. But, Venerable Brethren, this weapon will lose much of its efficacy or be altogether useless in the hands of men not accustomed to the interior life with Christ, not educated in the school of true and solid piety, not thoroughly inflamed with zeal for the glory of God and for the propagation of His kingdom. So keenly did Gregory feel this necessity that he used the greatest care in creating bishops and priests animated by a great desire for the divine glory and for the true welfare of souls. And this was the intent he had before him in his book on the Pastoral Rule, wherein are gathered together the laws regulating the formation of the clergy and the government of bishops - laws most suitable not for his times only but for our own. Like an "Argus full of light," says his biographer, "he moved all round the eyes of his pastoral solicitude through all the extent of the world" (Joann. Diac., lib ii. c. 55), to discover and correct the failings and the negligence of the clergy. Nay, he trembled at the very thought that barbarism and immortality might obtain a footing in the life of the clergy, and he was deeply moved and gave himself no peace whenever he learned of some infraction of the disciplinary laws of the Church, and immediately administered admonition and correction, threatening canonical penalties on transgressors, sometimes immediately applying these penalties himself, and again removing the unworthy from their offices without delay and without human respect.

28. Moreover, he inculcated the maxims which we frequently find in his writings in such form as this: "In what frame of mind does one enter upon the office of mediator between God and man who is not conscious of being familiar with

53

grace through a meritorious life?" (Reg. Past.i. 10). "U passion lives in his actions, with what presumption does he hasten to cure the wound, when he wears a scar on his very face?" (Reg. Past. i. 9). What fruit can be expected for the salvation of souls if the apostles "combat in their lives what they preach in their words?" (Reg. Past. i. 2). "Truly he cannot remove the delinquencies of others who is himself ravaged by the same" (Reg. Past. i. 11).

29. The picture of the true priest, as Gregory understands and describes him, is the man "who, dying to all passions of the flesh, already lives spiritually; who has no thought for the prosperity of the world; who has no fear of adversity; who desires only internal things; who does not permit himself to desire what belongs to others but is liberal of his own; who is all bowels of compassion and inclines to forgiveness, but in forgiveness never swerves unduly from the perfection of righteousness; who never commits unlawful actions, but deplores as though they were his own the unlawful actions of others; who with all affection of the heart compassionates the weakness of others, and rejoices in the prosperity of his neighbor as in his own profit; who in all his doings so renders himself a model for others as to have nothing whereof to be ashamed, at least, as regards his external actions; who studies so to live that he may be able to water the parched hearts of his neighbors with the waters of doctrine; who knows through the use of prayer and through his own experience that he can obtain from the Lord what he asks" (Reg. Past. i. 10).

30. How much thought, therefore, Venerable Brethren, must the Bishop seriously take with himself and in the presence of God before laying hands on young levites! "Let him never dare, either as an act of favor to anybody or in response to

petitions made to him, to promote any one to sacred orders whose life and actions do not furnish a guarantee of worthiness" (Registr. v 63 (58) ad universos episcopos per Hellad.) With what deliberation should he reflect before entrusting the work of the apostolate to newly ordained priests! If they be not duly tried under the vigilant guardianship of more prudent priests, if there be not abundant evidence of their morality, of their inclination for spiritual exercises, of their prompt obedience to all the norms of action which are suggested by ecclesiastical custom or proved by long experience, or imposed by those whom "the Holy Ghost has placed as bishops to rule the Church of God" (Acts xx. 28), they will exercise the sacerdotal ministry not for the salvation but for the ruin of the Christian people. For they will provoke discord, and excite rebellion, more or less tacit, thus offering to the world the sad spectacle of something like division amongst us, whereas in truth these deplorable incidents are but the pride and unruliness of a few. Oh! let those who stir up discord be altogether removed from every office. Of such apostles the Church has no need; they are not apostles of Jesus Christ Crucified but of themselves.

31. We seem to see still present before Our eyes the Holy Pontiff Gregory at the Lateran Council, surrounded by a great number of bishops from all parts of the world. Oh, how fruitful is the exhortation that falls from his lips on the duties of the clergy! How his heart is consumed with zeal! His words are as lightning rending the perverse, as scourges striking the indolent, as flames of divine love gently enfolding the most fervent. Read that wonderful homily of Gregory, Venerable Brethren, and have it read and meditated by your clergy, especially during the annual retreat (Hom. in Evang. i. 17).

32. Among other things, with unspeakable sorrow he exclaims: "Lo, the world is full of priests, but rare indeed it is to find a worker in the hands of God; we do indeed assume the priestly office, but the obligation of the office we do not fulfill" (Hom. in Evang. n. 3). What force the Church would have today could she count a worker in every priest! What abundant fruit would the supernatural life of the Church produce in souls were it efficaciously promoted by all. Gregory succeeded in his own times in strenuously stimulating this spirit of energetic action, and such was the impulse given by him that the same spirit was kept alive during the succeeding ages. The whole mediaeval period bears what may be called the Gregorian imprint; almost everything it had indeed came to it from the Pontiff - the rule of ecclesiastical government, the manifold phases of charity and philanthropy in its social institutions, the principles of the most perfect Christian asceticism and of monastic life, the arrangement of the liturgy and the art of sacred music.

33. The times are indeed greatly changed. But, as We have more than once repeated, nothing is changed in the life of the Church. From her Divine Founder she has inherited the virtue of being able to supply at all times, however much they may differ, all that is required not only for the spiritual welfare of souls, which is the direct object of her mission, but also everything that aids progress in true civilization, for this follows as a natural consequence of that same mission.

34. For it cannot be but that the truths of the supernatural order, of which the Church is the depository, promote also everything that is true, good, and beautiful in the order of nature, and this the more efficaciously in proportion as these truths are traced to the supreme principle of all truth, goodness and beauty, which is God.

35. Human science gains greatly from revelation, for the latter opens out new horizons and makes known sooner other truths of the natural order, and because it opens the true road to investigation and keeps it safe from errors of application and of method. Thus does the lighthouse show many things they otherwise would not see, while it points out the rocks on which the vessel would suffer shipwreck.

36. And since, for our moral discipline, the Divine Redeemer proposes as our supreme model of perfection His heavenly Father (Matthew v. 48), that is, the Divine goodness itself, who can fail to see the mighty impulse thence accruing to the ever more perfect observance of the natural law inscribed in our hearts, and consequently to the greater welfare of the individual, the family, and universal society? The ferocity of the barbarians was thus transformed to gentleness, woman was freed from subjection, slavery was repressed, order was restored in the due and reciprocal independence upon one another of the various classes of society, justice was recognized, the true liberty of souls was proclaimed, and social and domestic peace assured.

37. Finally, the arts modeled on the supreme exemplar of all beauty which is God Himself, from whom is derived all the beauty to be found in nature, are more securely withdrawn from vulgar concepts and more efficaciously rise towards the ideal, which is the life of all art. And how fruitful of good has been the principle of employing them in the service of divine worship and of offering to the Lord everything that is deemed to be worthy of him, by reason of its richness, its goodness, its elegance of form. This principle has created sacred art, which became and still continues to be the foundation of all profane art. We have recently touched upon this in a special motu proprio, when speaking of the restoration

57

of the Roman Chant according to the ancient tradition and of sacred music. And the same rules are applicable to the other arts, each in its own sphere, so that what has been said of the Chant may also be said of painting, sculpture, architecture; and towards all these most noble creations of genius the Church has been lavish of inspiration and encouragement. The whole human race, fed on this sublime ideal, raises magnificent temples, and here in the House of God, as in its own house, lifts up its heart to heavenly things in the midst of the treasures of all beautiful art, with the majesty of liturgical ceremony, and to the accompaniment of the sweetest of song.

38. All these benefits, We repeat, the action of the Pontiff St. Gregory succeeded in attaining in his own time and in the centuries that followed; and these, too, it will be possible to attain today, by virtue of the intrinsic efficacy of the principles which should guide us and of the means we have at our disposal, while preserving with all zeal the good which by the grace of God is still left us and "restoring in Christ" (Ephes. i. 10) all that has unfortunately lapsed from the right rule.

39. We are glad to be able to close these Our Letters with the very words with which St. Gregory concluded his memorable exhortation in the Lateran Council: "These things, Brethren, you should meditate with all solicitude yourselves and at the same time propose for the meditation of your neighbor. Prepare to restore to God the fruit of the ministry you have received. But everything we have indicated for you we shall obtain much better by prayer than by our discourse. Let us pray: O God, by whose will we have been called as pastors among the people, grant, we beseech Thee, that we may enabled to be in Thy sight what we are said to be by the

mouths of men" (Hom. cit., ii. 18).

40. And while We trust by the intercession of the holy Pontiff Gregory that God may graciously hear Our prayer, We impart to all of you, Venerable Brethren, and to your clergy and people the Apostolic benediction with all the affection of Our heart, as a pledge of heavenly favors and in token of Our paternal good will.

Given at Rome at St. Peter's on March 12, of the year 1904, on the feast of St. Gregory I. Pope and Doctor of the Church, in the first year of Our Pontificate.

PIUS X

ACERBO NIMIS
ENCYCLICAL OF POPE PIUS X
ON TEACHING CHRISTIAN DOCTRINE

TO THE PATRIARCHS, PRIMATES, ARCHBISHOPS, BISHOPS, AND OTHER ORDINARIES IN PEACE AND COMMUNION WITH THE APOSTOLIC SEE

Venerable Brethren,
Health and the Apostolic Blessing.

At this very troublesome and difficult time, the hidden designs of God have conducted Our poor strength to the office of Supreme pastor, to rule the entire flock of Christ. The enemy has, indeed, long been prowling about the fold and attacking it with such subtle cunning that now, more than ever before, the prediction of the Apostle to the elders of the Church of Ephesus seems to be verified: "I know that . . . fierce wolves will get in among you, and will not spare the flock." Those who still are zealous for the glory of God are seeking the causes and reasons for this decline in religion. Coming to a different explanation, each points out, according to his own view, a different plan for the protection and restoration of the kingdom of God on earth. But it seems to Vs, Venerable Brethren, that while we should not overlook other considerations, We are forced to agree with those who hold that the chief cause of the present indifference and, as it were, infirmity of soul, and the serious evils that result from it, is to be found above all in ignorance of things divine. This is fully in accord with what God Himself declared through the Prophet Osee: "And there is no knowledge of God in the land. Cursing and lying and killing and theft and adultery have overflowed: and blood hath touched blood. Thereafter shall the land mourn, and everyone that dwelleth in it shall languish."

2. It is a common complaint, unfortunately too well founded, that there are large numbers of Christians in our own time who are entirely ignorant of those truths necessary for salvation. And when we mention Christians, We refer not only to the masses or to those in the lower walks of life - for these find some excuse for their ignorance in the fact that the demands of their harsh employers hardly leave them time to take care of themselves or of their dear ones - but We refer to those especially who do not lack culture or talents and, indeed, are possessed of abundant knowledge regarding things of the world but live rashly and imprudently with regard to religion. It is hard to find words to describe how profound is the darkness in which they are engulfed and, what is most deplorable of all, how tranquilly they repose there. They rarely give thought to God, the Supreme Author and Ruler of all things, or to the teachings of the faith of Christ. They know nothing of the Incarnation of the Word of God, nothing of the perfect restoration of the human race which He accomplished. Grace, the greatest of the helps for attaining eternal things, the Holy Sacrifice and the Sacraments by which we obtain grace, are entirely unknown to them. They have no conception of the malice and baseness of sin; hence they show no anxiety to avoid sin or to renounce it. And so they arrive at life's end in such a condition that, lest all hope of salvation be lost, the priest is obliged to give in the last few moments of life a summary teaching of religion, a time which should be devoted to stimulating the soul to greater love for God. And even this as too often happens only when the dying man is not so sinfully ignorant as to look upon the ministration of the priest as useless, and then calmly faces the fearful passage to eternity without making his peace with God. And so Our Predecessor, Benedict XIV, had just cause

to write: "We declare that a great number of those who are condemned to eternal punishment suffer that everlasting calamity because of ignorance of those mysteries of faith which must be known and believed in order to be numbered among the elect."

3. There is then, Venerable Brethren, no reason for wonder that the corruption of morals and depravity of life is already so great, and ever increasingly greater, not only among uncivilized peoples but even in those very nations that are called Christian. The Apostle Paul, writing to the Ephesians, repeatedly admonished them in these words: "But immorality and every uncleanness or covetousness, let it not even be named among you, as become saints; or obscenity or foolish talk." He also places the foundation of holiness and sound morals upon a knowledge of divine things - which holds in check evil desires: "See to it therefore, brethren, that you walk with care: not as unwise but as wise. . . Therefore, do not become foolish, but understand what the will of the Lord is." And rightly so. For the will of man retains but little of that divinely implanted love of virtue and righteousness by which it was, as it were, attracted strongly toward the real and not merely apparent good. Disordered by the stain of the first sin, and almost forgetful of God, its Author, it improperly turns every affection to a love of vanity and deceit. This erring will, blinded by its own evil desires, has need therefore of a guide to lead it back to the paths of justice whence it has so unfortunately strayed. The intellect itself is this guide, which need not be sought elsewhere, but is provided by nature itself. It is a guide, though, that, if it lack its companion light, the knowledge of divine things, will be only an instance of the blind leading the blind so that both will fall into the pit. The holy king David, praising God for the light of truth with which He had illumined the intel-

lect, exclaimed: "The light of Thy countenance, O Lord, is signed upon us." Then he described the effect of this light by adding: "Thou hast given gladness in my heart," gladness, that is, which enlarges our heart so that it runs in the way of God's Commandments.

4. All this becomes evident on a little reflection. Christian teaching reveals God and His infinite perfection with far greater clarity than is possible by the human faculties alone. Nor is that all. This same Christian teaching also commands us to honor God by faith, which is of the mind, by hope, which is of the will, by love, which is of the heart; and thus the whole man is subjected to the supreme Maker and Ruler of all things. The truly remarkable dignity of man as the son of the heavenly Father, in Whose image he is formed, and with Whom he is destined to live in eternal happiness, is also revealed only by the doctrine of Jesus Christ. From this very dignity, and from man's knowledge of it, Christ showed that men should love one another as brothers, and should live here as become children of light, "not of revelry and drunkenness, not in debauchery and wantonness, not in strife and jealousy." He also bids us to place all our anxiety and care in the hands of God, for He will provide for us; He tells us to help the poor, to do good to those who hate us, and to prefer the eternal welfare of the soul to the temporal goods of this life. Without wishing to touch on every detail, nevertheless is it not true that the proud man is urged and commanded by the teaching of Christ to strive for humility, the source of true glory? "Whoever, therefore, humbles himself. . . he is the greatest in the kingdom of heaven." From that same teaching we learn prudence of the spirit, and thereby we avoid prudence of the flesh; we learn justice, by which we give to every man his due; fortitude, which prepares us to endure all things and with steadfast heart suffer all things for

the sake of God and eternal happiness; and, last of all, temperance through which we cherish even poverty borne out of love for God, nay, we even glory in the cross itself, unmindful of its shame. In fine, Christian teaching not only bestows on the intellect the light by which it attains truth, but from it our will draws that ardor by which we are raised up to God and joined with Him in the practice of virtue.

5. We by no means wish to conclude that a perverse will and unbridled conduct may not be joined with a knowledge of religion. Would to God that facts did not too abundantly prove the contrary! But We do maintain that the will cannot be upright nor the conduct good when the mind is shrouded in the darkness of crass ignorance. A man who walks with open eyes may, indeed, turn aside from the right path, but a blind man is in much more imminent danger of wandering away. Furthermore, there is always some hope for a reform of perverse conduct so long as the light of faith is not entirely extinguished; but if lack of faith is added to depraved morality because of ignorance, the evil hardly admits of remedy, and the road to ruin lies open.

6. How many and how grave are the consequences of ignorance in matters of religion! And on the other hand, how necessary and how beneficial is religious instruction! It is indeed vain to expect a fulfillment of the duties of a Christian by one who does not even know them.

7. We must now consider upon whom rests the obligation to dissipate this most pernicious ignorance and to impart in its stead the knowledge that is wholly indispensable. There can be no doubt, Venerable Brethren, that this most important duty rests upon all who are pastors of souls. On them, by command of Christ, rest the obligations of knowing and

of feeding the flocks committed to their care; and to feed implies, first of all, to teach. "I will give you pastors according to my own heart," God promised through Jeremias, "and they shall feed you with knowledge and doctrine." Hence the Apostle Paul said: "Christ did not send me to baptize, but to preach the gospel," thereby indicating that the first duty of all those who are entrusted in any way with the government of the Church is to instruct the faithful in the things of God.

8. We do not think it necessary to set forth here the praises of such instruction or to point out how meritorious it is in God's sight. If, assuredly, the alms with which we relieve the needs of the poor are highly praised by the Lord, how much more precious in His eyes, then, will be the zeal and labor expended in teaching and admonishing, by which we provide not for the passing needs of the body but for the eternal profit of the soul! Nothing, surely, is more desirable, nothing more acceptable to Jesus Christ, the Savior of souls, Who testifies of Himself through Isaias: "To bring good news to the poor he has sent me."

9. Here then it is well to emphasize and insist that for a priest there is no duty more grave or obligation more binding than this. Who, indeed, will deny that knowledge should be joined to holiness of life in the priest? "For the lips of the priest shall keep knowledge." The Church demands this knowledge of those who are to be ordained to the priesthood. Why? Because the Christian people expect from them knowledge of the divine law, and it was for that end that they were sent by God. "And they shall seek the law at his mouth; because he is the angel of the Lord of hosts." Thus the bishop speaking to the candidates for the priesthood in the ordination ceremony says: "Let your teaching be a spiritual remedy for God's people; may they be worthy fellow-

workers of our order; and thus meditating day and night on His law, they may believe what they read, and teach what they shall believe."

10. If what We have just said is applicable to all priests, does it not apply with much greater force to those who possess the title and the authority of parish priests, and who, by virtue of their rank and in a sense by virtue of a contract, hold the office of pastors of souls? These are, to a certain extent, the pastors and teachers appointed by Christ in order that the faithful might not be as "children, tossed to and fro and carried about by every wind of doctrine devised in the wickedness of men," but that practicing "the truth in love," they may, "grow up in all things in him who is the head, Christ."
11. For this reason the Council of Trent, treating of the duties of pastors of souls, decreed that their first and most important work is the instruction of the faithful. It therefore prescribes that they shall teach the truths of religion on Sundays and on the more solemn feast days; moreover during the holy seasons of Advent and Lent they are to give such instruction every day or at least three times a week. This, however, was not considered enough. The Council provided for the instruction of youth by adding that the pastors, either personally or through others, must explain the truths of religion at least on Sundays and feast days to the children of the parish, and inculcate obedience to God and to their parents. When the Sacraments are to be administered, it enjoins upon pastors the duty to explain their efficacy in plain and simple language.

12. These prescriptions of the Council of Trent have been summarized and still more clearly defined by Our Predecessor, Benedict XIV, in his Constitution Esti minime. "Two chief obligations," he wrote, "have been imposed by the

Council of Trent on those who have the care of souls: first, that of preaching the things of God to the people on the feast days; and second, that of teaching the rudiments of faith and of the divine law to the youth and others who need such instruction." Here the wise Pontiff rightly distinguishes between these two duties: one is what is commonly known as the explanation of the Gospel and the other is the teaching of Christian doctrine. Perhaps there are some who, wishing to lessen their labors, would believe that the homily on the Gospel can take the place of catechetical instruction. But for one who reflects a moment, such is obviously impossible. The sermon on the holy Gospel is addressed to those who should have already received knowledge of the elements of faith. It is, so to speak, bread broken for adults. Catechetical instruction, on the other hand, is that milk which the Apostle Peter wished the faithful to desire in all simplicity like new-born babes.

13. The task of the catechist is to take up one or other of the truths of faith or of Christian morality and then explain it in all its parts; and since amendment of life is the chief aim of his instruction, the catechist must needs make a comparison between what God commands us to do and what is our actual conduct. After this, he will use examples appropriately taken from the Holy Scriptures, Church history, and the lives of the saints - thus moving his hearers and clearly pointing out to them how they are to regulate their own conduct. He should, in conclusion, earnestly exhort all present to dread and avoid vice and to practice virtue.

14. We are indeed aware that the work of teaching the Catechism is unpopular with many because as a rule it is deemed of little account and for the reason that it does not lend itself easily to the winning of public praise. But this in Our opin-

ion is a judgment based on vanity and devoid of truth. We do not disapprove of those pulpit orators who, out of genuine zeal for the glory of God, devote themselves to defense of the faith and to its spread, or who eulogize the saints of God. But their labor presupposes labor of another kind, that of the catechist. And so if this be lacking, then the foundation is wanting; and they labor in vain who build the house. Too often it happens that ornate sermons which receive the applause of crowded congregations serve but to tickle the ears and fail utterly to touch the hearts of the hearers. Catechetical instruction, on the other hand, plain and simple though it be, is the word of which God Himself speaks through the lips of the prophet Isaias: "And as the rain and the snow come down from heaven, and return no more thither, but soak the earth and water it, and make it to spring and give seed to the sower and bread to the eater: so shall my word be, which shall go forth from my mouth. It shall not return to me void, but it shall do whatsoever I please and shall prosper in the things for which I sent it." We believe the same may be said of those priests who work hard to produce books which explain the truths of religion. They are surely to be commended for their zeal, but how many are there who read these works and take from them a fruit commensurate with the labor and intention of the writers? The teaching of the Catechism, on the other hand, when rightly done, never fails to profit those who listen to it.

15. In order to enkindle the zeal of the ministers of God, We again insist on the need to reach the ever-increasing numbers of those who know nothing at all of religion, or who possess at most only such knowledge of God and Christian truths as befits idolaters. How many there are, alas, not only among the young, but among adults and those advanced in years, who know nothing of the chief mysteries of faith; who on

hearing the name of Christ can only ask? "Who is he. . . that I may believe in him?" In consequence of this ignorance, they do not consider it a crime to excite and nourish hatred against their neighbor, to enter into most unjust contracts, to do business in dishonest fashion, to hold the funds of others at an exorbitant interest rate, and to commit other iniquities no less reprehensible. They are, moreover, ignorant of the law of Christ which not only condemns immoral actions but also forbids deliberate immoral thoughts and desires. Even when for some reason or other they avoid sensual pleasures, they nevertheless entertain evil thoughts without the least scruple, thereby multiplying their sins above the number of the hairs of the head. These persons are found, we deem it necessary to repeat, not merely among the poorer classes of the people or in sparsely settled districts, but also among those in the higher walks of life, even, indeed, among those puffed up with learning, who, relying upon a vain erudition, feel free to ridicule religion and to "deride whatever they do not know."

16. Now, if we cannot expect to reap a harvest when no seed has been planted, how can we hope to have a people with sound morals if Christian doctrine has not been imparted to them in due time? It follows, too, that if faith languishes in our days, if among large numbers it has almost vanished, the reason is that the duty of catechetical teaching is either fulfilled very superficially or altogether neglected. It will not do to say, in excuse, that faith is a free gift of God bestowed upon each one at Baptism. True enough, when we are baptized in Christ, the habit of faith is given, but this most divine seed, if left entirely to itself, by its own power, so to speak, is not like the mustard seed which "grows up. . . and puts out great branches." Man has the faculty of understanding at his birth, but he also has need of his mother's

word to awaken it, as it were, and to make it active. So too, the Christian, born again of water and the Holy Spirit, has faith within him, but he requires the word of the teaching Church to nourish and develop it and to make it bear fruit. Thus wrote the Apostle: "Faith then depends on hearing, and hearing on the word of Christ"; and to show the necessity of instruction, he added, "How are they to hear, if no one preaches?"

17. What We have said so far demonstrates the supreme importance of religious instruction. We ought, therefore, to do all that lies in our power to maintain the teaching of Christian doctrine with full vigor, and where such is neglected, to restore it; for in the words of Our Predecessor, Benedict XIV, "There is nothing more effective than catechetical instruction to spread the glory of God and to secure the salvation of souls."

18. We, therefore, Venerable Brethren, desirous of fulfilling this most important obligation of Our Teaching Office, and likewise wishing to introduce uniformity everywhere in so weighty a matter, do by Our Supreme Authority enact the following regulations and strictly command that they be observed and carried out in all dioceses of the world.

19. I. On every Sunday and holy day, with no exception, throughout the year, all parish priests and in general all those having the care of souls, shall instruct the boys and girls, for the space of an hour from the text of the Catechism on those things they must believe and do in order to attain salvation.

20. II. At certain times throughout the year, they shall prepare boys and girls to receive properly the Sacraments of Penance and Confirmation, by a continued instruction over a

period of days.

21. III. With a very special zeal, on every day in Lent and, if necessary, on the days following Easter, they shall instruct with the use of apt illustrations and exhortations the youth of both sexes to receive their first Communion in a holy manner.

22. IV. In each and every parish the society known as the Confraternity of Christian Doctrine is to be canonically established. Through this Confraternity, the pastors, especially in places where there is a scarcity of priests, will have lay helpers in the teaching of the Catechism, who will take up the work of imparting knowledge both from a zeal for the glory of God and in order to gain the numerous Indulgences granted by the Sovereign Pontiffs.

23. V. In the larger cities, and especially where universities, colleges and secondary schools are located, let classes in religion be organized to instruct in the truths of faith and in the practice of Christian life the youths who attend the public schools from which all religious teaching is banned.

24. VI. Since it is a fact that in these days adults need instruction no less than the young, all pastors and those having the care of souls shall explain the Catechism to the people in a plain and simple style adapted to the intelligence of their hearers. This shall be carried out on all holy days of obligation, at such time as is most convenient for the people, but not during the same hour when the children are instructed, and this instruction must be in addition to the usual homily on the Gospel which is delivered at the parochial Mass on Sundays and holy days. The catechetical instruction shall be based on the Catechism of the Council of Trent; and the mat-

ter is to be divided in such a way that in the space of four or five years, treatment will be given to the Apostles' Creed, the Sacraments, the Ten Commandments, the Lord's Prayer and the Precepts of the Church.

25. Venerable Brethren, We decree and command this by virtue of Our Apostolic Authority. It now rests with you to put it into prompt and complete execution in your respective dioceses, and by the power of your authority to see to it that these prescriptions of Ours be not neglected or, what amounts to the same thing, that they be not carried out carelessly or superficially. That this may be avoided, you must exhort and urge your pastors not to impart these instructions without having first prepared themselves in the work. Then they will not merely speak words of human wisdom, but "in simplicity and godly sincerity," imitating the example of Jesus Christ, Who, though He revealed "things hidden since the foundation of the world," yet spoke "all . . . things to the crowds in parables, and without parables . . . did not speak to them." We know that the Apostles, who were taught by the Lord, did the same; for of them Pope Saint Gregory wrote: "They took supreme care to preach to the uninstructed simple truths easy to understand, not things deep and difficult." In matters of religion, the majority of men in our times must be considered uninstructed.

26. We do not, however, wish to give the impression that this studied simplicity in imparting instruction does not require labor and meditation - on the contrary, it demands both more than any other kind of preaching. It is much easier to find a preacher capable of delivering an eloquent and elaborate discourse than a catechist who can impart a catechetical instruction which is praiseworthy in every detail. No matter what natural facility a person may have in ideas and lan-

guage, let him always remember that he will never be able to teach Christian doctrine to children or to adults without first giving himself to very careful study and preparation. They are mistaken who think that because of inexperience and lack of training of the people the work of catechizing can be performed in a slipshod fashion. On the contrary, the less educated the hearers, the more zeal and diligence must be used to adapt the sublime truths to their untrained minds; these truths, indeed, far surpass the natural understanding of the people, yet must be known by all - the uneducated and the cultured - in order that they may arrive at eternal happiness.

27. And now, Venerable Brethren, permit Us to close this letter by addressing to you these words of Moses: "If any man be on the Lord's side, let him join with me." We pray and entreat you to reflect on the great loss of souls due solely to ignorance of divine things. You have doubtless accomplished many useful and most praiseworthy works in your respective dioceses for the good of the flock entrusted to your care, but before all else, and with all possible zeal and diligence and care, see to it and urge on others that the knowledge of Christian doctrine pervades and imbues fully and deeply the minds of all. Here, using the words of the Apostle Peter, We say, "According to the gift that each has received, administer it to one another as good stewards of the manifold grace of God."

28. Through the intercession of the Most Blessed Immaculate Virgin, may your diligent efforts be made fruitful by the Apostolic Blessing which, in token of Our affection and as a pledge of heavenly favors, We wholeheartedly impart to you and to your clergy and people.

Given at Rome, at Saint Peter's, on the fifteenth day of April, 1905, in the second year of Our Pontificate.

PIUS X

IL FERMO PROPOSITO
ENCYCLICAL OF POPE PIUS X
ON CATHOLIC ACTION IN ITALY

TO THE BISHOPS OF ITALY

Venerable Brethren,
Health and the Apostolic Blessing.

1. The firm purpose and desire which We resolved upon at
the beginning of Our Pontificate to consecrate all the energy
which the good Lord deigns to grant Us in the work of restoring all things in Christ, reawakens in Our heart a great
trust in the all-powerful grace of God. Without that grace We
can neither plan nor undertake anything great or fruitful for
the good of souls here below. At the same time, however, We
feel more than ever the need of being upheld unanimously
and constantly in this venture both by you, Venerable Brethren, called to participate in Our pastoral office, as well as
by all the clergy and faithful committed to your care. Truly,
all of us in the Church are called to form that unique Body,
whose Head is Christ; "closely joined," as the Apostle Paul
teaches, "and knit together through every joint of the system
according to the functioning in due measure of each single
part." In such a way the Body increases and gradually per-
fects itself in the bond of charity. Now, if in this work of
"building up the body of Christ" it is Our primary duty to
teach, to point out the correct way to follow, to propose the
means to be used, to admonish and paternally exhort, it is
also the duty of Our beloved children, dispersed throughout
the world, to heed Our words, to carry them out first of all
in their own lives, and to aid in their effective fulfillment
in others, each one according to the grace of God received,
according to his state in life and duties, and according to the

zeal which inflames his heart.

2. Here We wish to recall those numerous works of zeal for the good of the Church, society, and individuals under the general name of "Catholic Action," which by the grace of God flourish throughout the world as well as in Our Italy. You well know, Venerable Brethren, how dear they are to Us and how fervently We long to see them strengthened and promoted. Not only have We spoken to not a few of you on many occasions as well as to their special representatives in Italy when they presented Us with the homage of their devotion and filial affection, but We have also published, or have had published by Our authority, various acts of which you already know. It is true that some of these, as the circumstances - truly sorrowful for Us - demanded, were directed at removing obstacles which hindered the progress of Catholic Action and caused great harm, by undisciplined tendencies, to the common good. For that reason We hesitated to offer a paternal word of comfort and encouragement to all throughout the world, in order that, only after We had removed as much as We possibly could all dangers throughout the world, the good would be able to increase and spread abroad. We are now, therefore, very happy to do so by this present letter in order to encourage everyone, for We are certain that Our words will be heard in a spirit of docility and obeyed by all.

3. The field of Catholic Action is extremely vast. In itself it does not exclude anything, in any manner, direct or indirect, which pertains to the divine mission of the Church. Accordingly one can plainly see how necessary it is for everyone to cooperate in such an important work, not only for the sanctification of his own soul, but also for the extension and increase of the Kingdom of God in individuals, families, and society; each one working according to his energy for the

good of his neighbor by the propagation of revealed truth, by the exercise of Christian virtues, by the exercise of the corporal and spiritual works of mercy. Such is the conduct worthy of God to which Saint Paul exhorts us, so as to please Him in all things, bringing forth fruits of all good works, and increasing in the knowledge of God. "May you walk worthily of God and please him in all things, bearing fruit in every good work and growing in the knowledge of God."

4. Over and above spiritual goods, however, there are many goods of the natural order over which the Church has no direct mission, although they flow as a natural consequence from her divine mission. The light of Catholic revelation is of such a nature that it diffuses itself with the greatest brilliance on every science. The force of the evangelical counsels is so powerful that it strengthens and firmly establishes the precepts of the natural law. The fruitfulness of the doctrine and morality taught by Jesus Christ is so limitless that providentially it sustains and promotes the material welfare of the individual, the family, and society. The Church, even in preaching Jesus Christ crucified, "stumbling block and foolishness to the world," has become the foremost leader and protector of civilization. She brought it wherever her apostles preached. She preserved and protected the good elements of the ancient pagan civilizations, disentangling from barbarism and educating for a new civilization the peoples who flocked to her maternal bosom. She endowed every civilization, gradually, but with a certain and always progressive step, with that excellent mark which is today universally preserved. The civilization of the world is Christian. The more completely Christian it is, the more true, more lasting and more productive of genuine fruit it is. On the other hand, the further it draws away from the Christian ideal, the more seriously the social order is endangered. By the very nature

of things, the Church has consequently become the guardian and protector of Christian society. That fact was universally recognized and admitted in other periods of history. In truth, it formed a solid foundation for civil legislation. On that very fact rested the relations between Church and State; the public recognition of the authority of the Church in those matters which touched upon conscience in any manner, the subordination of all the laws of the State to the Divine laws of the Gospel; the harmony of the two powers in securing the temporal welfare of the people in such a way that their eternal welfare did not suffer.

5. We have no need to tell you, Venerable Brethren, what prosperity and well-being, what peace and harmony, what respectful subjection to authority and what excellent government would be obtained and maintained in the world if one could see in practice the perfect ideal of Christian civilization. Granting, however, the continual battle of the flesh against the spirit, darkness against light, Satan against God, such cannot be hoped for, at least in all its fullness. Hence, raids are continually being made on the peaceful conquests of the Church. The sadness and pain these cause is accentuated by the fact that society tends more and more to be governed by principles opposed to that very Christian ideal, and is even in danger of completely falling away from God.

6. This fact, however, is no reason to lose courage. The Church well knows that the gates of hell will not prevail against her. Furthermore, she knows that she will be sorely afflicted; that her apostles are sent as lambs among wolves; that her followers will always bear the brunt of hatred and contempt, just as her Divine Founder received hatred and contempt. So the Church advances unafraid, spreading the Kingdom of God wherever she preaches and studying every

possible means she can use in regaining the losses in the kingdom already conquered. "To restore all things in Christ" has always been the Church's motto, and it is especially Our Own during these fearful moments through which we are now passing. "To restore all things" - not in any haphazard fashion, but "in Christ"; and the Apostle adds, "both those in the heavens and those on the earth." "To restore all things in Christ" includes not only what properly pertains to the divine mission of the Church, namely, leading souls to God, but also what We have already explained as flowing from that divine mission, namely, Christian civilization in each and every one of the elements composing it.

7. Since We particularly dwell on this last part of the desired restoration, you clearly see, Venerable Brethren, the services rendered to the Church by those chosen bands of Catholics who aim to unite all their forces in combating anti-Christian civilization by every just and lawful means. They use every means in repairing the serious disorders caused by it. They seek to restore Jesus Christ to the family, the school and society by re-establishing the principle that human authority represents the authority of God. They take to heart the interests of the people, especially those of the working and agricultural classes, not only by inculcating in the hearts of everybody a true religious spirit (the only true fount of consolation among the troubles of this life) but also by endeavoring to dry their tears, to alleviate their sufferings, and to improve their economic condition by wise measures. They strive, in a word, to make public laws conformable to justice and amend or suppress those which are not so. Finally, they defend and support in a true Catholic spirit the rights of God in all things and the no less sacred rights of the Church.

8. All these works, sustained and promoted chiefly by lay Catholics and whose form varies according to the needs of each country, constitute what is generally known by a distinctive and surely a very noble name: "Catholic Action," or the "Action of Catholics." At all times it came to the aid of the Church, and the Church has always cherished and blessed such help, using it in many ways according to the exigencies of the age.

9. In passing it is well to remark that it is impossible today to re-establish under the same form all the institutions which have been useful and even the only effective ones in past centuries, so numerous the new needs which changing circumstances keep producing. But the Church in its long history and on every occasion has wisely shown that she possesses the marvelous power of adapting herself to the changing conditions of civil society. Thus, while preserving the integrity and immutability of faith and morals and upholding her sacred rights, she easily bends and accommodates herself to all the unessential and accidental circumstances belonging to various stages of civilization and to the new requirements of civil society.

10. "Godliness," says Saint Paul, "is profitable in all respects, since it has the promise of the present life as well as of that which is to come." Even though Catholic Action changes in its external forms and in the means that it adapts, it always remains the same in the principles that direct it and the noble goal that it pursues. In order that Catholic Action may reach its goal, it is important to consider at this point the conditions it imposes, its nature and its goal.

11. Above all, one must be firmly convinced that the instrument is of little value if it is not adapted to the work at hand.

In regard to the things We mentioned above, Catholic Action, inasmuch as it proposes to restore all things in Christ, constitutes a real apostolate for the honor and glory of Christ Himself. To carry it out right one must have divine grace, and the apostle receives it only if he is united to Christ. Only when he has formed Jesus Christ in himself shall he more easily be able to restore Him to the family and society. Therefore, all who are called upon to direct or dedicate themselves to the Catholic cause, must be sound Catholics, firm in faith, solidly instructed in religious matters, truly submissive to the Church and especially to this supreme Apostolic See and the Vicar of Jesus Christ. They must be men of real piety, of manly virtue, and of a life so chaste and fearless that they will be a guiding example to all others. If they are not so formed it will be difficult to arouse others to do good and practically impossible to act with a good intention. The strength needed to persevere in continually bearing the weariness of every true apostolate will fail. The calumnies of enemies, the coldness and frightfully little cooperation of even good men, sometimes even the jealousy of friends and fellow workers (excusable, undoubtedly, on account of the weakness of human nature, but also harmful and a cause of discord, offense and quarrels) - all these will weaken the apostle who lacks divine grace. Only virtue, patient and firm and at the same time mild and tender, can remove or diminish these difficulties in such a way that the works undertaken by Catholic forces will not be compromised. The will of God, Saint Peter wrote the early Christians, is that by your good works you silence the foolish. "For such is the will of God, that by doing good you should put to silence the ignorance of foolish men."

12. It is also important to define clearly the works which the Catholic forces must energetically and constantly undertake.

These works must be of such evident importance that they will be appreciated by everybody. They must bear such a relation to the needs of modern society and be so well adapted to moral and material interests, especially those of the people and the poorer classes, that, while arousing in promoters of Catholic Action the greatest activity for obtaining the important and certain results which are to be looked for, they may also be readily understood and gladly welcomed by all. Since the serious problems of modern social life demand a prompt and definite solution, everyone is anxious to know and understand the different ways in which these solutions can be put into practice. Discussions of one kind or another are more and more numerous and rapidly published by the press. It is, therefore, of the greatest importance that Catholic Action seize the present moment and courageously propose its own solution, strengthening it by means of solid propaganda which at the same time will be active, intelligent, disciplined and organized against all erroneous doctrine. The goodness and justice of Christian principles, the true morality which Catholics profess, their evident unconcern for their own welfare while wishing nothing but the supreme good of others, and their open and sincere ability to foster better than all others the true economic interests of the people - these qualities cannot fail to make an impression on the minds and hearts of all who hear them, and to swell their ranks so as to form a strong and compact corps, capable of boldly resisting the opposing current and of commanding the respect of their enemies.

13. Our Predecessor, Leo XIII, of blessed memory, has pointed out, especially in that memorable encyclical "Rerum Novarum" and in later documents, the object to which Catholic Action should be particularly devoted, namely, "the practical solution of the social question according to Chris-

tian principles." Following these wise rules, We Ourselves in Our motu proprio of December 18, 1903, concerning Popular Christian Action-which in itself embraces the whole Catholic social movement - We Ourselves have laid down fundamental principles which should serve as a practical rule of action as well as a bond of harmony and charity. On these documents, therefore and within their most holy and necessary scope, Catholic Action, although varied and multiple in form while directed toward the same social good, must be regulated and united.

14. In order that this social action may continue and prosper by a necessary union of the various activities comprising it, Catholics above all must preserve a spirit of peace and harmony which can come only from a unity in understanding. On this point there cannot exist the least shadow or peradventure of a doubt, so clear and obvious are the teachings handed down by this Apostolic See, so brilliant is the light which most illustrious Catholics of every country have spread by their writings, so praiseworthy is the example of Catholics of other countries who, because of this harmony and unity of understanding, in a short time have reaped an abundant harvest.

15. To arrive at this end, in some places several of these praiseworthy works have called into being an institution of a general character which goes by the name of the "Popular Union." Experience has shown that this has been most effective. The purpose of the Popular Union has been to gather all Catholics, and especially the masses, around a common center of doctrine, propaganda, and social organization. Since, in fact, it answers a need felt in almost every country and its constitution is founded upon the very nature of things, it cannot be said to belong any more to one nation than an-

other, but is suitable to every place where the same needs are present and the same dangers arise. Its extremely popular character causes it to be most desirable and acceptable. It neither disturbs nor hinders the work of existing institutions but, on the contrary, increases their strength and efficiency. Because of its strictly personal organization, it spurs individuals to enter particular institutions, training them to perform practical and useful work, and uniting them all together in one common aim and desire.

16. Once the social center is thus established, all other institutions of an economic character concerned in various ways with the social problem will find themselves spontaneously united by their common end. At the same time, however, they will preserve their own individual structure, and in providing various needs they will still remain within the boundaries which their sphere of influence demands. At this point We are pleased to express Our satisfaction with the great good which in this regard has already been accomplished in Italy, and We feel certain that, with the help of God, much more will be done by this kind of zeal in the future to strengthen and increase the good already accomplished. The work of the Catholic Congresses and Committees is of singular merit, thanks to the intelligent activity of those capable men who plan and direct them. Such economic centers and unions, however, as We have previously stated at the end of the above mentioned Congresses, must continue to carry on in the same way and under the same expert direction.

17. For Catholic Action to be most effective it is not enough that it adapt itself to social needs only. It must also employ all those practical means which the findings of social and economic studies place in its hands. It must profit from the experience gained elsewhere. It must be vitally aware of the

conditions of civil society, and the public life of states. Otherwise it runs the risk of wasting time in searching for novelties and hazardous theories while overlooking the good, safe and tried means at hand. Again, perhaps it may propose institutions and methods belonging to other times but no longer understood by the people of the present day. Or, finally, it may go only half way, failing to use, in the measure in which they are granted, those civil rights which modern constitutions today offer all, and therefore also Catholics. In particular, the present constitution of states offers indiscriminately to all the right to influence public opinion, and Catholics, with due respect for the obligations imposed by the law of God and the precepts of the Church, can certainly use this to their advantage. In such a way they can prove themselves as capable as others (in fact, more capable than others) by cooperating in the material and civil welfare of the people. In so doing they shall acquire that authority and prestige which will make them capable of defending and promoting a higher good, namely, that of the soul.

18. These civil rights are of various kinds, even to the extent of directly participating in the political life of the country by representing the people in the legislative halls. Most serious reasons, however, dissuade Us, Venerable Brethren, from departing from that norm which Our Predecessor, Leo XIII, of blessed memory, decreed during his Pontificate. According to his decree it was universally forbidden in Italy for Catholics to participate in the legislative power. Other reasons equally grave, however, founded upon the supreme good of society which must be preserved at all costs demand that in particular cases a dispensation from the law be granted especially when you, Venerable Brethren, recognize the strict necessity of it for the good of souls and the interest of your churches, and you request such a dispensation.

19. This concession places a duty on all Catholics to prepare themselves prudently and seriously for political life in case they may be called to it. Hence it is of the utmost importance that the same activity (previously so praiseworthily planned by Catholics for the purpose of preparing themselves by means of good electoral organization for the administrative life of common and provincial councils) be extended to a suitable preparation and organization for political life. This was already recommended by the Circular of December 3, 1904, issued by the general Presidency of Economic Works in Italy. At the same time the other principles which regulate the conscience of every true Catholic must be inculcated and put into practice. Above all else he must remember to be and to act in every circumstance as a true Catholic, accepting and fulfilling public offices with the firm and constant resolution of promoting by every means the social and economic welfare of the country and particularly of the people, according to the maxims of a truly Christian civilization, and at the same time defending the supreme interests of the Church, which are those of religion and justice.

20. Such, Venerable Brethren, are the characteristics, the aim and conditions of Catholic Action, considered in its most important function, namely, the solution of the social question. For that reason it demands the most energetic attention of all the Catholic forces. By no means, however, does this exclude the existence of other activities nor does it mean that other organizations should not flourish and be promoted, for each one is directed to different particular goods of society and of the people. All are united in the work of restoring Christian civilization under its various aspects. These works, rising out of the zeal of particular persons, spreading throughout many dioceses, are sometimes grouped into federations. Since the end they foster is praiseworthy, the Chris-

tian principles they follow solid, and the means they adopt just, they are to be praised and encouraged in every way. At the same time, they must be permitted a certain freedom of organization (since it is impossible for so many people to be formed in the same mold and placed under the same direction). Organization, therefore, must arise spontaneously from the works themselves, otherwise it will only be an ephemeral building of fine architecture, but lacking a solid foundation and therefore quite unstable. Particular characteristics of different people must also be taken into consideration. Different uses, different tendencies are found in different places. It is of primary importance that the work be built on a good foundation of solid principles and maintained with earnestness and constancy. If this is the case, the method used and the form the various works take will be accidental.

21. In order to renew and increase in all the Catholic works necessary enthusiasm; in order to offer an occasion for the promoters and members of these works to see each other and become better acquainted; in order to strengthen the bond of charity, to inspire one another with a great zeal for fruitful activity, and to provide for the greater solidity and propagation of the works themselves, it will be very useful from time to time to hold general and particular Congresses of Italian Catholics, according to the norms already laid down by this Holy See. These Congresses, however, must be a solemn manifestation of the Catholic Faith and a festival of mutual harmony and peace.

22. We must touch, Venerable Brethren, on another point of extreme importance, namely, the relation of all the works of Catholic Action to ecclesiastical authority. If the teachings unfolded in the first part of this letter are thoughtfully considered it will be readily seen that all those works which

directly come to the aid of the spiritual and pastoral ministry of the Church and which labor religiously for the good of souls must in every least thing be subordinated to the authority of the Church and also to the authority of the Bishops placed by the Holy Spirit to rule the Church of God in the dioceses assigned to them. Moreover, the other works which, as We have said, are primarily designed for the restoration and promotion of true Christian civilization and which, as explained above, constitute Catholic Action, by no means may be considered as independent of the counsel and direction of ecclesiastical authority, especially since they must all conform to the principles of Christian faith and morality. At the same time it is impossible to imagine them as in opposition, more or less openly, to that same authority. Such works, however, by their very nature, should be directed with a reasonable degree of freedom, since responsible action is especially theirs in the temporal and economic affairs as well as in those matters of public administration and political life. These affairs are alien to the purely spiritual ministry. Since Catholics, on the other hand, are to raise always the banner of Christ, by that very fact they also raise the banner of the Church. Thus it is no more than right that they receive it from the hands of the Church, that the Church guard its immaculate honor, and that Catholics submit as docile, loving children to this maternal vigilance.

23. For these reasons it is evident how terribly wrong those few were who in Italy, and under Our very eyes, wanted to undertake a mission which they received neither from Us nor from any of Our Brethren in the episcopate. They promoted it not only without due homage to authority but even openly against the will of that authority, seeking to rationalize their disobedience by foolish distinctions. They said that they were undertaking their cause in the name of Christ; but

such a cause could not be Christ's since it was not built on the doctrine of the Divine Redeemer. How truly these words apply: "He who hears you, hears me; and he who rejects you, rejects me." "He who is not with me is against me; and he who does not gather with me scatters." This is a doctrine of humility, submission, filial respect. With extreme regret We had to condemn this tendency and halt by Our authority this pernicious movement which was rapidly gaining momentum. Our sorrow was increased when We saw many young people of excellent character and fervent zeal and capable of performing much good if properly directed, and who are also very dear to Us, carelessly attracted to such an erroneous program.

24. While pointing out the true nature of Catholic Action, Venerable Brethren, We cannot minimize the grave danger to which the clergy may find themselves exposed because of the conditions of the time. They may attach such importance to the material interests of the people that they will forget those more important duties of the sacred ministry.

25. The priest, raised above all men in order to accomplish the mission he has from God, must also remain above all human interests, all conflicts, all classes of society. His proper field of action is the Church. There, as ambassador of God, he preaches the truth, teaching along with respect for the rights of God respect also for the rights of every creature. In such a work he neither exposes himself to any opposition nor appears as a man of factions, ally to one group and adversary to others. In such a way he will not place himself in the danger of dissimulating the truth, of keeping silence in the conflict of certain tendencies, or of irritating exasperated souls by repeated arguments. In all these cases he would fail in his real duty. It is unnecessary to add that while treating

so often of material affairs he may find himself obligated to perform tasks harmful to himself and to the dignity of his office. He may take part in these associations, therefore, only after mature deliberation, with the consent of his Bishop, and then only in those cases when his assistance will be free from every danger and will be obviously useful.

26. This does-not diminish his zeal. The true apostle must make himself "all things to all men" in order to save all. Like the Divine Redeemer, he ought to be moved with compassion, "seeing the crowds . . . bewildered and dejected, like sheep without a shepherd." By means of the printed and spoken word, by direct participation in the above-mentioned cases, he can labor on behalf of the people according to the principles of justice and charity by favoring and promoting those institutions which propose to protect the masses from the invasion of Socialism, saving them at the same time from both economic ruin and moral and religious chaos. In this way the assistance of the clergy in the works of Catholic Action has a truly religious purpose. It will then not be a hindrance, but rather a help, to the spiritual ministry by enlarging its sphere and multiplying its results.

27. You see now, Venerable Brethren, how much We have desired to explain and inculcate these principles concerning Catholic Action which is to be sustained and promoted in Italy. It is not sufficient to point out the good; it also must be put into practice. Your own exhortations and paternal interest will render an inestimable service to the cause. Although the beginnings are humble, as is the case in all beginnings, divine grace will cause it to grow and prosper in a short time. All Our children who dedicate themselves to Catholic Action should once again listen to the advice which arises so spontaneously from Our heart. Amid the bitter sorrows which

daily surround Us, We will say with Saint Paul, "if . . . there is any comfort in Christ, any encouragement from charity, any fellowship in the Spirit, any feelings of mercy, fill up my joy by thinking alike, having the same charity, with one soul and one mind. Do nothing out of contentiousness or out of vainglory, but in humility let each one regard the others as his superiors, each one looking not to his own interests but to those of others. Have this mind in you which was also in Christ Jesus." Let Him be the beginning of all your undertakings: "Whatever you do in word or in work, do all in the name of the Lord Jesus Christ." Let Him be the end of your every word: "For from him and through him and unto him are all things. To him be the glory forever." On this day which is so reminiscent of that when the Apostles, full of the Holy Spirit, went out of the Cenacle to preach to the world the Kingdom of Christ, may the power of that same Spirit descend upon all of you. "May He bend whatever is rigid, inflame whatever has grown cold, and bring back whatever has gone astray."

28. May the Apostolic Blessing which We impart from the bottom of Our heart to you, Venerable Brethren, and your clergy and the Italian people, be a sign of divine favor and a pledge of Our very special affection.

Given at Saint Peter's, Rome, on the Feast of Pentecost, June 11, 1905, the second year of Our Pontificate.
PIUS X

VEHEMENTER NOS
ENCYCLICAL OF POPE PIUS X
ON THE FRENCH LAW OF SEPARATION

To Our Well-beloved Sons, Francois Marie Richard, Cardinal Archbishop of Paris; Victor Lucien Lecot, Cardinal Archbishop of Bordeaux; Pierre Hector Couillie, Cardinal Archbishop of Lyons; Joseph Guillaume Laboure, Cardinal Archbishop of Rennes; and to all Our Venerable Brethren, the Archbishops and Bishops, and to all the Clergy and People of France.

Venerable Brethren, Well Beloved Sons, Health and the Apostolic Benediction.

Our soul is full of sorrowful solicitude and Our heart overflows with grief, when Our thoughts dwell upon you. How, indeed, could it be otherwise, immediately after the promulgation of that law which, by sundering violently the old ties that linked your nation with the Apostolic See, creates for the Catholic Church in France a situation unworthy of her and ever to be lamented? That is, beyond question, an event of the gravest import, and one that must be deplored by all the right-minded, for it is as disastrous to society as it is to religion; but it is an event which can have surprised nobody who has paid any attention to the religious policy followed in France of late years. For you, Venerable Brethren, it will certainly have been nothing new or strange, witnesses as you have been of the many dreadful blows aimed from time to time by the public authority at religion. You have seen the sanctity and the inviolability of Christian marriage outraged by legislative acts in formal contradiction with them; the schools and hospitals laicized; clerics torn from their studies and from ecclesiastical discipline to be subjected to military service; the religious congregations dispersed and despoiled, and their members for the most part reduced to the last stage of destitution. Other legal measures which you all know have followed: the law ordaining public prayers at the beginning of each Parliamentary Session and of the assizes has been abolished; the signs of mourning traditionally observed on board the ships on Good Friday suppressed; the religious character effaced from the judicial oath; all actions and emblems serving in any way to recall the idea of religion banished from the courts, the schools, the army, the navy, and in a word from all public establishments. These measures and others still which, one after another really separated the Church from the State, were but so many steps designedly made to arrive at complete and official separation, as the authors of them have publicly and frequently admitted.

2. On the other hand the Holy See has spared absolutely no means to avert this great calamity. While it was untiring in warning those who were at the head of affairs in France, and in conjuring them over and over again to weigh well the immensity of the evils that would infallibly result from their separatist policy, it at the same time lavished upon France the most striking proofs of indulgent affection. It has then reason to hope that gratitude would have stayed those politicians on their downward path, and brought them at last to relinquish their designs. But all has been in vain - the attentions, good offices, and efforts of Our Predecessor and Ourself. The enemies of religion have succeeded at last in effecting by violence what they have long desired, in defiance of your rights as a Catholic nation and of the wishes of all who think rightly. At a moment of such gravity for the Church, therefore, filled with the sense of Our Apostolic responsibility, We have considered it Our duty to raise Our voice and to open Our heart to you, Venerable Brethren, and to your

clergy and people - to all of you whom We have ever cherished with special affection but whom We now, as is only right, love more tenderly than ever.

3. That the State must be separated from the Church is a thesis absolutely false, a most pernicious error. Based, as it is, on the principle that the State must not recognize any religious cult, it is in the first place guilty of a great injustice to God; for the Creator of man is also the Founder of human societies, and preserves their existence as He preserves our own. We owe Him, therefore, not only a private cult, but a public and social worship to honor Him. Besides, this thesis is an obvious negation of the supernatural order. It limits the action of the State to the pursuit of public prosperity during this life only, which is but the proximate object of political societies; and it occupies itself in no fashion (on the plea that this is foreign to it) with their ultimate object which is man's eternal happiness after this short life shall have run its course. But as the present order of things is temporary and subordinated to the conquest of man's supreme and absolute welfare, it follows that the civil power must not only place no obstacle in the way of this conquest, but must aid us in effecting it. The same thesis also upsets the order providentially established by God in the world, which demands a harmonious agreement between the two societies. Both of them, the civil and the religious society, although each exercises in its own sphere its authority over them. It follows necessarily that there are many things belonging to them in common in which both societies must have relations with one another. Remove the agreement between Church and State, and the result will be that from these common matters will spring the seeds of disputes which will become acute on both sides; it will become more difficult to see where the truth lies, and great confusion is certain to arise. Finally, this thesis inflicts

great injury on society itself, for it cannot either prosper or last long when due place is not left for religion, which is the supreme rule and the sovereign mistress in all questions touching the rights and the duties of men. Hence the Roman Pontiffs have never ceased, as circumstances required, to refute and condemn the doctrine of the separation of Church and State. Our illustrious predecessor, Leo XIII, especially, has frequently and magnificently expounded Catholic teaching on the relations which should subsist between the two societies. "Between them," he says, "there must necessarily be a suitable union, which may not improperly be compared with that existing between body and soul. - Quaedam intercedat necesse est ordinata colligatio (inter illas) quae quidem conjunctioni non immerito comparatur, per quam anima et corpus in homine copulantur."He proceeds: "Human societies cannot, without becoming criminal, act as if God did not exist or refuse to concern themselves with religion, as though it were something foreign to them, or of no purpose to them.... As for the Church, which has God Himself for its author, to exclude her from the active life of the nation, from the laws, the education of the young, the family, is to commit a great and pernicious error. - Civitates non possunt, citra scellus, gerere se tamquam si Deus omnino non esset, aut curam religionis velut alienam nihilque profuturam abjicere.... Ecclesiam vero, quam Deus ipse constituit, ab actione vitae excludere, a legibus, ab institutione adolescentium, a societate domestica, magnus et perniciousus est error."

4. And if it is true that any Christian State does something eminently disastrous and reprehensible in separating itself from the Church, how much more deplorable is it that France, of all nations in the world, would have entered on this policy; France which has been during the course of centuries the object of such great and special predilection

on the part of the Apostolic See whose fortunes and glories have ever been closely bound up with the practice of Christian virtue and respect for religion. Leo XIII had truly good reason to say: "France cannot forget that Providence has united its destiny with the Holy See by ties too strong and too old that she should ever wish to break them. And it is this union that has been the source of her real greatness and her purest glories.... To disturb this traditional union would be to deprive the nation of part of her moral force and great influence in the world."

5. And the ties that consecrated this union should have been doubly inviolable from the fact that they were sanctioned by sworn treaties. The Concordat entered upon by the Sovereign Pontiff and the French Government was, like all treaties of the same kind concluded between States, a bilateral contract binding on both parties to it. The Roman Pontiff on the one side and the Head of the French Nation on the other solemnly stipulated both for themselves and their successors to maintain inviolate the pact they signed. Hence the same rule applied to the Concordat as to all international treaties, viz., the law of nations which prescribes that it could not be in any way annulled by one alone of the contracting parties. The Holy See has always observed with scrupulous fidelity the engagements it has made, and it has always required the same fidelity from the State. This is a truth which no impartial judge can deny. Yet today the State, by its sole authority, abrogates the solemn pact it signed. Thus it violates its sworn promise. To break with the Church, to free itself from her friendship, it has stopped at nothing, and has not hesitated to outrage the Apostolic See by this violation of the law of nations, and to disturb the social and political order itself - for the reciprocal security of nations in their relations with one another depends mainly on the inviolable fidelity and

the sacred respect with which they observe their treaties.

6. The extent of the injury inflicted on the Apostolic See by the unilateral abrogation of the Concordat is notably aggravated by the manner in which the State has effected this abrogation. It is a principle admitted without controversy, and universally observed by all nations, that the breaking of a treaty should be previously and regularly notified, in a clear and explicit manner, to the other contracting party by the one which intends to put an end to the treaty. Yet not only has no notification of this kind been made to the Holy See, but no indication whatever on the subject has been conveyed to it. Thus the French Government has not hesitated to treat the Apostolic See without ordinary respect and without the courtesy that is never omitted even in dealing with the smallest States. Its officials, representatives though they were of a Catholic nation, have heaped contempt on the dignity and power of the Sovereign Pontiff, the Supreme Head of the Church, whereas they should have shown more respect to this power than to any other political power - and a respect all the greater from the fact that the Holy See is concerned with the eternal welfare of souls, and that its mission extends everywhere.

7. If We now proceed to examine in itself the law that has just been promulgated, We find, therein, fresh reason for protesting still more energetically. When the State broke the links of the Concordat, and separated itself from the Church, it ought, as a natural consequence, to have left her independence, and allowed her to enjoy peacefully that liberty, granted by the common law, which it pretended to assign to her. Nothing of the kind has been done. We recognize in the law many exceptional and odiously restrictive provisions, the effect of which is to place the Church under the domina-

tion of the civil power. It has been a source of bitter grief to Us to see the State thus encroach on matters which are within the exclusive jurisdiction of the Church; and We bewail this all the more from the fact that the State, dead to all sense of equity and justice, has thereby created for the Church of France a situation grievous, crushing, and oppressive of her most sacred rights.

8. For the provisions of the new law are contrary to the constitution on which the Church was founded by Jesus Christ. The Scripture teaches us, and the tradition of the Fathers confirms the teaching, that the Church is the mystical body of Christ, ruled by the Pastors and Doctors (I Ephes. iv. II sqq.) - a society of men containing within its own fold chiefs who have full and perfect powers for ruling, teaching and judging (Matt. xxviii. 18-20; xvi. 18, 19; xviii. 17; Tit. ii. 15; 11. Cor. x. 6; xiii. 10. & c.) It follows that the Church is essentially an unequal society, that is, a society comprising two categories of per sons, the Pastors and the flock, those who occupy a rank in the different degrees of the hierarchy and the multitude of the faithful. So distinct are these categories that with the pastoral body only rests the necessary right and authority for promoting the end of the society and directing all its members towards that end; the one duty of the multitude is to allow themselves to be led, and, like a docile flock, to follow the Pastors. St. Cyprian, Martyr, expresses this truth admirably when he writes: "Our Lord, whose precepts we must revere and observe, in establishing the episcopal dignity and the nature of the Church, addresses Peter thus in the gospel: Ego dico tibi, quia tu es Petrus, etc. Hence, through all the vicissitudes of time and circumstance, the plan of the episcopate and the constitution of the Church have always been found to be so framed that the Church rests on the Bishops, and that all its acts are ruled by

them. - Dominus Noster, cujus praecepta metuere et servare debemus, episcopi honorem et ecclesiae suae rationem disponens, in evangelio loquitur et dicit Petro: Ego dico tibi quia tu es Petrus, etc.... Inde per temporum et successionum vices Episcoporum ordinatio et Ecclesiae ratio decurrit, ut Ecclesia super Episcopos constituatur et omnis actus Ecclesiae per eosdem praepositos gubernetur" (St. Cyprian, Epist. xxvii.-xxviii. ad Lapsos ii. i.) St. Cyprian affirms that all this is based on Divine law, divina lege fundatum. The Law of Separation, in opposition to these principles, assigns the administration and the supervision of public worship not to the hierarchical body divinely instituted by Our Savior, but to an association formed of laymen. To this association it assigns a special form and a juridical personality, and considers it alone as having rights and responsibilities in the eyes of the law in all matters appertaining to religious worship. It is this association which is to have the use of the churches and sacred edifices, which is to possess ecclesiastical property, real and personal, which is to have at its disposition (though only for a time) the residences of the Bishops and priests and the seminaries; which is to administer the property, regulate collections, and receive the alms and the legacies destined for religious worship. As for the hierarchical body of Pastors, the law is completely silent. And if it does prescribe that the associations of worship are to be constituted in harmony with the general rules of organization of the cult whose existence they are designed to assure, it is none the less true that care has been taken to declare that in all disputes which may arise relative to their property the Council of State is the only competent tribunal. These associations of worship are therefore placed in such a state of dependence on the civil authority that the ecclesiastical authority will, clearly, have no power over them. It is obvious at a glance that all these provisions seriously violate the rights of the Church, and are in opposition with her Divine constitution. Moreover, the law on these points is not set forth in clear and precise terms, but is left so vague and so open to arbitrary decisions that its mere interpretation is well calculated to be productive of the greatest trouble.

9. Besides, nothing more hostile to the liberty of the Church than this Law could well be conceived. For, with the existence of the associations of worship, the Law of Separation hinders the Pastors from exercising the plenitude of their authority and of their office over the faithful; when it attributes to the Council of State supreme jurisdiction over these associations and submits them to a whole series of prescriptions not contained in the common law, rendering their formation difficult and their continued existence more difficult still; when, after proclaiming the liberty of public worship, it proceeds to restrict its exercise by numerous exceptions; when it despoils the Church of the internal regulation of the churches in order to invest the State with this function; when it thwarts the preaching of Catholic faith and morals and sets up a severe and exceptional penal code for clerics - when it sanctions all these provisions and many others of the same kind in which wide scope is left to arbitrary ruling, does it not place the Church in a position of humiliating subjection and, under the pretext of protecting public order, deprive peaceable citizens, who still constitute the vast majority in France, of the sacred right of practicing their religion? Hence it is not merely by restricting the exercise of worship (to which the Law of Separation falsely reduces the essence of religion) that the State injures the Church, but by putting obstacles to her influence, always a beneficent influence over the people, and by paralyzing her activity in a thousand different ways. Thus, for instance, the State has not been satisfied with depriving the Church of the Religious Orders,

those precious auxiliaries of hers in her sacred mission, in teaching and education, in charitable works, but it must also deprive her of the resources which constitute the human means necessary for her existence and the accomplishment of her mission.

10. In addition to the wrongs and injuries to which we have so far referred, the Law of Separation also violates and tramples underfoot the rights of property of the Church. In defiance of all justice, it despoils the Church of a great portion of a patrimony which belongs to her by titles as numerous as they are sacred; it suppresses and annuls all the pious foundations consecrated, with perfect legality, to divine worship and to suffrages for the dead. The resources furnished by Catholic liberality for the maintenance of Catholic schools, and the working of various charitable associations connected with religion, have been transferred to lay associations in which it would be idle to seek for a vestige of religion. In this it violates not only the rights of the Church, but the formal and explicit purpose of the donors and testators. It is also a subject of keen grief to Us that the law, in contempt of all right, proclaims as property of the State, Departments or Communes the ecclesiastical edifices dating from before the Concordat. True, the Law concedes the gratuitous use, for an indefinite period, of these to the associations of worship, but it surrounds the concession with so many and so serious reserves that in reality it leaves to the public powers the full disposition of them. Moreover, We entertain the gravest fears for the sanctity of those temples, the august refuges of the Divine Majesty and endeared by a thousand memories to the piety of the French people. For they are certainly in danger of profanation if they fall into the hands of laymen.

11. When the law, by the suppression of the Budget of Public Worship, exonerates the State from the obligation of providing for the expenses of worship, it violates an engagement contracted in a diplomatic convention, and at the same time commits a great injustice. On this point there cannot be the slightest doubt, for the documents of history offer the clearest confirmation of it. When the French Government assumed in the Concordat the obligation of supplying the clergy with a revenue sufficient for their decent subsistence and for the requirements of public worship, the concession was not a merely gratuitous one - it was an obligation assumed by the State to make restitution, at least in part, to the Church whose property had been confiscated during the first Revolution. On the other hand when the Roman Pontiff in this same Concordat bound himself and his successors, for the sake of peace, not to disturb the possessors of property thus taken from the Church, he did so only on one condition: that the French Government should bind itself in perpetuity to endow the clergy suitably and to provide for the expenses of divine worship.

12. Finally, there is another point on which We cannot be silent. Besides the injury it inflicts on the interests of the Church, the new law is destined to be most disastrous to your country. For there can be no doubt but that it lamentably destroys union and concord. And yet without such union and concord no nation can live long or prosper. Especially in the present state of Europe, the maintenance of perfect harmony must be the most ardent wish of everybody in France who loves his country and has its salvation at heart. As for Us, following the example of Our Predecessor and inheriting from him a special predilection for your nation, We have not confined Ourself to striving for the preservation of full rights of the religion of your forefathers, but We have always,

with that fraternal peace of which religion is certainly the strongest bond ever before Our eyes, endeavored to promote unity among you. We cannot, therefore, without the keenest sorrow observe that the French Government has just done a deed which inflames on religious grounds passions already too dangerously excited, and which, therefore, seems to be calculated to plunge the whole country into disorder.

13. Hence, mindful of Our Apostolic charge and conscious of the imperious duty incumbent upon Us of defending and preserving against all assaults the full and absolute integrity of the sacred and inviolable rights of the Church, We do, by virtue of the supreme authority which God has confided to Us, and on the grounds above set forth, reprove and condemn the law voted in France for the separation of Church and State, as deeply unjust to God whom it denies, and as laying down the principle that the Republic recognizes no cult. We reprove and condemn it as violating the natural law, the law of nations, and fidelity to treaties; as contrary to the Divine constitution of the Church, to her essential rights and to her liberty; as destroying justice and trampling underfoot the rights of property which the Church has acquired by many titles and, in addition, by virtue of the Concordat. We reprove and condemn it as gravely offensive to the dignity of this Apostolic See, to Our own person, to the Episcopacy, and to the clergy and all the Catholics of France. Therefore, We protest solemnly and with all Our strength against the introduction, the voting and the promulgation of this law, declaring that it can never be alleged against the imprescriptible rights of the Church.

14. We had to address these grave words to you, Venerable Brethren, to the people of France and of the whole Christian world, in order to make known in its true light what has been

done. Deep indeed is Our distress when We look into the future and see there the evils that this law is about to bring upon a people so tenderly loved by Us. And We are still more grievously affected by the thought of the trials, sufferings and tribulations of all kinds that are to be visited on you, Venerable Brethren, and on all your clergy. Yet, in the midst of these crushing cares, We are saved from excessive affliction and discouragement when Our mind turns to Divine Providence, so rich in mercies, and to the hope, a thousand times verified, that Jesus Christ will not abandon His Church or ever deprive her of His unfailing support. We are, then, far from feeling any fear for the Church. Her strength and her stability are Divine, as the experience of ages triumphantly proves. The world knows of the endless calamities, each more terrible than the last, that have fallen upon her during this long course of time - but where all purely human institutions must inevitably have succumbed, the Church has drawn from her trials only fresh strength and richer fruitfulness. As to the persecuting laws passed against her, history teaches, even in recent times, and France itself confirms the lesson, that though forged by hatred, they are always at last wisely abrogated, when they are found to be prejudicial to the interests of the State. God grant those who are at present in power in France may soon follow the example set for them in this matter by their predecessors. God grant that they may, amid the applause of all good people, make haste to restore to religion, the source of civilization and prosperity, the honor which is due to her together with her liberty.

15. Meanwhile, and as long as oppressive persecution continues, the children of the Church, putting on the arms of light, must act with all their strength in defense of Truth and justice - it is their duty always, and today more than ever. To this holy contest you, Venerable Brethren, who are to be the

teachers and guides, will bring all the force of that vigilant and indefatigable zeal of which the French Episcopate has, to its honor, given so many well-known proofs. But above all things We wish, for it is of the greatest importance, that in all the plans you undertake for the defense of the Church, you to endeavor to ensure the most perfect union of hearts and wills. It is Our firm intention to give you at a fitting time practical instructions which shall serve as a sure rule of conduct for you amid the great difficulties of the present time. And We are certain in advance that you will faithfully adopt them. Meanwhile continue the salutary work you are doing; strive to kindle piety among the people as much as possible; promote and popularize more and more the teaching of Christian doctrine; preserve the souls entrusted to you from the errors and seductions they meet on all sides; instruct, warn, encourage, console your flocks, and perform for them all the duties imposed on you by your pastoral office. In this work you will certainly find indefatigable collaborators in your clergy. They are rich in men remarkable for piety, knowledge, and devotion to the Holy See, and We know that they are always ready to devote themselves unreservedly under your direction to the cause of the triumph of the Church and the eternal salvation of souls. The clergy will also certainly understand that during the present turmoil they must be animated by the sentiments professed long ago by the Apostles, rejoicing that they are found worthy to suffer opprobrium for the name of Jesus, "Gaudentes quoniam digni habiti sunt pro nomine Jesu contumeliam pati" (Rom. xiii. 12). They will therefore stoutly stand up for the rights and liberty of the Church, but without offense to anybody. Nay more, in their earnestness to preserve charity, as the ministers of Jesus Christ are especially bound to do, they will reply to iniquity with justice, to outrage with mildness, and to ill-treatment with benefits.

16. And now We turn to you, Catholics of France, asking you to receive Our words as a testimony of that most tender affection with which We have never ceased to love your country, and as comfort to you in the midst of the terrible calamities through which you will have to pass. You know the aim of the impious sects which are placing your heads under their yoke, for they themselves have proclaimed with cynical boldness that they are determined to "de Catholicise" France. They want to root out from your hearts the last vestige of the faith which covered your fathers with glory, which made your country great and prosperous among nations, which sustains you in your trials, which brings tranquility and peace to your homes, and which opens to you the way to eternal happiness. You feel that you must defend this faith with your whole souls. But be not deluded - all labor and effort will be useless if you endeavor to repulse the assaults made on you without being firmly united. Remove, therefore, any causes of disunion that may exist among you. And do what is necessary to ensure that your unity may be as strong as it should be among men who are fighting for the same cause, especially when this cause is of those for the triumph of which everybody should be willing to sacrifice something of his own opinions. If you wish, within the limits of your strength and according to your imperious duty, to save the religion of your ancestors from the dangers to which it is exposed, it is of the first importance that you show a large degree of courage and generosity. We feel sure that you will show this generosity; and by being charitable towards God's ministers, you will incline God to be more and more charitable toward yourselves.

17. As for the defense of religion, if you wish to undertake it in a worthy manner, and to carry it on perseveringly and efficaciously, two things are first of all necessary: you must

model yourselves so faithfully on the precepts of the Christian law that all your actions and your entire lives may do honor to the faith you profess, and then you must be closely united with those whose special office it is to watch over religion, with your priests, your bishops, and above all with this Apostolic See, which is the pivot of the Catholic faith and of all that can be done in its name. Thus armed for the fray, go forth fearlessly for the defense of the Church; but take care that your trust is placed entirely in God, for whose cause you are working, and never cease to pray to Him for help.

18. For Us, as long as you have to struggle against danger, We will be heart and soul in the midst of you; labors, pains, sufferings - We will share them all with you; and pouring forth to God, who has founded the Church and ever preserves her, Our most humble and instant prayers, We will implore Him to bend a glance of mercy on France, to save her from the storms that have been let loose upon her, and, by the intercession of Mary Immaculate, to restore soon to her the blessings of calm and peace.

19. As a pledge of these heavenly gifts and a proof of Our special predilection, We impart with all Our heart the Apostolic Benediction to you, Venerable Brethren, to your clergy and to the entire French people.

Given at Rome, at St. Peter's, on February 11 in the year 1906, the third of Our Pontificate.
PIUS X

TRIBUS CIRCITER
ENCYCLICAL OF POPE PIUS X
ON THE MARIAVITES OR
MYSTIC PRIESTS OF POLAND

TO OUR VENERABLE BRETHREN,
THE ARCHBISHOPS OF WARSAW, AND BISHOPS OF
PLOTSK AND LUBLIN AMONG THE POLES

Venerable Brethren, Health and the Apostolic Benediction.

About three years ago this Apostolic See was duly informed that some priests, especially among the junior clergy of your dioceses, had founded, without permission from their lawful Superiors, a kind of pseudo-monastic society, known as the Mariavites or Mystic Priests, the members of which, little by little, turned aside from the right road and from the obedience they owe the Bishops "whom the Holy Ghost has placed to rule the Church of God," and became vain in their thoughts.

2. To a certain woman, whom they proclaimed to be most holy, marvelously endowed with heavenly gifts, divinely enlightened about many things, and providentially given for the salvation of a world about to perish, they did not hesitate to entrust themselves without reserve, and to obey her every wish.

3. Relying on an alleged mandate from God, they set themselves to promote without discrimination and of their own initiative among the people frequent exercises of piety (highly commendable when rightly carried out,) especially the adoration of the Most Holy Sacrament and the practice of frequent communion; but at the same time they made the

gravest charges against all priests and bishops who ventured to express any doubt about the sanctity and divine election of the woman, or showed any hostility to the society of the Mariavites. Such a pass did matters reach that there was reason to fear that many of the faithful in their delusion were about to abandon their lawful pastors.

4. Hence, on the advice of Our Venerable Brethren the Cardinals of the General Inquisition, We had a decree issued, as you are aware, under date of September 4, 1904, suppressing the above-named society of priests, and commanding them to break off absolutely all relations with the woman. But the priests in question, notwithstanding that they signed a document expressing their subjection to the authority of their bishops and that perhaps they did, as they say they did, partly break off their relations with the woman, still failed to abandon their undertaking and to renounce sincerely the condemned association. Not only did they condemn your exhortations and inhibitions, not only did many of them sign as audacious declaration in which they rejected communion with their bishops, not only in more places than one did they incite the deluded people to drive away their lawful pastors, but, like the enemies of the Church, asserted that she has fallen from truth and justice, and hence has been abandoned by the Holy Spirit, and that to themselves alone, the Mariavite priests, was it divinely given to instruct the faithful in true piety.

5. Nor is this all. A few weeks ago two of these priests came to Rome: Romanus Prochniewsky and Joannes Kowalski, the latter of whom is recognized, in virtue of some kind of delegation from the woman referred to, as their Superior by all the members of the Society. Both of them, in a petition alleged by them to have been written by the express

order of Our Lord Jesus Christ, ask the Supreme Pastor of the Church, or the Congregation of the Holy Office in his name, to issue a document conceived in these terms: "That Maria Francesca (the woman mentioned above) has been made most holy by God, that she is the mother of mercy for all men called and elected to salvation by God in these days; and that all Mariavite priests are commanded by God to promote throughout the world devotion to the Most Holy Sacrament and to the Blessed Virgin Mary of Perpetual Succor, free from all restriction of ecclesiastical or human law or custom, and from all ecclesiastical and human power whatsoever. . ."

6. From these words We were disposed to believe that the priests in question were blinded not so much by conscious pride as by ignorance and delusion, like those false prophets of whom Ezechiel writes: "They see vain things and they foretell lies, saying: The Lord saith: whereas the Lord hath not sent them: and they have persisted to confirm what they have said. Have you not seen a vain vision and spoken a lying divination: and you say: The Lord saith: whereas I have not spoken" (Ezechiel xiii. 6, 7). We therefore received them with piety, exhorted them to put away the deceits of vain revelation, to subject themselves and their works to the salutary authority of their Superiors, and to hasten the return of the faithful of Christ to the safe path of obedience and reverence towards their pastors; and finally to leave to the vigilance of the Holy See and the other competent authorities the task of confirming such pious customs as might seem best adapted for the fuller increase of Christian life in many parishes in your dioceses, and at the same time to admonish any priests who were found guilty of speaking abusively or contemptuously of devout practices and exercises approved by the Church. And We were consoled to see the two priests,

moved by Our fatherly kindness, throw themselves at Our feet and express their firm resolution to carry out Our wishes with the devotedness of sons. They then caused to be transmitted to Us a written statement which increased Our hope that these deluded sons would sincerely abandon past illusions and return to the right road:

7. "We (these are their words), always ready to fulfill the will of God, which has now been made so clear to us by His Vicar, do most sincerely and joyfully revoke our letter, which we sent on February 1 of the present year to the Archbishop of Warsaw, and in which we declared that we separated from him. Moreover, we do most sincerely and with the greatest joy profess that we wish to be always united with our Bishops, and especially with the Archbishop of Warsaw, as far as your Holiness will order this of us. Furthermore, as we are now acting in the name of all the Mariavites, we do make this profession of our entire obedience and subjection in the name not only of all the Mariavites, but of all the Adorers of the Most Holy Sacrament. We make this profession in a special way in the name of the Mariavites of Plotsk who, for the same cause as the Mariavites of Warsaw, handed their Bishop a declaration of separation from him. Wherefore, all of us without exception prostrate at the feet of your Holiness, professing again and again our love and obedience to the Holy See, and in a most special way to your Holiness, most humbly ask pardon for any pain we may have caused your fatherly heart. Finally, we declare that we will at once set to work with all our energy to restore peace between the people and their Bishops immediately. Nay, we can affirm that this peace will be really restored very soon."

8. It was, therefore, very pleasant for Us to be able to believe that these sons of Ours, thus pardoned, would at once on

their return to Poland give effect to their promises, and on this account We hastened to advise you, Venerable Brethren, to receive them and their companions, now that they professed entire obedience to your authority, with equal mercy and to restore them legally, if their acts corresponded with their promises, to their faculties for exercising their priestly functions.

But the event has deceived Our hopes; for We have learnt by recent documents that they have again opened their minds to lying revelations, and that since their return to Poland, they not only have not yet shown you, Venerable Brethren, the respect and obedience they promised, but that they have written to their companions a letter quite opposed to truth and genuine obedience.

9. But their profession of fidelity to the Vicar of Christ is vain in those who, in fact, do not cease to violate the authority of their Bishops. For "by far the most august part of the Church consists of the Bishops, (as Our Predecessor Leo XIII of holy memory wrote in his letter of December 17, 1888, to the Archbishop), inasmuch as this part by divine right teaches and rules men; hence, whoever resists them or pertinaciously refuses obedience to them puts himself apart from the Church. . . On the other hand, to pass judgment upon or to rebuke the acts of Bishops does not at all belong to private individuals - that comes within the province only of those higher than they in authority and especially of the Sovereign Pontiff, for to him Christ entrusted the charge of feeding not only His lambs, but His sheep throughout the world. At most, it is allowed in matters of grave complaint to refer the whole case to the Roman Pontiff, and this with prudence and moderation as zeal for the common good requires, not clamorously or abusively, for in this way dissensions and

hostilities are bred, or certainly increased."

10. Idle and deceitful too is the exhortation of the priest Johannes Kowalski to his companions in error on behalf of peace, while he persists in his foolish talk and incitements to rebellion against legitimate pastors and in brazen violation of episcopal commands.

11. Wherefore, that the faithful of Christ and all the so-called Mariavite priests who are in good faith may no longer be led astray by the delusions of the woman above-mentioned and of the priest Johannes Kowalski, We again confirm the decree whereby the society of Mariavites, unlawfully and invalidly founded, is entirely suppressed, and We declare it suppressed and condemned, and We proclaim that the pro-hibition is still in force which forbids all priests, with the exception of the one whom the Bishop of Plotsk shall in his prudence depute to be her confessor, to have anything what-ever to do on any pretext with the woman.

12. You, Venerable Brethren, We earnestly exhort to em-brace with paternal charity erring priests immediately they sincerely repent, and not to refuse to call them again, under your direction, to their priestly duties, when they have been duly proved worthy. But should they, which may God forbid, reject your exhortations and persevere in their contumacy, it will be Our care to see that they are severely dealt with. Study to lead back to the right path the faithful of Christ who are now laboring under a delusion that may be pardoned; and foster in your dioceses those practices of piety, recently or long since approved in numerous documents issued by the Apostolic See, and do this with all the more alacrity now when by the blessing of God priests among you are enabled to exercise their ministry and the faithful to emulate the ex-

ample of piety of their fathers.

13. Meanwhile as a pledge of heavenly favors and in evidence of Our paternal good will we bestow most lovingly in the Lord the Apostolic Benediction on you, Venerable Brethren, and on all the clergy and people entrusted to your care and vigilance.

Given at Rome, at St. Peter's, the fifth day of April, 1906, in the third year of Our Pontificate.
PIUS X

PIENI L'ANIMO
ENCYCLICAL OF POPE PIUS X
ON THE CLERGY IN ITALY

TO THE VENERABLE BRETHREN, THE ARCHBISH-OPS, AND BISHOPS OF ITALY

Venerable Brethren, Health and the Apostolic Blessing.

Our soul is fearful of the strict rendering that We shall one day be called upon to make to Jesus Christ, the Prince of Pastors, concerning the flock He entrusted to Our care. We pass each day with great solicitude in preserving as much as possible the faithful from the dangerous evils that afflict society at the present time. Therefore, We consider addressed to Us the words of the Prophet: "Cry, cease not, lift up thy voice like a trumpet." Accordingly, sometimes by speech and sometimes by letter We constantly warn, beseech, and censure, arousing, above all, the zeal of Our Brethren in the Episcopate so that each one of them will exercise the most solicitous vigilance in that portion of the flock over which the Holy Spirit has placed him.

2. The cause which now moves Us to raise Our voice is of very serious importance. It demands all the attention of your mind and all the energy of your pastoral office to counteract the disorder which has already produced the most destructive effects. If this disorder is not radically removed with a firm hand, even more fatal consequences will be felt in the coming years. In fact, Venerable Brethren, We have letters, full of sadness and tears, from several of you, in which you deplore the spirit of insubordination and independence displayed here and there among the clergy. Most assuredly, a poisonous atmosphere corrupts men's minds to a great extent

today, and the deadly effects are those which the Apostolic Saint Jude formerly described: "These men also defile the flesh, disregard authority, deride majesty." That is to say, over and above the most degrading corruption of manners there is also an open contempt for authority and for those who exercise it. What overwhelms Us with grief, however, is the fact that this spirit should creep into the sanctuary even in the least degree, infecting those to whom the words of Ecclesiasticus should most fittingly be applied: "Their generation, obedience and love." This unfortunate spirit is doing the damage especially among young priests, spreading among them new and reprehensible theories concerning the very nature of obedience. In order to recruit new members for this growing troop of rebels, what is even more serious is the fact that such maxims are being more or less secretly propagated among youths preparing for the priesthood within the enclosure of the seminaries.

3. We therefore consider it Our duty, Venerable Brethren, to appeal to your conscience to see that you do not spare any effort and with a firm hand and constant resolve you do not hesitate to destroy this evil seed which carries with it such destructive consequences. Never forget that the Holy Spirit has placed you to rule. Remember Saint Paul's command to Titus: "Rebuke with all authority. Let no one despise thee." Be firm in demanding that obedience from your priests and clerics which is a matter of absolute obligation for all the faithful, and constitutes the most important part of the sacred duty of priests.

4. Take the proper means necessary for the diminution of these quarrelsome souls. Bear well in mind, Venerable Brethren, the Apostle's warning to Timothy: "Do not lay hands hastily upon anyone." In fact, haste in admitting men

to Sacred Orders naturally opens the way to a multiplication of people in the sanctuary who do not increase joy. We know that there are cities and dioceses where, far from there being any reason to lament the dearth of clergy, the clergy greatly exceed the needs of the faithful. Venerable Brethren, what reason is there for imposing hands so frequently? In those places where the lack of clergy is no sufficient reason for haste in so important a matter and the clergy are more numerous than the requirements demand, nothing excuses from the most delicate caution and the greatest exactitude in selecting those who are to receive the sacerdotal honor. The eagerness of the aspirants is no excuse for haste. The priesthood that Jesus Christ instituted for the salvation of souls is by no means a human profession or office which anyone desiring it for any reason can say he has a right to receive. Therefore, let the Bishops call young men to sacred orders, not according to the desires or pretexts of the aspirants, but, as the Council of Trent prescribes, according to the needs of the dioceses. In this task they can select only those who are really suitable and dismiss those who have inclinations contrary to the priestly vocation. The most dangerous of these inclinations are a disregard for discipline and that pride of mind which fosters it.

5. In order that young men who display qualities suitable for the sacred ministry may not be lacking, Venerable Brethren, We wish to insist most earnestly on what We have already frequently pointed out. That is to say, you have a very serious obligation before God of guarding and fostering most solicitously the proper conduct of the seminaries. Your priests will be as you have trained them. The letter of December 8, 1902, which Our most prudent Predecessor addressed to you as a testament from his long Pontificate is very important. We desire to add nothing new to it; We

shall merely remind you of the rules it lays down. We especially recommend the immediate execution of Our orders, published through the Sacred Congregation of Bishops and Regulars, on the concentration of the seminaries especially for the study of philosophy and theology. In this way the great advantage resulting from the separation of the major and minor seminaries and the no less great advantage of the necessary instruction of the clergy will be secured.

6. Let the seminaries be jealously guarded in order that a proper atmosphere will be maintained. Let them always be destined exclusively for preparing youths, not for civil careers, but for the noble vocation of being ministers of Christ. Let philosophy, theology, and the related sciences, especially Sacred Scripture, be studied along the lines of pontifical directives: according to the teaching of Saint Thomas which Our venerable Predecessor so often recommended, and We Ourselves recommended in the Apostolic Letter of January 23, 1904. Therefore, let the Bishops exercise the most prudent vigilance towards the professors' teachings. Let them recall those who run after certain dangerous novelties to their sense of duty. If they do not profit from these warnings, let them be removed - cost what it may - from their teaching position. Young clerics are forbidden to frequent the universities unless the Bishops think there are very good reasons and necessary precautions have been taken. Seminarians are absolutely forbidden to take part in external activities. Accordingly. We forbid them to read newspapers and periodicals, excepting, in the case of the latter, those with solid principles and which the Bishop deems suitable for their study. Let discipline continue to be fostered with renewed vigor and vigilance. Finally, in every seminary there must be a spiritual director. He is to be a man of extraordinary prudence and experienced in the ways of Christian perfec-

tion. With untiring zeal he must train the young men in solid piety, the primary foundation of the spiritual life. Venerable Brethren, if these rules are conscientiously and religiously followed they will be your sure guarantee of seeing a clergy growing up around you which will be your joy and your crown.

7. If these instructions are not observed, the problem of insubordination and independence which We now lament will be even more aggravated by some of the younger clergy and cause even more harm. This is especially so since those who are subject to this reprobate spirit are not lacking, and, abusing the sacred office of preaching, they are its outspoken promoters and apostles, to the detriment and scandal of the faithful.

8. On July 31, 1894, Our Predecessor, through the Sacred Congregation of Bishops and Regulars, called the Bishops' attention to this very serious problem. The regulations and norms set up in that Pontifical document We now affirm and renew, commanding the Bishops to form their conscience according to it, lest the words of the Prophet Nahum might be applied to any of them: "Thy shepherds have slumbered." No one can have the faculty of preaching "unless he first be approved of in life, knowledge and morals." Priests of other dioceses should not be allowed to preach unless they have testimonial letters from their own Bishop. Let the subject of their sermons be that which the Divine Savior indicated when He said: "Preach the gospel . . . teaching them to observe all that I commanded you." Or, according to the Council of Trent, "announcing to them the vices they should avoid and the virtues they should follow in order to escape eternal punishment and attain heavenly glory." Therefore, let those arguments better suited to journalistic campaigns and

lecture halls be completely banished from the holy place. Let moral preaching be preferred to sermons which are, to say the least, fruitless. Let the preacher speak "not in the persuasive words of wisdom, but in the demonstration of the Spirit and of power." The principal source, therefore, from which preaching will derive its strength will be the Sacred Scriptures, understood not according to the private judgment of minds very frequently blinded by passions, but according to the traditions of the Church and the interpretations of the holy Fathers and Councils.

9. According to these rules, Venerable Brethren, you should judge those to whom you will entrust the ministry of the divine word. Whenever you find any of them departing from these rules, being more concerned with their own interests than those of Jesus Christ and more anxious for worldly applause than the welfare of souls, warn and correct them. If that proves insufficient, be firm in removing them from an office for which they have proven themselves unworthy. You should be especially diligent in employing this vigilance and severity since the ministry of preaching belongs in a special way to you, and is one of the chief functions of the Episcopal Office. Whoever outside your rank preaches, he does so only in your name and in your place. It follows, therefore, that you are always responsible before God for the way in which the bread of the divine word is distributed to the faithful. In order to remove all responsibility from Our shoulders, We notice and command all Ordinaries to discontinue or suspend, after charitable warnings, any preacher, be he secular or regular, and even if it be during a course of sermons, who does not completely obey the regulations laid down in the above-mentioned Instruction of the Congregation of Bishops and Regulars. Better by far would it be if the faithful were satisfied with the simple homilies and explanations of

the Catechism their parish priests offer them than to attend sermons that do more harm than good.

10. Another field where the junior clergy find a wide scope and great stimulus for maintaining and advocating exemption from every bond of legitimate authority is the so-called Popular Christian Action. This action, Venerable Brethren, is not in itself reprehensible, nor by its nature does it lead to contempt of authority. Many, however, misunderstanding its nature, have voluntarily abandoned the rules laid down for its promotion by Our Predecessor of immortal memory.

11. You are aware that We are referring to the Instruction on Popular Christian Action which, by command of Leo XIII, the Sacred Congregation of Extraordinary Ecclesiastical Affairs issued on January 27, 1902, and which was sent to each one of you to carry out in your dioceses. For Our part, We maintain and, with the fullness of Our power, We renew these instructions with each and every one of their regulations. Similarly We confirm and renew all the orders We issued in the motu proprio of December 18, 1903, on Popular Christian Action along with the Circular Letter dated July 28, 1904, of Our beloved son, the Cardinal Secretary of State.

12. Concerning the founding and directing of newspapers and periodicals, the clergy must faithfully follow Article 42 of the Apostolic Constitution Officiorum, namely, "Clerics are forbidden to direct newspapers or periodicals without the previous consent of the Ordinaries." Similarly, without the previous consent of the Ordinary, no cleric can publish any kind of writing, be it concerned with a religious, moral, or merely technical subject. Before the founding of circles and societies their rules and constitutions must be examined and

approved by the Ordinary. No priest or cleric can lecture on Popular Christian Action or any other subject without the permission of the Ordinary of the place. Language which might inspire aversion for the higher classes is, and can only be regarded as, altogether contrary to the true spirit of Christian charity. Likewise, all terms smacking of an unhealthy novelty in Catholic publications are condemnable, such as those deriding the piety of the faithful, or pointing out a new orientation of the Christian life, new directions of the Church, new aspirations of the modern soul, a new social vocation of the clergy, or a new Christian civilization.

13. While it is a very praiseworthy thing for the clergy, and especially the younger clergy, to go to the people, nevertheless, they must proceed in this matter with due obedience to authority and the commands of their ecclesiastical superiors. In devoting themselves according to this submission to the cause of Popular Christian Action, their noble duty must be "to rescue the children of the people from ignorance of spiritual and eternal things, encouraging them by their kindness to live honestly and virtuously; to strengthen adults in the faith, fortifying them in the practice of the Christian life by removing all contrary influences; to foster among the Catholic laity those institutions which are really instrumental in improving the moral and material welfare of the masses; and above all, to defend the principles of evangelical justice and charity, applying equally to everyone the rights and duties of civil society. . . . Let them, moreover, be ever mindful that even among the people the priest should inviolately preserve his novel character as a minister of God, being placed at the head of his brethren for their salvation. In devoting himself to the people should he do anything contrary to the dignity of the priesthood or ecclesiastical duties or discipline, he must be rebuked."

14. Moreover, Venerable Brethren, in order to erect an effective bulwark against this extravagance of thought and extension of the spirit of independence, by Our authority, We absolutely forbid all clerics and priests to give their names in the future to any society that does not have Episcopal approbation. In a very special manner, under penalty of exclusion from Sacred Orders for clerics and suspension ipso facto a divinis for priests, We forbid them to become members of the National Democratic League, whose program was issued from Roma-Torrette on October 20, 1905. Its statutes were published the same year by the Provisional Committee of Bologna without the name of their author.

15. Being concerned about the present state of the Italian clergy and the importance of the subject, the solicitude of Our Apostolic Office demanded Us to issue these directives. We must now once again arouse your zeal, Venerable Brethren, in order that these arrangements and regulations will be quickly and fully carried out in your dioceses. Prevent the evil where fortunately it has not yet appeared. Suppress it immediately where it is beginning to spring up. Wipe it out with a firm and resolute hand where unfortunately it has already ripened. Making this a matter of conscience for you, We pray that God will fill you with the spirit of prudence and necessary firmness. For that reason, from the bottom of Our heart, We impart to you the Apostolic Blessing.

Given at Saint Peter's, Rome, on July 28, 1906, the third
year of Our Pontificate.
PIUS X

GRAVISSIMO OFFICII MUNERE
ENCYCLICAL OF POPE PIUS X
ON FRENCH ASSOCIATIONS OF WORSHIP

TO OUR VENERABLE BRETHREN,
THE ARCHBISHOPS, AND BISHOPS OF FRANCE

Venerable Brethren, Health and the Apostolic Benediction.

We are about to discharge today a very grave obligation of Our office, an obligation which We assumed towards you when We announced, after the promulgation of the law creating a rupture between the French Republic and the Church, that We should indicate at a fitting time what it might seem to Us ought to be done to defend and preserve religion in your country. We have allowed you to wait until today for the satisfaction of your desires, by reason not only of the importance of this great question, but also and above all by reason of the quite special charity which binds Us to you and to all your interests because of the unforgettable services rendered to the Church by your nation.

2. Therefore, after having condemned, as was Our duty, this iniquitous law, We have examined with greatest care whether the articles of the said law would leave Us any means of organizing religious life in France in such a way as to safeguard from injury the sacred principles on which Holy Church reposes. To this end it appeared good to Us both to take the counsel of the assembled episcopate and to prescribe for your general assembly the points which ought to be the principal objects of your deliberations. And now, knowing your views as well as those of several cardinals, and after having maturely reflected and implored by the most fervent prayers the Father of Lights, We see that We

ought to confirm fully by Our Apostolic authority the almost unanimous decision of your assembly.

3. It is for this reason that, with reference to the associations for public worship as the law establishes them, we decree that it is absolutely impossible for them to be formed without a violation of the sacred rights pertaining to the very life of the Church.

4. Putting aside, therefore, these associations which the knowledge of Our duty forbids us to approve, it might appear opportune to examine whether it is lawful to make trial in their place of some other sort of associations at once legal and canonical, and thus to preserve the Catholics of France from the grave complications which menace them. Of a certainty, nothing so engrosses and distresses Us as these eventualities; and would to Heaven that We had some hope of being able, without infringing the rights of God, to make this essay, and thus to deliver Our well-beloved sons from the fear of such manifold and such great trials.

5. But as this hope fails Us while the law remains what it is, We declare that it is not permissible to try this other kind of association as long as it is not established in a sure and legal manner that the Divine constitution of the Church, the immutable rights of the Roman Pontiff and of the Bishops, as well as their authority over the necessary property of the Church and particularly over the sacred edifices, shall be irrevocably placed in the said associations in full security. To desire the contrary is impossible for us, without betraying the sanctity of Our office and bringing about the ruin of the Church of France.

6. It remains, therefore, for you, Venerable Brethren, to set yourselves to work and to employ all means which the law recognizes as within the rights of all citizens to arrange for and organize religious worship. In a matter so important and so arduous you will never have to wait for Our assistance. Absent in body, We shall be with you in thought and in heart, and We shall aid you on every occasion with Our counsel and with Our authority. Take up with courage the burden We impose upon you under the inspiration of Our love for the Church and for your country, and entrust the result to the all-foreseeing goodness of God, Whose help, We are firmly convinced, will not, in His own good time, be wanting to France.

7. It is not difficult to foresee the nature of the recriminations which the enemies of the Church will make against Our present decree and Our orders. They will endeavor to persuade the people that We have not had the interests of the Church of France solely in view; that We have had another design foreign to religion; that the form of the Republic in France is hateful to Us, that in order to overthrow it We are seconding the efforts of the parties hostile to it; and that We refuse to France what the Holy See has without difficulties accorded to other nations. These recriminations, with others of the same sort, which, as can be foreseen from certain indications, will be disseminated among the public in order to excite irritation, We denounce now and henceforth with the utmost indignation as false; and it is incumbent upon you, Venerable Brethren, as upon all good men, to refute them in order that they may not deceive simple and ignorant people.

8. With reference to the special charge against the Church of having been more accommodating in a similar case outside France, you should explain that the Church has acted in this

way because the situations were quite different, and above all because the Divine attributes of the hierarchy were, in a certain measure, safeguarded. If any State has separated from the Church, while leaving to her the resource of the liberty common to all and the free disposal of her property, that State has without doubt, and on more than one ground, acted unjustly; but nevertheless, it could not be said that it has created for the Church a situation absolutely intolerable.

9. But it is quite otherwise today in France; there the makers of this unjust law wished to make it a law, not of separation, but of oppression. Thus they affirmed their desire for peace, and promised an understanding; and they are now waging an atrocious war against the religion of the country and hurling the brand of the most violent discords, and thus inciting the citizens against each other, to the great detriment, as everyone sees, of the public welfare itself.

10. Assuredly they will tax their ingenuity to throw upon Us the blame for this conflict and for the evils resulting therefrom. But whoever loyally examines the facts of which We have spoken in the Encyclical Vehementer Nos will be able to see whether We have deserved the least reproach - We, who, after having patiently borne with injustice upon injustice in Our love for the beloved French nation, finally find Ourselves summoned to go beyond the last holy limits of Our Apostolic duty, and We declare that We will not go beyond them - or rather whether the fault does not lie entirely with those who in hate of the Apostolic name have gone to such extremities.

11. Therefore, if they desire to show Us their submission and their devotion, let the Catholic men of France struggle for the Church in accordance with the directions We have

already given them, that is to say, with perseverance and energy, and yet without acting in a seditious and violent manner. It is not by violence, but by firmness, that, fortifying themselves in their good right as within a citadel, they will succeed in breaking the obstinacy of their enemies; let them well understand, as We have said and as we repeat that their efforts will be useless unless they unite in a perfect understanding for the defense of religion.

12. They now know Our verdict on the subject of this nefarious law: they should wholeheartedly conform to it, and whatever the opinions of some or others of them may have been hitherto during the discussion of the question, We entreat them all that no one shall permit himself to wound anyone whomsoever on the pretext that his own way of seeing things is the best. What can be done by concord of will and union of forces, let them learn from their adversaries; and just as the latter were able to impose on the nation the stigma of this criminal law, so by their united action will our people be able to eliminate and remove it.

13. In this hard trial of France, if all those who wish to defend with all their power the supreme interests of their country work as they ought to do in union among themselves with their Bishops and with Ourselves for the cause of religion, far from despairing of the welfare of the Church of France, it is to be hoped, on the contrary, that she will be restored to her former prosperity and dignity. We in no way doubt that the Catholics will fully comply with Our directions, and conform with Our desires: and We shall ardently seek to obtain for them by the intercession of Mary, the Immaculate Virgin, the aid of the Divine goodness.

14. As a pledge of heavenly gifts and in testimony of Our

paternal benevolence, We impart with all Our heart the Apostolic Benediction to you, Venerable Brethren, and to the whole French nation.

Given at Rome, at St. Peter's, on August 10, the Feast of St. Lawrence, the Martyr, in the year 1906, and the fourth of Our Pontificate.

PIUS X

UNE FOIS ENCORE
ENCYCLICAL OF POPE PIUS X
ON THE SEPARATION OF CHURCH AND STATE

TO OUR VENERABLE BRETHREN, THE CARDINALS,
ARCHBISHOPS, AND BISHOPS OF FRANCE
AND TO THE FRENCH CLERGY AND PEOPLE

Venerable Brethren and Beloved Sons, Health and Apostolic
Benediction.

Once again the serious events which have been precipitated
in your noble country compel Us to write to the Church
of France to sustain her in her trials, and to comfort her in
her sorrow. When the children are suffering the heart of the
Father ought more than ever to go out to them. And so, now
that We see you suffer, from the depths of our fatherly heart
floods of tenderness break forth more copiously than ever,
and flow to you with the greater comfort and sweetness.

2. These sufferings, Venerable Brethren and beloved sons,
now find a sorrowful echo throughout the whole Catholic
Church; but We feel them more deeply still and We sympa-
thize with a pity which grows with your trials and seems to
increase day by day.

3. But with these cruel sorrows the Master has, it is true,
mingled a consolation than which none can be dearer to
our heart. It springs from your unshakable attachment to
the Church, from your unfailing fidelity to this Apostolic
See, and from the firm and deeply founded unity that reigns
amongst you. On this fidelity and union We confidently reck-
oned from the first, for we were too well aware of the noble-
ness and generosity of the French heart to have any fear that

on the field of battle disunion would find its way into your ranks. Equally great is the joy that We feel at the magnificent spectacle you are now giving to the world; and with our high praise of you before the whole Church, We give thanks from the depths of Our heart to the Father of mercies, the Author of all good.

4. Recourse to God, so infinitely good, is all the more necessary because, far from abating, the struggle grows fiercer and expands unceasingly. It is no longer only the Christian faith that they would uproot at all costs from the hearts of the people; it is any belief which lifting man above the horizon of this world would supernaturally bring back his wearied eyes to heaven. Illusion on the subject is no longer possible. War has been declared against everything supernatural, because behind the supernatural stands God, and because it is God that they want to tear out of the mind and heart of man.

5. The war will be bitter and without respite on the part of those who wage it. That as it goes on harder trials than those which you have hitherto known await you is possible and even probable. Common prudence calls on each of you to prepare for them. And this you will do simply, valiantly, and full of confidence, sure that however fiercely the fight may rage, victory will in the end remain in your hands.

6. The pledge of this victory is your union first of all amongst yourselves, and secondly with this Apostolic See. This twofold union will make you invincible, and against it all efforts will break.

7. Our enemies have on this been under no misapprehensions. From the outset, and with the greatest clearness of vision, they determined on their objective; first to separate

you from Us and the Chair of Peter, and then to sow disorder among you. From then till now they have made no change in their tactics; they have pursued their end without rest and by every means; some with comprehensive and catching formulas; others with the most brutal cynicism. Specious promises, dishonorable bribes offered to schism, threats and violence, all these have been brought into play and employed. But your clear-sighted fidelity has wrecked all these attempts. There upon, thinking that the best way to separate you from Us was to shatter your confidence in the Apostolic See, they have not hesitated, from the tribune and in the press, to throw discredit upon Our acts by misrepresenting and sometimes even by calumniating Our intentions.

8. The Church, they said, is seeking to arouse religious war in France, and is summoning to her aid the violent persecution which has been the object of her prayers. What a strange accusation! Founded by Him who came to bring peace to the world and to reconcile man with God, a Messenger of peace upon earth, the Church could only seek religious war by repudiating her high mission and belying it before the eyes of all. To this mission of patient sweetness and love she rests and will remain always faithful. Besides, the whole world now knows that if peace of conscience is broken in France that is not the work of the Church but of her enemies. Fairminded men, even though not of our faith, recognize that if there is a struggle on the question of religion in your beloved country, it is not because the Church was the first to unfurl the flag, but because war was declared against her. During the last twenty-five years she has had to undergo this warfare. That is the truth and the proof of it is seen in the declarations made and repeated over and over again in the Press, at meetings, at Masonic congresses, and even in Parliament, as well as in the attacks which have been progressively and

systematically directed against her. These facts are undeniable, and no argument can ever make away with them. The Church then does not wish for war, and religious war least of all. To affirm the contrary is an outrageous calumny.

9. Nor has she any desire for violent persecution. She knows what persecution is, for she has suffered it in all times and in all places. Centuries passed in bloodshed give her the right to say with a holy boldness that she does not fear it, and that as often as may be necessary she will be able to meet it. But persecution is in itself an evil, for it is injustice and prevents man from worshipping God in freedom. The Church then cannot desire it, even with a view to the good which Providence in its infinite wisdom ever draws out of it. Besides, persecution is not only evil, it is also suffering, and there we have a fresh reason why the Church, who is the best of mothers, will never seek it.

10. This persecution which she is reproached as having provoked, and which they declare they have refused, is now being actually inflicted upon her. Have they not within these last days evicted from their houses even the Bishops who are most venerable by their age and virtues, driven the seminarists from the grands and petits seminaries, and entered upon the expulsion of the cures from their presbyteries? The whole Catholic world has watched this spectacle with sadness, and has not hesitated to give the name which they deserved to such acts of violence.

11. As for the ecclesiastical property which we are accused of having abandoned, it is important to remark that this property was partly the patrimony of the poor and the patrimony, more sacred still, of the dead. It was not permissible to the Church to abandon or surrender it; she could only let

it be taken from her by violence. Nobody will believe that she has deliberately abandoned, except under the pressure of the most overwhelming motives, what was confided to her keeping, and what was so necessary for the exercise of worship, for the maintenance of sacred edifices, for the instruction of her clergy, and for the support of her ministers. It was only when perfidiously placed in the position of having to choose between material ruin and consent to the violation of her constitution, which is of divine origin, that the Church refused, at the cost of poverty, to allow the work of God to be touched by her. Her property, then, has been wrested from her; it was not she that abandoned it. Consequently, to declare ecclesiastical property unclaimed on a given date unless the Church had by then created within herself a new organism; to subject this creation to conditions in rank opposition to the divine constitution of the Church, which was thus compelled to reject them; to transfer this property to third parties as if it had become "sans maitre," and finally to assert that in thus acting there was no spoliation of the Church but only a disposal of the property abandoned by her - this is not merely argument of transparent sophistry but adding insult to the most cruel spoliation. This spoliation is undeniable in spite of vain attempts at palliating it by declaring that no moral person existed to whom the property might be handed over; for the state has power to confer civil personality on whomsoever the public good demands that it should be granted to, establishments that are Catholic as well as others. In any case it would have been easy for the state not to have subjected the formation of associations cultuelles to conditions in direct opposition to the divine constitution of the Church which they were supposed to serve.

12. And yet that is precisely what was done in the matter of the associations cultuelles. They were organized under

the law in such a way that its dispositions on this subject ran directly counter to those rights which, derived from her constitution, are essential to the Church, notably as affecting the ecclesiastical hierarchy, the inviolable base given to His work by the Divine Master himself. Moreover, the law conferred on these associations powers which are the exclusive prerogative of ecclesiastical authority both in the matter of the exercise of worship and of the proprietorship and administration of property. And lastly, not only are these associations withdrawn from ecclesiastical jurisdiction but they are made judicially answerable to the civil authority. These are the reasons which have driven Us in Our previous Encyclicals to condemn these associations cultuelles in spite of the heavy sacrifices which such condemnation involved.

13. We have also been accused of prejudice and inconsistency. It has been said that We had refused to approve in France what We had approved in Germany. But this charge is equally lacking in foundation and justice. For although the German law was blameable on many points, and has been merely tolerated in order to avoid greater evils, the cases were quite different, for that law contained an express recognition of the Catholic hierarchy, which the French law does not do.

14. As regards the annual declaration demanded for the exercise of worship, it did not offer the full legal security which one had a right to desire. Nevertheless - though in principle gatherings of the faithful in church have none of the constituent elements proper to public meetings, and it would, in fact, be odious to attempt to assimilate them - the Church could, in order to avoid greater evils, have brought herself to tolerate this declaration. But by providing that the "cure or officiating priest would no longer," in his church, "be

anything more than an occupier without any judicial title or power to perform any acts of administration," there has been imposed on ministers of religion in the very exercise of their ministry a situation so humiliating and vague that, under such conditions, it was impossible to accept the declaration. There remains for consideration the law recently voted by the two Chambers.

15. From the point of view of ecclesiastical property, this law is a law of spoliation and confiscation, and it has completed the stripping of the Church. Although her Divine Founder was born poor in a manger, and died poor on the Cross, although she herself has known poverty from her cradle, the property that came to her was nonetheless hers, and no one had the right to deprive her of it. Her ownership, indisputable from every point of view, had been, moreover, officially sanctioned by the state, which could not consequently violate it. From the point of view of the exercise of worship, this law has organized anarchy; it is the consecration of uncertainty and caprice. Uncertainty whether places of worship, always liable to be diverted from their purpose, are meanwhile to be placed, or not placed, at the disposition of the clergy and faithful; uncertainty whether they shall be reserved from them or not, and for how long; whilst an arbitrary administrative regulates the conditions of their use, which is rendered eminently precarious. Public worship will be in as many diverse situations as the other. On the other hand, there is an obligation to meet all sorts of heavy charges, whilst at the same time there are draconian restrictions upon the resources by which they are to be met. Thus, though but of yesterday, this law has already evoked manifold and severe criticisms from men belonging indiscriminately to all political parties and all shades of religious belief. These criticisms alone are sufficient judgment of the

law.

16. It is easy to see, Venerable Brethren and beloved sons, from what We have just recalled to you, that this law is an aggravation of the Law of Separation, and we cannot therefore do otherwise than condemn it.

17. The vague and ambiguous wording of some of its articles places the end pursued by our enemies in a new light. Their object is, as we have already pointed out, the destruction of the Church and the dechristianization of France, but without people's attending to it or even noticing it. If their enterprise had been really popular, as they pretend it to be, they would not have hesitated to pursue it with visor raised and to take the whole responsibility. But instead of assuming that responsibility, they try to clear themselves of it and deny it, and in order to succeed the better, fling it upon the Church their victim. This is the most striking of all the proofs that their evil work does not respond to the wishes of the country.

18. It is in vain that after driving Us to the cruel necessity of rejecting the laws that have been made - seeing the evils they have drawn down upon the country, and feeling the universal reprobation which, like a slow tide, is rising round them - they seek to lead public opinion astray and to make the responsibility for these evils fall upon Us. Their attempt will not succeed.

19. As for Ourselves, We have accomplished Our duty, as every other Roman Pontiff would have done. The high charge with which it has pleased Heaven to invest Us, in spite of Our unworthiness, as also the Christian faith itself, which you profess with Us, dictated to Us Our conduct. We could not have acted otherwise without trampling under foot

Our conscience, without being false to the oath which We took on mounting the chair of Peter, and without violating the Catholic hierarchy, the foundation given to the Church by our Savior Jesus Christ.

We await, then, without fear, the verdict of history. History will tell how We, with Our eyes fixed immutably upon the defense of the higher rights of God, have neither wished to humiliate the civil power, nor to combat a form of government, but to safeguard the inviolable work of Our Lord and Master Jesus Christ. It will say that We have defended you, Our beloved sons, with all the strength of Our great love; that what We have demanded and now demand for the Church, of which the French Church is the elder daughter and an integral part, is respect for its hierarchy and inviolability of its property and liberty; that if Our demand had been granted religious peace would not have been troubled in France, and that, the day it is listened to that peace so much desired will be restored in the country.

20. And, lastly, history will say, that if, sure beforehand of your magnanimous generosity. We have not hesitated to tell you that the hour for sacrifice had struck, it is to remind the world, in the name of the Master of all things, that men here below should feed their minds upon thoughts of a higher sort than those of the perishable contingencies of life, and that the supreme and intangible joy of the human soul on earth is that of duty supernaturally carried out, cost what it may and so God honored, served and loved, in spite of all.

21. Confident that the Immaculate Virgin, Daughter of the Father, Mother of the Word, and Spouse of the Holy Ghost, will obtain for you from the most holy and adorable Trinity better days, and as a token of the calm which We firmly hope

will follow the storm, it is from the depths of Our heart that We impart Our Apostolic Blessing to you, Venerable Brethren, as well as to your clergy and the whole French people.

Given at Rome, at St. Peter's on the Feast of the Epiphany, January 6, 1907, the fourth year of Our pontificate.
PIUS X

PASCENDI DOMINICI GREGIS
ENCYCLICAL OF POPE PIUS X
ON THE DOCTRINES OF THE MODERNISTS

To the Patriarchs, Primates, Archbishops, Bishops
and other Local Ordinaries in Peace

and Communion with the Apostolic See.

Venerable Brethren, Health and Apostolic Benediction.
The office divinely committed to Us of feeding the Lord's
flock has especially this duty assigned to it by Christ, namely, to guard with the greatest vigilance the deposit of the
faith delivered to the saints, rejecting the profane novelties
of words and oppositions of knowledge falsely so called.
There has never been a time when this watchfulness of the
supreme pastor was not necessary to the Catholic body; for,
owing to the efforts of the enemy of the human race, there
have never been lacking "men speaking perverse things"
(Acts xx. 30), "vain talkers and seducers" (Tit. i. 10), "erring and driving into error" (2 Tim. iii. 13). Still it must be
confessed that the number of the enemies of the cross of
Christ has in these last days increased exceedingly, who are
striving, by arts, entirely new and full of subtlety, to destroy
the vital energy of the Church, and, if they can, to overthrow
utterly Christ's kingdom itself. Wherefore We may no longer be silent, lest We should seem to fail in Our most sacred
duty, and lest the kindness that, in the hope of wiser counsels, We have hitherto shown them, should be attributed to
forgetfulness of Our office.

Gravity of the Situation

2. That We make no delay in this matter is rendered neces-

sary especially by the fact that the partisans of error are to be sought not only among the Church's open enemies; they lie hid, a thing to be deeply deplored and feared, in her very bosom and heart, and are the more mischievous, the less conspicuously they appear. We allude, Venerable Brethren, to many who belong to the Catholic laity, nay, and this is far more lamentable, to the ranks of the priesthood itself, who, feigning a love for the Church, lacking the firm protection of philosophy and theology, nay more, thoroughly imbued with the poisonous doctrines taught by the enemies of the Church, and lost to all sense of modesty, vaunt themselves as reformers of the Church; and, forming more boldly into line of attack, assail all that is most sacred in the work of Christ, not sparing even the person of the Divine Redeemer, whom, with sacrilegious daring, they reduce to a simple, mere man.

3. Though they express astonishment themselves, no one can justly be surprised that We number such men among the enemies of the Church, if, leaving out of consideration the internal disposition of soul, of which God alone is the judge, he is acquainted with their tenets, their manner of speech, their conduct. Nor indeed will he err in accounting them the most pernicious of all the adversaries of the Church. For as We have said, they put their designs for her ruin into operation not from without but from within; hence, the danger is present almost in the very veins and heart of the Church, whose injury is the more certain, the more intimate is their knowledge of her. Moreover they lay the axe not to the branches and shoots, but to the very root, that is, to the faith and its deepest fires. And having struck at this root of immortality, they proceed to disseminate poison through the whole tree, so that there is no part of Catholic truth from which they hold their hand, none that they do not strive to corrupt. Further, none is more skilful, none more astute

141

than they, in the employment of a thousand noxious arts; for they double the parts of rationalist and Catholic, and this so craftily that they easily lead the unwary into error; and since audacity is their chief characteristic, there is no conclusion of any kind from which they shrink or which they do not thrust forward with pertinacity and assurance. To this must be added the fact, which indeed is well calculated to deceive souls, that they lead a life of the greatest activity, of assiduous and ardent application to every branch of learning, and that they possess, as a rule, a reputation for the strictest morality. Finally, and this almost destroys all hope of cure, their very doctrines have given such a bent to their minds, that they disdain all authority and brook no restraint; and relying upon a false conscience, they attempt to ascribe to a love of truth that which is in reality the result of pride and obstinacy. Once indeed We had hopes of recalling them to a better sense, and to this end we first of all showed them kindness as Our children, then we treated them with severity, and at last We have had recourse, though with great reluctance, to public reproof. But you know, Venerable Brethren, how fruitless has been Our action. They bowed their head for a moment, but it was soon uplifted more arrogantly than ever. If it were a matter which concerned them alone, We might perhaps have overlooked it: but the security of the Catholic name is at stake. Wherefore, as to maintain it longer would be a crime, We must now break silence, in order to expose before the whole Church in their true colours those men who have assumed this bad disguise.

Division of the Encyclical

4. But since the Modernists (as they are commonly and rightly called) employ a very clever artifice, namely, to present their doctrines without order and systematic arrangement

into one whole, scattered and disjointed one from another, so as to appear to be in doubt and uncertainty, while they are in reality firm and steadfast, it will be of advantage, Venerable Brethren, to bring their teachings together here into one group, and to point out the connexion between them, and thus to pass to an examination of the sources of the errors, and to prescribe remedies for averting the evil.

ANALYSIS OF MODERNIST TEACHING

5. To proceed in an orderly manner in this recondite subject, it must first of all be noted that every Modernist sustains and comprises within himself many personalities; he is a philosopher, a believer, a theologian, an historian, a critic, an apologist, a reformer. These roles must be clearly distinguished from one another by all who would accurately know their system and thoroughly comprehend the principles and the consequences of their doctrines.

Agnosticism its Philosophical Foundation

6. We begin, then, with the philosopher. Modernists place the foundation of religious philosophy in that doctrine which is usually called Agnosticism. According to this teaching human reason is confined entirely within the field of phenomena, that is to say, to things that are perceptible to the senses, and in the manner in which they are perceptible; it has no right and no power to transgress these limits. Hence it is incapable of lifting itself up to God, and of recognizing His existence, even by means of visible things. From this it is inferred that God can never be the direct object of science, and that, as regards history, He must not be considered as an historical subject. Given these premises, all will readily perceive what becomes of Natural Theology, of the motives

of credibility, of external revelation. The Modernists simply make away with them altogether; they include them in Intellectualism, which they call a ridiculous and long ago defunct system. Nor does the fact that the Church has formally condemned these portentous errors exercise the slightest restraint upon them. Yet the Vatican Council has defined, "If anyone says that the one true God, our Creator and Lord, cannot be known with certainty by the natural light of human reason by means of the things that are made, let him be anathema" (De Revel., can. I); and also: "If anyone says that it is not possible or not expedient that man be taught, through the medium of divine revelation, about God and the worship to be paid Him, let him be anathema" (Ibid., can. 2); and finally, "If anyone says that divine revelation cannot be made credible by external signs, and that therefore men should be drawn to the faith only by their personal internal experience or by private inspiration, let him be anathema" (De Fide, can. 3). But how the Modernists make the transition from Agnosticism, which is a state of pure nescience, to scientific and historic Atheism, which is a doctrine of positive denial; and consequently, by what legitimate process of reasoning, starting from ignorance as to whether God has in fact intervened in the history of the human race or not, they proceed, in their explanation of this history, to ignore God altogether, as if He really had not intervened, let him answer who can. Yet it is a fixed and established principle among them that both science and history must be atheistic: and within their boundaries there is room for nothing but phenomena; God and all that is divine are utterly excluded. We shall soon see clearly what, according to this most absurd teaching, must be held touching the most sacred Person of Christ, what concerning the mysteries of His life and death, and of His Resurrection and Ascension into heaven.

Vital Immanence

7. However, this Agnosticism is only the negative part of the system of the Modernist: the positive side of it consists in what they call vital immanence. This is how they advance from one to the other. Religion, whether natural or supernatural, must, like every other fact, admit of some explanation. But when Natural theology has been destroyed, the road to revelation closed through the rejection of the arguments of credibility, and all external revelation absolutely denied, it is clear that this explanation will be sought in vain outside man himself. It must, therefore, be looked for in man; and since religion is a form of life, the explanation must certainly be found in the life of man. Hence the principle of religious immanence is formulated. Moreover, the first actuation, so to say, of every vital phenomenon, and religion, as has been said, belongs to this category, is due to a certain necessity or impulsion; but it has its origin, speaking more particularly of life, in a movement of the heart, which movement is called a sentiment. Therefore, since God is the object of religion, we must conclude that faith, which is the basis and the foundation of all religion, consists in a sentiment which originates from a need of the divine. This need of the divine, which is experienced only in special and favourable circumstances, cannot, of itself, appertain to the domain of consciousness; it is at first latent within the consciousness, or, to borrow a term from modern philosophy, in the subconsciousness, where also its roots lies hidden and undetected.

Should anyone ask how it is that this need of the divine which man experiences within himself grows up into a religion, the Modernists reply thus: Science and history, they say, are confined within two limits, the one external, namely, the visible world, the other internal, which is consciousness.

145

When one or other of these boundaries has been reached, there can be no further progress, for beyond is the unknowable. In presence of this unknowable, whether it is outside man and beyond the visible world of nature, or lies hidden within in the subconsciousness, the need of the divine, according to the principles of Fideism, excites in a soul with a propensity towards religion a certain special sentiment, without any previous advertence of the mind: and this sentiment possesses, implied within itself both as its own object and as its intrinsic cause, the reality of the divine, and in a way unites man with God. It is this sentiment to which Modernists give the name of faith, and this it is which they consider the beginning of religion.

8. But we have not yet come to the end of their philosophy, or, to speak more accurately, their folly. For Modernism finds in this sentiment not faith only, but with and in faith, as they understand it, revelation, they say, abides. For what more can one require for revelation? Is not that religious sentiment which is perceptible in the consciousness revelation, or at least the beginning of revelation? Nay, is not God Himself, as He manifests Himself to the soul, indistinctly it is true, in this same religious sense, revelation? And they add: Since God is both the object and the cause of faith, this revelation is at the same time of God and from God; that is, God is both the revealer and the revealed.

Hence, Venerable Brethren, springs that ridiculous proposition of the Modernists, that every religion, according to the different aspect under which it is viewed, must be considered as both natural and supernatural. Hence it is that they make consciousness and revelation synonymous. Hence the law, according to which religious consciousness is given as the universal rule, to be put on an equal footing with revelation, and to which all must submit, even the supreme authority of the Church, whether in its teaching capacity, or in that of legislator in the province of sacred liturgy or discipline.

Deformation of Religious History the Consequence

9. However, in all this process, from which, according to the Modernists, faith and revelation spring, one point is to be particularly noted, for it is of capital importance on account of the historico-critical corollaries which are deduced from it. - For the Unknowable they talk of does not present itself to faith as something solitary and isolated; but rather in close conjunction with some phenomenon, which, though it belongs to the realm of science and history yet to some extent oversteps their bounds. Such a phenomenon may be an act of nature containing within itself something mysterious; or it may be a man, whose character, actions and words cannot, apparently, be reconciled with the ordinary laws of history. Then faith, attracted by the Unknowable which is united with the phenomenon, possesses itself of the whole phenomenon, and, as it were, permeates it with its own life. From this two things follow. The first is a sort of transfiguration of the phenomenon, by its elevation above its own true conditions, by which it becomes more adapted to that form of the divine which faith will infuse into it. The second is a kind of disfigurement, which springs from the fact that faith, which has made the phenomenon independent of the circumstances of place and time, attributes to it qualities which it has not; and this is true particularly of the phenomena of the past, and the older they are, the truer it is. From these two principles the Modernists deduce two laws, which, when united with a third which they have already got from agnosticism, constitute the foundation of historical criticism. We will take an illustration from the Person of Christ. In the person of

Christ, they say, science and history encounter nothing that is not human. Therefore, in virtue of the first canon deduced from agnosticism, whatever there is in His history suggestive of the divine, must be rejected. Then, according to the second canon, the historical Person of Christ was transfigured by faith; therefore everything that raises it above historical conditions must be removed. Lately, the third canon, which lays down that the person of Christ has been disfigured by faith, requires that everything should be excluded, deeds and words and all else that is not in keeping with His character, circumstances and education, and with the place and time in which He lived. A strange style of reasoning, truly; but it is Modernist criticism.

10. Therefore the religious sentiment, which through the agency of vital immanence emerges from the lurking places of the subconsciousness, is the germ of all religion, and the explanation of everything that has been or ever will be in any religion. The sentiment, which was at first only rudimentary and almost formless, gradually matured, under the influence of that mysterious principle from which it originated, with the progress of human life, of which, as has been said, it is a form. This, then, is the origin of all religion, even supernatural religion; it is only a development of this religious sentiment. Nor is the Catholic religion an exception; it is quite on a level with the rest; for it was engendered, by the process of vital immanence, in the consciousness of Christ, who was a man of the choicest nature, whose like has never been, nor will be. - Those who hear these audacious, these sacrilegious assertions, are simply shocked! And yet, Venerable Brethren, these are not merely the foolish babblings of infidels. There are many Catholics, yea, and priests too, who say these things openly; and they boast that they are going to reform the Church by these ravings! There is no question

now of the old error, by which a sort of right to the supernatural order was claimed for the human nature. We have gone far beyond that: we have reached the point when it is affirmed that our most holy religion, in the man Christ as in us, emanated from nature spontaneously and entirely. Than this there is surely nothing more destructive of the whole supernatural order. Wherefore the Vatican Council most justly decreed: "If anyone says that man cannot be raised by God to a knowledge and perfection which surpasses nature, but that he can and should, by his own efforts and by a constant development, attain finally to the possession of all truth and good, let him be anathema" (De Revel., can. 3).

The Origin of Dogmas

11. So far, Venerable Brethren, there has been no mention of the intellect. Still it also, according to the teaching of the Modernists, has its part in the act of faith. And it is of importance to see how. - In that sentiment of which We have frequently spoken, since sentiment is not knowledge, God indeed presents Himself to man, but in a manner so confused and indistinct that He can hardly be perceived by the believer. It is therefore necessary that a ray of light should be cast upon this sentiment, so that God may be clearly distinguished and set apart from it. This is the task of the intellect, whose office it is to reflect and to analyse, and by means of which man first transforms into mental pictures the vital phenomena which arise within him, and then expresses them in words. Hence the common saying of Modernists: that the religious man must ponder his faith. - The intellect, then, encountering this sentiment directs itself upon it, and produces in it a work resembling that of a painter who restores and gives new life to a picture that has perished with age. The simile is that of one of the leaders of Modernism. The

operation of the intellect in this work is a double one: first by a natural and spontaneous act it expresses its concept in a simple, ordinary statement; then, on reflection and deeper consideration, or, as they say, by elaborating its thought, it expresses the idea in secondary propositions, which are derived from the first, but are more perfect and distinct. These secondary propositions, if they finally receive the approval of the supreme magisterium of the Church, constitute dogma.

12. Thus, We have reached one of the principal points in the Modernists' system, namely the origin and the nature of dogma. For they place the origin of dogma in those primitive and simple formulae, which, under a certain aspect, are necessary to faith; for revelation, to be truly such, requires the clear manifestation of God in the consciousness. But dogma itself they apparently hold, is contained in the secondary formulae.

To ascertain the nature of dogma, we must first find the relation which exists between the religious formulas and the religious sentiment. This will be readily perceived by him who realizes that these formulas have no other purpose than to furnish the believer with a means of giving an account of his faith to himself. These formulas therefore stand midway between the believer and his faith; in their relation to the faith, they are the inadequate expression of its object, and are usually called symbols; in their relation to the believer, they are mere instruments.

Its Evolution

13. Hence it is quite impossible to maintain that they express absolute truth: for, in so far as they are symbols, they are the

images of truth, and so must be adapted to the religious sentiment in its relation to man; and as instruments, they are the vehicles of truth, and must therefore in their turn be adapted to man in his relation to the religious sentiment. But the object of the religious sentiment, since it embraces that absolute, possesses an infinite variety of aspects of which now one, now another, may present itself. In like manner, he who believes may pass through different phases. Consequently, the formulae too, which we call dogmas, must be subject to these vicissitudes, and are, therefore, liable to change. Thus the way is open to the intrinsic evolution of dogma. An immense collection of sophisms this, that ruins and destroys all religion. Dogma is not only able, but ought to evolve and to be changed. This is strongly affirmed by the Modernists, and as clearly flows from their principles. For amongst the chief points of their teaching is this which they deduce from the principle of vital immanence; that religious formulas, to be really religious and not merely theological speculations, ought to be living and to live the life of the religious sentiment. This is not to be understood in the sense that these formulas, especially if merely imaginative, were to be made for the religious sentiment; it has no more to do with their origin than with number or quality; what is necessary is that the religious sentiment, with some modification when necessary, should vitally assimilate them. In other words, it is necessary that the primitive formula be accepted and sanctioned by the heart; and similarly the subsequent work from which spring the secondary formulas must proceed under the guidance of the heart. Hence it comes that these formulas, to be living, should be, and should remain, adapted to the faith and to him who believes. Wherefore if for any reason this adaptation should cease to exist, they lose their first meaning and accordingly must be changed. And since the character and lot of dogmatic formulas is so precarious, there is no

151

room for surprise that Modernists regard them so lightly and in such open disrespect. And so they audaciously charge the Church both with taking the wrong road from inability to distinguish the religious and moral sense of formulas from their surface meaning, and with clinging tenaciously and vainly to meaningless formulas whilst religion is allowed to go to ruin. Blind that they are, and leaders of the blind, inflated with a boastful science, they have reached that pitch of folly where they pervert the eternal concept of truth and the true nature of the religious sentiment; with that new system of theirs they are seen to be under the sway of a blind and unchecked passion for novelty, thinking not at all of finding some solid foundation of truth, but despising the holy and apostolic traditions, they embrace other vain, futile, uncertain doctrines, condemned by the Church, on which, in the height of their vanity, they think they can rest and maintain truth itself.

The Modernist as Believer:
Individual Experience and Religious Certitude

14. Thus far, Venerable Brethren, of the Modernist considered as Philosopher. Now if we proceed to consider him as Believer, seeking to know how the Believer, according to Modernism, is differentiated from the Philosopher, it must be observed that although the Philosopher recognizes as the object of faith the divine reality, still this reality is not to be found but in the heart of the Believer, as being an object of sentiment and affirmation; and therefore confined within the sphere of phenomena; but as to whether it exists outside that sentiment and affirmation is a matter which in no way concerns this Philosopher. For the Modernist .Believer, on the contrary, it is an established and certain fact that the divine reality does really exist in itself and quite independently of

the person who believes in it. If you ask on what foundation this assertion of the Believer rests, they answer: In the experience of the individual. On this head the Modernists differ from the Rationalists only to fall into the opinion of the Protestants and pseudo-mystics. This is their manner of putting the question: In the religious sentiment one must recognize a kind of intuition of the heart which puts man in immediate contact with the very reality of God, and infuses such a persuasion of God's existence and His action both within and without man as to excel greatly any scientific conviction. They assert, therefore, the existence of a real experience, and one of a kind that surpasses all rational experience. If this experience is denied by some, like the rationalists, it arises from the fact that such persons are unwilling to put themselves in the moral state which is necessary to produce it. It is this experience which, when a person acquires it, makes him properly and truly a believer.

How far off we are here from Catholic teaching we have already seen in the decree of the Vatican Council. We shall see later how, with such theories, added to the other errors already mentioned, the way is opened wide for atheism. Here it is well to note at once that, given this doctrine of experience united with the other doctrine of symbolism, every religion, even that of paganism, must be held to be true. What is to prevent such experiences from being met within every religion? In fact that they are to be found is asserted by not a few. And with what right will Modernists deny the truth of an experience affirmed by a follower of Islam? With what right can they claim true experiences for Catholics alone? Indeed Modernists do not deny but actually admit, some confusedly, others in the most open manner, that all religions are true. That they cannot feel otherwise is clear. For on what ground, according to their theories, could falsity be predicated of any religion whatsoever? It must be certainly on one of these two: either on account of the falsity of the religious sentiment or on account of the falsity of the formula pronounced by the mind. Now the religious sentiment, although it may be more perfect or less perfect, is always one and the same; and the intellectual formula, in order to be true, has but to respond to the religious sentiment and to the Believer, whatever be the intellectual capacity of the latter. In the conflict between different religions, the most that Modernists can maintain is that the Catholic has more truth because it is more living and that it deserves with more reason the name of Christian because it corresponds more fully with the origins of Christianity. That these consequences flow from the premises will not seem unnatural to anybody. But what is amazing is that there are Catholics and priests who, We would fain believe, abhor such enormities yet act as if they fully approved of them. For they heap such praise and bestow such public honour on the teachers of these errors as to give rise to the belief that their admiration is not meant merely for the persons, who are perhaps not devoid of a certain merit, but rather for the errors which these persons openly profess and which they do all in their power to propagate.

Religious Experience and Tradition

15. But this doctrine of experience is also under another aspect entirely contrary to Catholic truth. It is extended and applied to tradition, as hitherto understood by the Church, and destroys it. By the Modernists, tradition is understood as a communication to others, through preaching by means of the intellectual formula, of an original experience. To this formula, in addition to its representative value, they attribute a species of suggestive efficacy which acts both in the per-

son who believes, to stimulate the religious sentiment should it happen to have grown sluggish and to renew the experience once acquired, and in those who do not yet believe, to awake for the first time the religious sentiment in them and to produce the experience. In this way is religious experience propagated among the peoples; and not merely among contemporaries by preaching, but among future generations both by books and by oral transmission from one to another. Sometimes this communication of religious experience takes root and thrives, at other times it withers at once and dies. For the Modernists, to live is a proof of truth, since for them life and truth are one and the same thing. Hence again it is given to us to infer that all existing religions are equally true, for otherwise they would not live.

Faith and Science

16. Having reached this point, Venerable Brethren, we have sufficient material in hand to enable us to see the relations which Modernists establish between faith and science, including history also under the name of science. And in the first place it is to be held that the object of the one is quite extraneous to and separate from the object of the other. For faith occupies itself solely with something which science declares to be unknowable for it. Hence each has a separate field assigned to it: science is entirely concerned with the reality of phenomena, into which faith does not enter at all; faith on the contrary concerns itself with the divine reality which is entirely unknown to science. Thus the conclusion is reached that there can never be any dissension between faith and science, for if each keeps on its own ground they can never meet and therefore never be in contradiction. And if it be objected that in the visible world there are some things which appertain to faith, such as the human life of Christ,

the Modernists reply by denying this. For though such things come within the category of phenomena, still in as far as they are lived by faith and in the way already described have been by faith transfigured and disfigured, they have been removed from the world of sense and translated to become material for the divine. Hence should it be further asked whether Christ has wrought real miracles, and made real prophecies, whether He rose truly from the dead and ascended into heaven, the answer of agnostic science will be in the negative and the answer of faith in the affirmative - yet there will not be, on that account, any conflict between them. For it will be denied by the philosopher as philosopher, speaking to philosophers and considering Christ only in His historical reality; and it will be affirmed by the speaker, speaking to believers and considering the life of Christ as lived again by the faith and in the faith.

Faith Subject to Science

17. Yet, it would be a great mistake to suppose that, given these theories, one is authorized to believe that faith and science are independent of one another. On the side of science the independence is indeed complete, but it is quite different with regard to faith, which is subject to science not on one but on three grounds. For in the first place it must be observed that in every religious fact, when you take away the divine reality and the experience of it which the believer possesses, everything else, and especially the religious formulas of it, belongs to the sphere of phenomena and therefore falls under the control of science. Let the believer leave the world if he will, but so long as he remains in it he must continue, whether he like it or not, to be subject to the laws, the observation, the judgments of science and of history. Further, when it is said that God is the object of faith alone,

the statement refers only to the divine reality not to the idea of God. The latter also is subject to science which while it philosophizes in what is called the logical order soars also to the absolute and the ideal. It is therefore the right of philosophy and of science to form conclusions concerning the idea of God, to direct it in its evolution and to purify it of any extraneous elements which may become confused with it. Finally, man does not suffer a dualism to exist in him, and the believer therefore feels within him an impelling need so to harmonize faith with science, that it may never oppose the general conception which science sets forth concerning the universe.

Thus it is evident that science is to be entirely independent of faith, while on the other hand, and notwithstanding that they are supposed to be strangers to each other, faith is made subject to science. All this, Venerable Brothers, is in formal opposition with the teachings of Our Predecessor, Pius IX, where he lays it down that: In matters of religion it is the duty of philosophy not to command but to serve, but not to prescribe what is to be believed but to embrace what is to be believed with reasonable obedience, not to scrutinize the depths of the mysteries of God but to venerate them devoutly and humbly.

The Modernists completely invert the parts, and to them may be applied the words of another Predecessor of Ours, Gregory IX., addressed to some theologians of his time: Some among you, inflated like bladders with the spirit of vanity strive by profane novelties to cross the boundaries fixed by the Fathers, twisting the sense of the heavenly pages . . .to the philosophical teaching of the rationals, not for the profit of their hearer but to make a show of science . . . these, seduced by strange and eccentric doctrines, make the head of the tail and force the queen to serve the servant.

The Methods of Modernists

18. This becomes still clearer to anybody who studies the conduct of Modernists, which is in perfect harmony with their teachings. In the writings and addresses they seem not unfrequently to advocate now one doctrine now another so that one would be disposed to regard them as vague and doubtful. But there is a reason for this, and it is to be found in their ideas as to the mutual separation of science and faith. Hence in their books you find some things which might well be expressed by a Catholic, but in the next page you find other things which might have been dictated by a rationalist. When they write history they make no mention of the divinity of Christ, but when they are in the pulpit they profess it clearly; again, when they write history they pay no heed to the Fathers and the Councils, but when they catechize the people, they cite them respectfully. In the same way they draw their distinctions between theological and pastoral exegesis and scientific and historical exegesis. So, too, acting on the principle that science in no way depends upon faith, when they treat of philosophy, history, criticism, feeling no horror at treading in the footsteps of Luther, they are wont to display a certain contempt for Catholic doctrines, or the Holy Fathers, for the Ecumenical Councils, for the ecclesiastical magisterium; and should they be rebuked for this, they complain that they are being deprived of their liberty. Lastly, guided by the theory that faith must be subject to science, they continuously and openly criticize the Church because of her sheer obstinacy in refusing to submit and accommodate her dogmas to the opinions of philosophy; while they, on their side, after having blotted out the old theology, endeavour to introduce a new theology which shall follow the

vagaries of their philosophers.

The Modernist as Theologian:
His Principles, Immanence and Symbolism

19. And thus, Venerable Brethren, the road is open for us to study the Modernists in the theological arena - a difficult task, yet one that may be disposed of briefly. The end to be attained is the conciliation of faith with science, always, however, saving the primacy of science over faith. In this branch the Modernist theologian avails himself of exactly the same principles which we have seen employed by the Modernist philosopher, and applies them to the believer: the principles of immanence and symbolism. The process is an extremely simple one. The philosopher has declared: The principle of faith is immanent; the believer has added: This principle is God; and the theologian draws the conclusion: God is immanent in man. Thus we have theological immanence. So too, the philosopher regards as certain that the representations of the object of faith are merely symbolical; the believer has affirmed that the object of faith is God in Himself; and the theologian proceeds to affirm that: The representations of the divine reality are symbolical. And thus we have theological symbolism. Truly enormous errors both, the pernicious character of which will be seen clearly from an examination of their consequences. For, to begin with symbolism, since symbols are but symbols in regard to their objects and only instruments in regard to the believer, it is necessary first of all, according to the teachings of the Modernists, that the believer do not lay too much stress on the formula, but avail himself of it only with the scope of uniting himself to the absolute truth which the formula at once reveals and conceals, that is to say, endeavours to express but without succeeding in doing so. They would also have

the believer avail himself of the formulas only in as far as they are useful to him, for they are given to be a help and not a hindrance; with proper regard, however, for the social respect due to formulas which the public magisterium has deemed suitable for expressing the common consciousness until such time as the same magisterium provide otherwise. Concerning immanence it is not easy to determine what Modernists mean by it, for their own opinions on the subject vary. Some understand it in the sense that God working in man is more intimately present in him than man is in even himself, and this conception, if properly understood, is free from reproach. Others hold that the divine action is one with the action of nature, as the action of the first cause is one with the action of the secondary cause, and this would destroy the supernatural order. Others, finally, explain it in a way which savours of pantheism and this, in truth, is the sense which tallies best with the rest of their doctrines.

20. With this principle of immanence is connected another which may be called the principle of divine permanence. It differs from the first in much the same way as the private experience differs from the experience transmitted by tradition. An example will illustrate what is meant, and this example is offered by the Church and the Sacraments. The Church and the Sacraments, they say, are not to be regarded as having been instituted by Christ Himself. This is forbidden by agnosticism, which sees in Christ nothing more than a man whose religious consciousness has been, like that of all men, formed by degrees; it is also forbidden by the law of immanence which rejects what they call external application; it is further forbidden by the law of evolution which requires for the development of the germs a certain time and a certain series of circumstances; it is, finally, forbidden by history, which shows that such in fact has been the course of things.

Still it is to be held that both Church and Sacraments have been founded mediately by Christ. But how? In this way: All Christian consciences were, they affirm, in a manner virtually included in the conscience of Christ as the plant is included in the seed. But as the shoots live the life of the seed, so, too, all Christians are to be said to live the life of Christ. But the life of Christ is according to faith, and so, too, is the life of Christians. And since this life produced, in the courses of ages, both the Church and the Sacraments, it is quite right to say that their origin is from Christ and is divine. In the same way they prove that the Scriptures and the dogmas are divine. And thus the Modernistic theology may be said to be complete. No great thing, in truth, but more than enough for the theologian who professes that the conclusions of science must always, and in all things, be respected. The application of these theories to the other points We shall proceed to expound, anybody may easily make for himself.

Dogma and the Sacraments

21. Thus far We have spoken of the origin and nature of faith. But as faith has many shoots, and chief among them the Church, dogma, worship, the Books which we call "Sacred," of these also we must know what is taught by the Modernists. To begin with dogma, we have already indicated its origin and nature. Dogma is born of the species of impulse or necessity by virtue of which the believer is constrained to elaborate his religious thought so as to render it clearer for himself and others. This elaboration consists entirely in the process of penetrating and refining the primitive formula, not indeed in itself and according to logical development, but as required by circumstances, or vitally as the Modernists more abstrusely put it. Hence it happens that around the primitive formula secondary formulas gradu-

ally continue to be formed, and these subsequently grouped into bodies of doctrine, or into doctrinal constructions as they prefer to call them, and further sanctioned by the public magisterium as responding to the common consciousness, are called dogma. Dogma is to be carefully distinguished from the speculations of theologians which, although not alive with the life of dogma, are not without their utility as serving to harmonize religion with science and remove opposition between the two, in such a way as to throw light from without on religion, and it may be even to prepare the matter for future dogma. Concerning worship there would not be much to be said, were it not that under this head are comprised the Sacraments, concerning which the Modernists fall into the gravest errors. For them the Sacraments are the resultant of a double need - for, as we have seen, everything in their system is explained by inner impulses or necessities. In the present case, the first need is that of giving some sensible manifestation to religion; the second is that of propagating it, which could not be done without some sensible form and consecrating acts, and these are called sacraments. But for the Modernists the Sacraments are mere symbols or signs, though not devoid of a certain efficacy - an efficacy, they tell us, like that of certain phrases vulgarly described as having "caught on," inasmuch as they have become the vehicle for the diffusion of certain great ideas which strike the public mind. What the phrases are to the ideas, that the Sacraments are to the religious sentiment - that and nothing more. The Modernists would be speaking more clearly were they to affirm that the Sacraments are instituted solely to foster the faith - but this is condemned by the Council of Trent: If anyone say that these sacraments are instituted solely to foster the faith, let him be anathema.

The Holy Scriptures

22. We have already touched upon the nature and origin
of the Sacred Books. According to the principles of the
Modernists they may be rightly described as a collection of
experiences, not indeed of the kind that may come to anybody, but those extraordinary and striking ones which have
happened in any religion. And this is precisely what they
teach about our books of the Old and New Testament. But
to suit their own theories they note with remarkable ingenuity that, although experience is something belonging to the
present, still it may derive its material from the past and the
future alike, inasmuch as the believer by memory lives the
past over again after the manner of the present, and lives the
future already by anticipation. This explains how it is that
the historical and apocalyptical books are included among
the Sacred Writings. God does indeed speak in these books
- through the medium of the believer, but only, according
to Modernistic theology, by vital immanence and permanence. Do we inquire concerning inspiration? Inspiration,
they reply, is distinguished only by its vehemence from that
impulse which stimulates the believer to reveal the faith that
is in him by words or writing. It is something like what happens in poetical inspiration, of which it has been said: There
is God in us, and when he stirreth he sets us afire. And it is
precisely in this sense that God is said to be the origin of the
inspiration of the Sacred Books. The Modernists affirm, too,
that there is nothing in these books which is not inspired.
In this respect some might be disposed to consider them
as more orthodox than certain other moderns who somewhat restrict inspiration, as, for instance, in what have been
put forward as tacit citations. But it is all mere juggling of
words. For if we take the Bible, according to the tenets of
agnosticism, to be a human work, made by men for men, but

allowing the theologian to proclaim that it is divine by immanence, what room is there left in it for inspiration? General inspiration in the Modernist sense it is easy to find, but of inspiration in the Catholic sense there is not a trace.

The Church

23. A wider field for comment is opened when you come to treat of the vagaries devised by the Modernist school concerning the Church. You must start with the supposition that the Church has its birth in a double need, the need of the individual believer, especially if he has had some original and special experience, to communicate his faith to others, and the need of the mass, when the faith has become common to many, to form itself into a society and to guard, increase, and propagate the common good. What, then, is the Church? It is the product of the collective conscience, that is to say of the society of individual consciences which by virtue of the principle of vital permanence, all depend on one first believer, who for Catholics is Christ. Now every society needs a directing authority to guide its members towards the common end, to conserve prudently the elements of cohesion which in a religious society are doctrine and worship. Hence the triple authority in the Catholic Church, disciplinary, dogmatic, liturgical. The nature of this authority is to be gathered from its origin, and its rights and duties from its nature. In past times it was a common error that authority came to the Church from without, that is to say directly from God; and it was then rightly held to be autocratic. But his conception had now grown obsolete. For in the same way as the Church is a vital emanation of the collectivity of consciences, so too authority emanates vitally from the Church itself. Authority therefore, like the Church, has its origin in the religious conscience, and, that being so, is subject to it.

Should it disown this dependence it becomes a tyranny. For we are living in an age when the sense of liberty has reached its fullest development, and when the public conscience has in the civil order introduced popular government. Now there are not two consciences in man, any more than there are two lives. It is for the ecclesiastical authority, therefore, to shape itself to democratic forms, unless it wishes to provoke and foment an intestine conflict in the consciences of mankind. The penalty of refusal is disaster. For it is madness to think that the sentiment of liberty, as it is now spread abroad, can surrender. Were it forcibly confined and held in bonds, terrible would be its outburst, sweeping away at once both Church and religion. Such is the situation for the Modernists, and their one great anxiety is, in consequence, to find a way of conciliation between the authority of the Church and the liberty of believers.

The Relations Between Church and State

24. But it is not with its own members alone that the Church must come to an amicable arrangement - besides its relations with those within, it has others outside. The Church does not occupy the world all by itself; there are other societies in the world, with which it must necessarily have contact and relations. The rights and duties of the Church towards civil societies must, therefore, be determined, and determined, of course, by its own nature as it has been already described. The rules to be applied in this matter are those which have been laid down for science and faith, though in the latter case the question is one of objects while here we have one of ends. In the same way, then, as faith and science are strangers to each other by reason of the diversity of their objects, Church and State are strangers by reason of the diversity of their ends, that of the Church being spiritual while that of the

State is temporal. Formerly it was possible to subordinate the temporal to the spiritual and to speak of some questions as mixed, allowing to the Church the position of queen and mistress in all such, because the Church was then regarded as having been instituted immediately by God as the author of the supernatural order. But his doctrine is today repudiated alike by philosophy and history. The State must, therefore, be separated from the Church, and the Catholic from the citizen. Every Catholic, from the fact that he is also a citizen, has the right and the duty to work for the common good in the way he thinks best, without troubling himself about the authority of the Church, without paying any heed to its wishes, its counsels, its orders - nay, even in spite of its reprimands. To trace out and prescribe for the citizen any line of conduct, on any pretext whatsoever, is to be guilty of an abuse of ecclesiastical authority, against which one is bound to act with all one's might. The principles from which these doctrines spring have been solemnly condemned by our predecessor Pius VI. in his Constitution Auctorem fidei.

The Magisterium of the Church

25. But it is not enough for the Modernist school that the State should be separated from the Church. For as faith is to be subordinated to science, as far as phenomenal elements are concerned, so too in temporal matters the Church must be subject to the State. They do not say this openly as yet - but they will say it when they wish to be logical on this head. For given the principle that in temporal matters the State possesses absolute mastery, it will follow that when the believer, not fully satisfied with his merely internal acts of religion, proceeds to external acts, such for instance as the administration or reception of the sacraments, these will fall under the control of the State. What will then become

of ecclesiastical authority, which can only be exercised by external acts? Obviously it will be completely under the dominion of the State. It is this inevitable consequence which impels many among liberal Protestants to reject all external worship, nay, all external religious community, and makes them advocate what they call, individual religion. If the Modernists have not yet reached this point, they do ask the Church in the meanwhile to be good enough to follow spontaneously where they lead her and adapt herself to the civil forms in vogue. Such are their ideas about disciplinary authority. But far more advanced and far more pernicious are their teachings on doctrinal and dogmatic authority. This is their conception of the magisterium of the Church: No religious society, they say, can be a real unit unless the religious conscience of its members be one, and one also the formula which they adopt. But his double unity requires a kind of common mind whose office is to find and determine the formula that corresponds best with the common conscience, and it must have moreover an authority sufficient to enable it to impose on the community the formula which has been decided upon. From the combination and, as it were fusion of these two elements, the common mind which draws up the formula and the authority which imposes it, arises, according to the Modernists, the notion of the ecclesiastical magisterium. And as this magisterium springs, in its last analysis, from the individual consciences and possesses its mandate of public utility for their benefit, it follows that the ecclesiastical magisterium must be subordinate to them, and should therefore take democratic forms. To prevent individual consciences from revealing freely and openly the impulses they feel, to hinder criticism from impelling dogmas towards their necessary evolutions - this is not a legitimate use but an abuse of a power given for the public utility. So too a due method and measure must be observed in the exercise of authority. To condemn and prescribe a work without the knowledge of the author, without hearing his explanations, without discussion, assuredly savours of tyranny. And thus, here again a way must be found to save the full rights of authority on the one hand and of liberty on the other. In the meanwhile the proper course for the Catholic will be to proclaim publicly his profound respect for authority - and continue to follow his own bent. Their general directions for the Church may be put in this way: Since the end of the Church is entirely spiritual, the religious authority should strip itself of all that external pomp which adorns it in the eyes of the public. And here they forget that while religion is essentially for the soul, it is not exclusively for the soul, and that the honour paid to authority is reflected back on Jesus Christ who instituted it.

The Evolution of Doctrine

26. To finish with this whole question of faith and its shoots, it remains to be seen, Venerable Brethren, what the Modernists have to say about their development. First of all they lay down the general principle that in a living religion everything is subject to change, and must change, and in this way they pass to what may be said to be, among the chief of their doctrines, that of Evolution. To the laws of evolution everything is subject - dogma, Church, worship, the Books we revere as sacred, even faith itself, and the penalty of disobedience is death. The enunciation of this principle will not astonish anybody who bears in mind what the Modernists have had to say about each of these subjects. Having laid down this law of evolution, the Modernists themselves teach us how it works out. And first with regard to faith. The primitive form of faith, they tell us, was rudimentary and common to all men alike, for it had its origin in human nature

and human life. Vital evolution brought with it progress, not by the accretion of new and purely adventitious forms from without, but by an increasing penetration of the religious sentiment in the conscience. This progress was of two kinds: negative, by the elimination of all foreign elements, such, for example, as the sentiment of family or nationality; and positive by the intellectual and moral refining of man, by means of which the idea was enlarged and enlightened while the religious sentiment became more elevated and more intense. For the progress of faith no other causes are to be assigned than those which are adduced to explain its origin. But to them must be added those religious geniuses whom we call prophets, and of whom Christ was the greatest; both because in their lives and their words there was something mysterious which faith attributed to the divinity, and because it fell to their lot to have new and original experiences fully in harmony with the needs of their time. The progress of dogma is due chiefly to the obstacles which faith has to surmount, to the enemies it has to vanquish, to the contradictions it has to repel. Add to this a perpetual striving to penetrate ever more profoundly its own mysteries. Thus, to omit other examples, has it happened in the case of Christ: in Him that divine something which faith admitted in Him expanded in such a way that He was at last held to be God. The chief stimulus of evolution in the domain of worship consists in the need of adapting itself to the uses and customs of peoples, as well as the need of availing itself of the value which certain acts have acquired by long usage. Finally, evolution in the Church itself is fed by the need of accommodating itself to historical conditions and of harmonizing itself with existing forms of society. Such is religious evolution in detail. And here, before proceeding further, we would have you note well this whole theory of necessities and needs, for it is at the root of the entire system of the Modernists, and it is upon it that they will erect that famous method of theirs called the historical.

27. Still continuing the consideration of the evolution of doctrine, it is to be noted that Evolution is due no doubt to those stimulants styled needs, but, if left to their action alone, it would run a great risk of bursting the bounds of tradition, and thus, turned aside from its primitive vital principle, would lead to ruin instead of progress. Hence, studying more closely the ideas of the Modernists, evolution is described as resulting from the conflict of two forces, one of them tending towards progress, the other towards conservation. The conserving force in the Church is tradition, and tradition is represented by religious authority, and this both by right and in fact; for by right it is in the very nature of authority to protect tradition, and, in fact, for authority, raised as it is above the contingencies of life, feels hardly, or not at all, the spurs of progress. The progressive force, on the contrary, which responds to the inner needs lies in the individual consciences and ferments there - especially in such of them as are in most intimate contact with life. Note here, Venerable Brethren, the appearance already of that most pernicious doctrine which would make of the laity a factor of progress in the Church. Now it is by a species of compromise between the forces of conservation and of progress, that is to say between authority and individual consciences, that changes and advances take place. The individual consciences of some of them act on the collective conscience, which brings pressure to bear on the depositaries of authority, until the latter consent to a compromise, and, the pact being made, authority sees to its maintenance.

With all this in mind, one understands how it is that the Modernists express astonishment when they are reprimanded or punished. What is imputed to them as a fault they regard as a sacred duty. Being in intimate contact with consciences they know better than anybody else, and certainly better than the ecclesiastical authority, what needs exist - nay, they embody them, so to speak, in themselves. Having a voice and a pen they use both publicly, for this is their duty. Let authority rebuke them as much as it pleases - they have their own conscience on their side and an intimate experience which tells them with certainty that what they deserve is not blame but praise. Then they reflect that, after all there is no progress without a battle and no battle without its victim, and victims they are willing to be like the prophets and Christ Himself. They have no bitterness in their hearts against the authority which uses them roughly, for after all it is only doing its duty as authority. Their sole grief is that it remains deaf to their warnings, because delay multiplies the obstacles which impede the progress of souls, but the hour will most surely come when there will be no further chance for tergiversation, for if the laws of evolution may be checked for a while, they cannot be ultimately destroyed. And so they go their way, reprimands and condemnations notwithstanding, masking an incredible audacity under a mock semblance of humility. While they make a show of bowing their heads, their hands and minds are more intent than ever on carrying out their purposes. And this policy they follow willingly and wittingly, both because it is part of their system that authority is to be stimulated but not dethroned, and because it is necessary for them to remain within the ranks of the Church in order that they may gradually transform the collective conscience - thus unconsciously avowing that the common conscience is not with them, and that they have no right to claim to be its interpreters.

28. Thus then, Venerable Brethren, for the Modernists, both as authors and propagandists, there is to be nothing stable, nothing immutable in the Church. Nor indeed are they without precursors in their doctrines, for it was of these that Our Predecessor Pius IX wrote: These enemies of divine revelation extol human progress to the skies, and with rash and sacrilegious daring would have it introduced into the Catholic religion as if this religion were not the work of God but of man, or some kind of philosophical discovery susceptible of perfection by human efforts. On the subject of revelation and dogma in particular, the doctrine of the Modernists offers nothing new - we find it condemned in the Syllabus of Pius IX., where it is enunciated in these terms: Divine revelation is imperfect, and therefore subject to continual and indefinite progress, corresponding with the progress of human reason; and condemned still more solemnly in the Vatican Council: The doctrine of the faith which God has revealed has not been proposed to human intelligences to be perfected by them as if it were a philosophical system, but as a divine deposit entrusted to the Spouse of Christ to be faithfully guarded and infallibly interpreted. Hence the sense, too, of the sacred dogmas is that which our Holy Mother the Church has once declared, nor is this sense ever to be abandoned on plea or pretext of a more profound comprehension of the truth. Nor is the development of our knowledge, even concerning the faith, impeded by this pronouncement - on the contrary it is aided and promoted. For the same Council continues: Let intelligence and science and wisdom, therefore, increase and progress abundantly and vigorously in individuals and in the mass, in the believer and in the whole Church, throughout the ages and the centuries - but only in its own kind, that is, according to the same dogma, the same sense, the same acceptation.

29. After having studied the Modernist as philosopher, believer and theologian, it now remains for us to consider him as historian, critic, apologist, reformer.

30. Some Modernists, devoted to historical studies, seem to be greatly afraid of being taken for philosophers. About philosophy, they tell you, they know nothing whatever - and in this they display remarkable astuteness, for they are particularly anxious not to be suspected of being prejudiced in favour of philosophical theories which would lay them open to the charge of not being objective, to use the word in vogue. And yet the truth is that their history and their criticism are saturated with their philosophy, and that their historico-critical conclusions are the natural fruit of their philosophical principles. This will be patent to anybody who reflects. Their three first laws are contained in those three principles of their philosophy already dealt with: the principle of agnosticism, the principle of the transfiguration of things by faith, and the principle which We have called of disfiguration. Let us see what consequences flow from each of them. Agnosticism tells us that history, like every other science, deals entirely with phenomena, and the consequence is that God, and every intervention of God in human affairs, is to be relegated to the domain of faith as belonging to it alone. In things where a double element, the divine and the human, mingles, in Christ, for example, or the Church, or the sacraments, or the many other objects of the same kind, a division must be made and the human element assigned to history while the divine will go to faith. Hence we have that distinction, so current among the Modernists, between the Christ of history and the Christ of faith, between the sacraments of history and the sacraments of faith, and so on. Next

we find that the human element itself, which the historian has to work on, as it appears in the documents, has been by faith transfigured, that is to say raised above its historical conditions. It becomes necessary, therefore, to eliminate also the accretions which faith has added, to assign them to faith itself and to the history of faith: thus, when treating of Christ, the historian must set aside all that surpasses man in his natural condition, either according to the psychological conception of him, or according to the place and period of his existence. Finally, by virtue of the third principle, even those things which are not outside the sphere of history they pass through the crucible, excluding from history and relegating to faith everything which, in their judgment, is not in harmony with what they call the logic of facts and in character with the persons of whom they are predicated. Thus, they will not allow that Christ ever uttered those things which do not seem to be within the capacity of the multitudes that listened to Him. Hence they delete from His real history and transfer to faith all the allegories found in His discourses. Do you inquire as to the criterion they adopt to enable them to make these divisions? The reply is that they argue from the character of the man, from his condition of life, from his education, from the circumstances under which the facts took place - in short, from criteria which, when one considers them well, are purely subjective. Their method is to put themselves into the position and person of Christ, and then to attribute to Him what they would have done under like circumstances. In this way, absolutely a priori and acting on philosophical principles which they admit they hold but which they affect to ignore, they proclaim that Christ, according to what they call His real history, was not God and never did anything divine, and that as man He did and said only what they, judging from the time in which he lived, can admit Him to have said or done.

31. And as history receives its conclusions, ready-made, from philosophy, so too criticism takes its own from history. The critic, on the data furnished him by the historian, makes two parts of all his documents. Those that remain after the triple elimination above described go to form the real history; the rest is attributed to the history of the faith or as it is styled, to internal history. For the Modernists distinguish very carefully between these two kinds of history, and it is to be noted that they oppose the history of the faith to real history precisely as real. Thus we have a double Christ: a real Christ, and a Christ, the one of faith, who never really existed; a Christ who has lived at a given time and in a given place, and a Christ who has never lived outside the pious meditations of the believer - the Christ, for instance, whom we find in the Gospel of St. John, which is pure contemplation from beginning to end.

32. But the dominion of philosophy over history does not end here. Given that division, of which We have spoken, of the documents into two parts, the philosopher steps in again with his principle of vital immanence, and shows how everything in the history of the Church is to be explained by vital emanation. And since the cause or condition of every vital emanation whatsoever is to be found in some need, it follows that no fact can ante-date the need which produced it - historically the fact must be posterior to the need. See how the historian works on this principle. He goes over his documents again, whether they be found in the Sacred Books or elsewhere, draws up from them his list of the successive needs of the Church, whether relating to dogma or liturgy or other matters, and then he hands his list over to the critic. The critic takes in hand the documents dealing with

the history of faith and distributes them, period by period, so that they correspond exactly with the lists of needs, always guided by the principle that the narration must follow the facts, as the facts follow the needs. It may at times happen that some parts of the Sacred Scriptures, such as the Epistles, themselves constitute the fact created by the need. Even so, the rule holds that the age of any document can only be determined by the age in which each need had manifested itself in the Church. Further, a distinction must be made between the beginning of a fact and its development, for what is born one day requires time for growth. Hence the critic must once more go over his documents, ranged as they are through the different ages, and divide them again into two parts, and divide them into two lots, separating those that regard the first stage of the facts from those that deal with their development, and these he must again arrange according to their periods.

33. Then the philosopher must come in again to impose on the historian the obligation of following in all his studies the precepts and laws of evolution. It is next for the historian to scrutinize his documents once more, to examine carefully the circumstances and conditions affecting the Church during the different periods, the conserving force she has put forth, the needs both internal and external that have stimulated her to progress, the obstacles she has had to encounter, in a word everything that helps to determine the manner in which the laws of evolution have been fulfilled in her. This done, he finishes his work by drawing up in its broad lines a history of the development of the facts. The critic follows and fits in the rest of the documents with this sketch; he takes up his pen, and soon the history is made complete. Now we ask here: Who is the author of this history? The historian? The critic? Assuredly, neither of these but the

philosopher. From beginning to end everything in it is a priori, and a priori in a way that reeks of heresy. These men are certainly to be pitied, and of them the Apostle might well say: They became vain in their thoughts. . . professing themselves to be wise they became fools (Rom. i. 21, 22); but, at the same time, they excite just indignation when they accuse the Church of torturing the texts, arranging and confusing them after its own fashion, and for the needs of its cause. In this they are accusing the Church of something for which their own conscience plainly reproaches them.

How the Bible is Dealt With

34. The result of this dismembering of the Sacred Books and this partition of them throughout the centuries is naturally that the Scriptures can no longer be attributed to the authors whose names they bear. The Modernists have no hesitation in affirming commonly that these books, and especially the Pentateuch and the first three Gospels, have been gradually formed by additions to a primitive brief narration - by interpolations of theological or allegorical interpretation, by transitions, by joining different passages together. This means, briefly, that in the Sacred Books we must admit a vital evolution, springing from and corresponding with evolution of faith. The traces of this evolution, they tell us, are so visible in the books that one might almost write a history of them. Indeed this history they do actually write, and with such an easy security that one might believe them to have with their own eyes seen the writers at work through the ages amplifying the Sacred Books. To aid them in this they call to their assistance that branch of criticism which they call textual, and labour to show that such a fact or such a phrase is not in its right place, and adducing other arguments of the same kind. They seem, in fact, to have constructed for

themselves certain types of narration and discourses, upon which they base their decision as to whether a thing is out of place or not. Judge if you can how men with such a system are fitted for practicing this kind of criticism. To hear them talk about their works on the Sacred Books, in which they have been able to discover so much that is defective, one would imagine that before them nobody ever even glanced through the pages of Scripture, whereas the truth is that a whole multitude of Doctors, infinitely superior to them in genius, in erudition, in sanctity, have sifted the Sacred Books in every way, and so far from finding imperfections in them, have thanked God more and more the deeper they have gone into them, for His divine bounty in having vouchsafed to speak thus to men. Unfortunately, these great Doctors did not enjoy the same aids to study that are possessed by the Modernists for their guide and rule, - a philosophy borrowed from the negation of God, and a criterion which consists of themselves.

We believe, then, that We have set forth with sufficient clearness the historical method of the Modernists. The philosopher leads the way, the historian follows, and then in due order come internal and textual criticism. And since it is characteristic of the first cause to communicate its virtue to secondary causes, it is quite clear that the criticism We are concerned with is an agnostic, immanentist, and evolutionist criticism. Hence anybody who embraces it and employs it, makes profession thereby of the errors contained in it, and places himself in opposition to Catholic faith. This being so, one cannot but be greatly surprised by the consideration which is attached to it by certain Catholics. Two causes may be assigned for this: first, the close alliance, independent of all differences of nationality or religion, which the historians and critics of this school have formed among themselves;

second, the boundless effrontery of these men. Let one of them but open his mouth and the others applaud him in chorus, proclaiming that science has made another step forward; let an outsider but hint at a desire to inspect the new discovery with his own eyes, and they are on him in a body; deny it - and you are an ignoramus; embrace it and defend it - and there is no praise too warm for you. In this way they win over any who, did they but realize what they are doing, would shrink back with horror. The impudence and the domineering of some, and the thoughtlessness and imprudence of others, have combined to generate a pestilence in the air which penetrates everywhere and spreads the contagion. But let us pass to the apologist.

The Modernist as Apologist

35. The Modernist apologist depends in two ways on the philosopher. First, indirectly, inasmuch as his theme is history - history dictated, as we have seen, by the philosopher; and, secondly, directly, inasmuch as he takes both his laws and his principles from the philosopher. Hence that common precept of the Modernist school that the new apologetics must be fed from psychological and historical sources. The Modernist apologists, then, enter the arena by proclaiming to the rationalists that though they are defending religion, they have no intention of employing the data of the sacred books or the histories in current use in the Church, and composed according to old methods, but real history written on modern principles and according to rigorously modern methods. In all this they are not using an argumentum ad hominem, but are stating the simple fact that they hold, that the truth is to be found only in this kind of history. They feel that it is not necessary for them to dwell on their own sincerity in their writings - they are already known to and praised by

the rationalists as fighting under the same banner, and they not only plume themselves on these encomiums, which are a kind of salary to them but would only provoke nausea in a real Catholic, but use them as an offset to the reprimands of the Church.

But let us see how the Modernist conducts his apologetics. The aim he sets before himself is to make the non-believer attain that experience of the Catholic religion which, according to the system, is the basis of faith. There are two ways open to him, the objective and the subjective. The first of them proceeds from agnosticism. It tends to show that religion, and especially the Catholic religion, is endowed with such vitality as to compel every psychologist and historian of good faith to recognize that its history hides some unknown element. To this end it is necessary to prove that this religion, as it exists today, is that which was founded by Jesus Christ; that is to say, that it is the product of the progressive development of the germ which He brought into the world. Hence it is imperative first of all to establish what this germ was, and this the Modernist claims to be able to do by the following formula: Christ announced the coming of the kingdom of God, which was to be realized within a brief lapse of time and of which He was to become the Messiah, the divinely-given agent and ordainer. Then it must be shown how this germ, always immanent and permanent in the bosom of the Church, has gone on slowly developing in the course of history, adapting itself successively to the different mediums through which it has passed, borrowing from them by vital assimilation all the dogmatic, cultural, ecclesiastical forms that served its purpose; whilst, on the other hand , it surmounted all obstacles, vanquished all enemies, and survived all assaults and all combats. Anybody who well and duly considers this mass of obstacles, adversaries, attacks, combats, and the vitality and fecundity which the Church has shown throughout them all, must admit that if the laws of evolution are visible in her life they fail to explain the whole of her history - the unknown rises forth from it and presents itself before us. Thus do they argue, never suspecting that their determination of the primitive germ is an a priori of agnostic and evolutionist philosophy, and that the formula of it has been gratuitously invented for the sake of buttressing their position.

36. But while they endeavour by this line of reasoning to secure access for the Catholic religion into souls, these new apologists are quite ready to admit that there are many distasteful things in it. Nay, they admit openly, and with ill-concealed satisfaction, that they have found that even its dogma is not exempt from errors and contradictions. They add also that this is not only excusable but - curiously enough - even right and proper. In the Sacred Books there are many passages referring to science or history where manifest errors are to be found. But the subject of these books is not science or history but religion and morals. In them history and science serve only as a species of covering to enable the religious and moral experiences wrapped up in them to penetrate more readily among the masses. The masses understood science and history as they are expressed in these books, and it is clear that had science and history been expressed in a more perfect form this would have proved rather a hindrance than a help. Then, again, the Sacred Books being essentially religious, are consequently necessarily living. Now life has its own truth and its own logic, belonging as they do to a different order, viz., truth of adaptation and of proportion both with the medium in which it exists and with the end towards which it tends. Finally the Modernists, losing all sense of control, go so far as to proclaim as true and legitimate every-

thing that is explained by life.

We, Venerable Brethren, for whom there is but one and only truth, and who hold that the Sacred Books, written under the inspiration of the Holy Ghost, have God for their author (Conc. Vat., De Revel., c. 2) declare that this is equivalent to attributing to God Himself the lie of utility or officious lie, and We say with St. Augustine: In an authority so high, admit but one officious lie, and there will not remain a single passage of those apparently difficult to practice or to believe, which on the same most pernicious rule may not be explained as a lie uttered by the author willfully and to serve a purpose. (Epist. 28). And thus it will come about, the holy Doctor continues, that everybody will believe and refuse to believe what he likes or dislikes. But the Modernists pursue their way gaily. They grant also that certain arguments adduced in the Sacred Books, like those, for example, which are based on the prophecies, have no rational foundation to rest on. But they will defend even these as artifices of preaching, which are justified by life. Do they stop here? No, indeed, for they are ready to admit, nay, to proclaim that Christ Himself manifestly erred in determining the time when the coming of the Kingdom of God was to take place, and they tell us that we must not be surprised at this since even Christ was subject to the laws of life! After this what is to become of the dogmas of the Church? The dogmas brim over with flagrant contradictions, but what matter that since, apart from the fact that vital logic accepts them, they are not repugnant to symbolical truth. Are we not dealing with the infinite, and has not the infinite an infinite variety of aspects? In short, to maintain and defend these theories they do not hesitate to declare that the noblest homage that can be paid to the Infinite is to make it the object of contradictory propositions! But when they justify even contradiction, what is it that they will refuse to justify?

Subjective Arguments

37. But it is not solely by objective arguments that the non-believer may be disposed to faith. There are also subjective ones at the disposal of the Modernists, and for those they return to their doctrine of immanence. They endeavour, in fact, to persuade their non-believer that down in the very deeps of his nature and his life lie the need and the desire for religion, and this not a religion of any kind, but the specific religion known as Catholicism, which, they say, is absolutely postulated by the perfect development of life. And here We cannot but deplore once more, and grievously, that there are Catholics who, while rejecting immanence as a doctrine, employ it as a method of apologetics, and who do this so imprudently that they seem to admit that there is in human nature a true and rigorous necessity with regard to the supernatural order - and not merely a capacity and a suitability for the supernatural, order - and not merely a capacity and a suitability for the supernatural, such as has at all times been emphasized by Catholic apologists. Truth to tell it is only the moderate Modernists who make this appeal to an exigency for the Catholic religion. As for the others, who might be called intergralists, they would show to the non-believer, hidden away in the very depths of his being, the very germ which Christ Himself bore in His conscience, and which He bequeathed to the world. Such, Venerable Brethren, is a summary description of the apologetic method of the Modernists, in perfect harmony, as you may see, with their doctrines - methods and doctrines brimming over with errors, made not for edification but for destruction, not for the formation of Catholics but for the plunging of Catholics into heresy; methods and doctrines that would be fatal to any

religion.

The Modernist as Reformer

38. It remains for Us now to say a few words about the Modernist as reformer. From all that has preceded, some idea may be gained of the reforming mania which possesses them: in all Catholicism there is absolutely nothing on which it does not fasten. Reform of philosophy, especially in the seminaries: the scholastic philosophy is to be relegated to the history of philosophy among obsolete systems, and the young men are to be taught modern philosophy which alone is true and suited to the times in which we live. Reform of theology; rational theology is to have modern philosophy for its foundation, and positive theology is to be founded on the history of dogma. As for history, it must be for the future written and taught only according to their modern methods and principles. Dogmas and their evolution are to be harmonized with science and history. In the Catechism no dogmas are to be inserted except those that have been duly reformed and are within the capacity of the people. Regarding worship, the number of external devotions is to be reduced, or at least steps must be taken to prevent their further increase, though, indeed, some of the admirers of symbolism are disposed to be more indulgent on this head. Ecclesiastical government requires to be reformed in all its branches, but especially in its disciplinary and dogmatic parts. Its spirit with the public conscience, which is not wholly for democracy; a share in ecclesiastical government should therefore be given to the lower ranks of the clergy, and even to the laity, and authority should be decentralised. The Roman Congregations, and especially the index and the Holy Office, are to be reformed. The ecclesiastical authority must change its line of conduct in the social and political world; while keep-

ing outside political and social organization, it must adapt itself to those which exist in order to penetrate them with its spirit. With regard to morals, they adopt the principle of the Americanists, that the active virtues are more important than the passive, both in the estimation in which they must be held and in the exercise of them. The clergy are asked to return to their ancient lowliness and poverty, and in their ideas and action to be guided by the principles of Modernism; and there are some who, echoing the teaching of their Protestant masters, would like the suppression of ecclesiastical celibacy. What is there left in the Church which is not to be reformed according to their principles?

Modernism and All the Heresies

39. It may be, Venerable Brethren, that some may think We have dwelt too long on this exposition of the doctrines of the Modernists. But it was necessary, both in order to refute their customary charge that We do not understand their ideas, and to show that their system does not consist in scattered and unconnected theories but in a perfectly organized body, all the parts of which are solidly joined so that it is not possible to admit one without admitting all. For this reason, too, We have had to give this exposition a somewhat didactic form and not to shrink from employing certain uncouth terms in use among the Modernists. And now, can anybody who takes a survey of the whole system be surprised that We should define it as the synthesis of all heresies? Were one to attempt the task of collecting together all the errors that have been broached against the faith and to concentrate the sap and substance of them all into one, he could not better succeed than the Modernists have done. Nay, they have done more than this, for, as we have already intimated, their system means the destruction not of the Catholic religion alone

but of all religion. With good reason do the rationalists applaud them, for the most sincere and the frankest among the rationalists warmly welcome the modernists as their most valuable allies.

For let us return for a moment, Venerable Brethren, to that most disastrous doctrine of agnosticism. By it every avenue that leads the intellect to God is barred, but the Modernists would seek to open others available for sentiment and action. Vain efforts! For, after all, what is sentiment but the reaction of the soul on the action of the intelligence or the senses. Take away the intelligence, and man, already inclined to follow the senses, becomes their slave. Vain, too, from another point of view, for all these fantasias on the religious sentiment will never be able to destroy common sense, and common sense tells us that emotion and everything that leads the heart captive proves a hindrance instead of a help to the discovery of truth. We speak, of course, of truth in itself - as for that other purely subjective truth, the fruit of sentiment and action, if it serves its purpose for the jugglery of words, it is of no use to the man who wants to know above all things whether outside himself there is a God into whose hands he is one day to fall. True, the Modernists do call in experience to eke out their system, but what does this experience add to sentiment? Absolutely nothing beyond a certain intensity and a proportionate deepening of the conviction of the reality of the object. But these two will never make sentiment into anything but sentiment, nor deprive it of its characteristic which is to cause deception when the intelligence is not there to guide it; on the contrary, they but confirm and aggravate this characteristic, for the more intense sentiment is the more it is sentimental. In matters of religious sentiment and religious experience, you know, Venerable Brethren, how necessary is prudence and how necessary, too, the science which directs prudence. You know it from your own dealings with sounds, and especially with souls in whom sentiment predominates; you know it also from your reading of ascetical books - books for which the Modernists have but little esteem, but which testify to a science and a solidity very different from theirs, and to a refinement and subtlety of observation of which the Modernists give no evidence. Is it not really folly, or at least sovereign imprudence, to trust oneself without control to Modernist experiences? Let us for a moment put the question: if experiences have so much value in their eyes, why do they not attach equal weight to the experience that thousands upon thousands of Catholics have that the Modernists are on the wrong road? It is, perchance, that all experiences except those felt by the Modernists are false and deceptive? The vast majority of mankind holds and always will hold firmly that sentiment and experience alone, when not enlightened and guided by reason, do not lead to the knowledge of God. What remains, then, but the annihilation of all religion, - atheism? Certainly it is not the doctrine of symbolism - will save us from this. For if all the intellectual elements, as they call them, of religion are pure symbols, will not the very name of God or of divine personality be also a symbol, and if this be admitted will not the personality of God become a matter of doubt and the way opened to Pantheism? And to Pantheism that other doctrine of the divine immanence leads directly. For does it, We ask, leave God distinct from man or not? If yes, in what does it differ from Catholic doctrine, and why reject external revelation? If no, we are at once in Pantheism. Now the doctrine of immanence in the Modernist acceptation holds and professes that every phenomenon of conscience proceeds from man as man. The rigorous conclusion from this is the identity of man with God, which means Pantheism. The same conclusion follows from the distinction Modernists make between science and faith. The object of science they say is the reality of the knowable; the object of faith, on the contrary, is the reality of the unknowable. Now what makes the unknowable unknowable is its disproportion with the intelligible - a disproportion which nothing whatever, even in the doctrine of the Modernist, can suppress. Hence the unknowable remains and will eternally remain unknowable to the believer as well as to the man of science. Therefore if any religion at all is possible it can only be the religion of an unknowable reality. And why this religion might not be that universal soul of the universe, of which a rationalist speaks, is something We do see. Certainly this suffices to show superabundantly by how many roads Modernism leads to the annihilation of all religion. The first step in this direction was taken by Protestantism; the second is made by Modernism; the next will plunge headlong into atheism.

THE CAUSE OF MODERNISM

40. To penetrate still deeper into Modernism and to find a suitable remedy for such a deep sore, it behooves Us, Venerable Brethren, to investigate the causes which have engendered it and which foster its growth. That the proximate and immediate cause consists in a perversion of the mind cannot be open to doubt. The remote causes seem to us to be reduced to two: curiosity and pride. Curiosity by itself, if not prudently regulated, suffices to explain all errors. Such is the opinion of Our Predecessor, Gregory XVI., who wrote: A lamentable spectacle is that presented by the aberrations of human reason when it yields to the spirit of novelty, when against the warning of the Apostle it seeks to know beyond what it is meant to know, and when relying too much on itself it thinks it can find the fruit outside the Church wherein

truth is found without the slightest shadow of error (Ep. Encycl. Singulari nos, 7 Kal. Jul. 1834).

But it is pride which exercises an incomparably greater sway over the soul to blind it and plunge it into error, and pride sits in Modernism as in its own house, finding sustenance everywhere in its doctrines and an occasion to flaunt itself in all its aspects. It is pride which fills Modernists with that confidence in themselves and leads them to hold themselves up as the rule for all, pride which puffs them up with that vainglory which allows them to regard themselves as the sole possessors of knowledge, and makes them say, inflated with presumption, We are not as the rest of men, and which, to make them really not as other men, leads them to embrace all kinds of the most absurd novelties; it is pride which rouses in them the spirit of disobedience and causes them to demand a compromise between authority and liberty; it is pride that makes of them the reformers of others, while they forget to reform themselves, and which begets their absolute want of respect for authority, not excepting the supreme authority. No, truly, there is no road which leads so directly and so quickly to Modernism as pride. When a Catholic laymen or a priest forgets that precept of the Christian life which obliges us to renounce ourselves if we would follow Jesus Christ and neglects to tear pride from his heart, ah! but he is a fully ripe subject for the errors of Modernism. Hence, Venerable Brethren, it will be your first duty to thwart such proud men, to employ them only in the lowest and obscurest offices; the higher they try to rise, the lower let them be placed, so that their lowly position may deprive them of the power of causing damage. Sound your young clerics, too, most carefully, by yourselves and by the directors of your seminaries, and when you find the spirit of pride among any of them reject them without compunction from the priesthood. Would to God that this had always been done with the proper vigilance and constancy.

41. If we pass from the moral to the intellectual causes of Modernism, the first which presents itself, and the chief one, is ignorance. Yes, these very Modernists who pose as Doctors of the Church, who puff out their cheeks when they speak of modern philosophy, and show such contempt for scholasticism, have embraced the one with all its false glamour because their ignorance of the other has left them without the means of being able to recognise confusion of thought, and to refute sophistry. Their whole system, with all its errors, has been born of the alliance between faith and false philosophy.

Methods of Propagandism

42. If only they had displayed less zeal and energy in propagating it! But such is their activity and such their unwearying capacity for work on behalf of their cause, that one cannot but be pained to see them waste such labour in endeavouring to ruin the Church when they might have been of such service to her had their efforts been better employed. Their articles to delude men's minds are of two kinds, the first to remove obstacles from their path, the second to devise and apply actively and patiently every instrument that can serve their purpose. They recognize that the three chief difficulties for them are scholastic philosophy, the authority of the fathers and tradition, and the magisterium of the Church, and on these they wage unrelenting war. For scholastic philosophy and theology they have only ridicule and contempt. Whether it is ignorance or fear, or both, that inspires this conduct in them, certain it is that the passion for novelty is always united in them with hatred of scholasti-

cism, and there is no surer sign that a man is on the way to Modernism than when he begins to show his dislike for this system. Modernists and their admirers should remember the proposition condemned by Pius IX: The method and principles which have served the doctors of scholasticism when treating of theology no longer correspond with the exigencies of our time or the progress of science (Syll. Prop. 13). They exercise all their ingenuity in diminishing the force and falsifying the character of tradition, so as to rob it of all its weight. But for Catholics the second Council of Nicea will always have the force of law, where it condemns those who dare, after the impious fashion of heretics, to deride the ecclesiastical traditions, to invent novelties of some kind . . . or endeavour by malice or craft to overthrow any one of the legitimate traditions of the Catholic Church; and Catholics will hold for law, also, the profession of the fourth Council of Constantinople: We therefore profess to conserve and guard the rules bequeathed to the Holy Catholic and Apostolic Church by the Holy and most illustrious Apostles, by the orthodox Councils, both general and local, and by every one of those divine interpreters the Fathers and Doctors of the Church. Wherefore the Roman Pontiffs, Pius IV. and Pius IX., ordered the insertion in the profession of faith of the following declaration: I most firmly admit and embrace the apostolic and ecclesiastical traditions and other observances and constitutions of the Church. The Modernists pass the same judgment on the most holy Fathers of the Church as they pass on tradition; decreeing, with amazing effrontery that, while personally most worthy of all veneration, they were entirely ignorant of history and criticism, for which they are only excusable on account of the time in which they lived. Finally, the Modernists try in every way to diminish and weaken the authority of the ecclesiastical magisterium itself by sacrilegiously falsifying its origin, character, and rights, and by freely repeating the calumnies of its adversaries. To all the band of Modernists may be applied those words which Our Predecessor wrote with such pain: To bring contempt and odium on the mystic Spouse of Christ, who is the true light, the children of darkness have been wont to cast in her face before the world a stupid calumny, and perverting the meaning and force of things and words, to depict her as the friend of darkness and ignorance, and the enemy of light, science, and progress (Motu-proprio, Ut mysticum, 14 March, 1891). This being so, Venerable Brethren, no wonder the Modernists vent all their gall and hatred on Catholics who sturdily fight the battles of the Church. But of all the insults they heap on them those of ignorance and obstinacy are the favourites. When an adversary rises up against them with an erudition and force that render him redoubtable, they try to make a conspiracy of silence around him to nullify the effects of his attack, while in flagrant contrast with this policy towards Catholics, they load with constant praise the writers who range themselves on their side, hailing their works, excluding novelty in every page, with choruses of applause; for them the scholarship of a writer is in direct proportion to the recklessness of his attacks on antiquity, and of his efforts to undermine tradition and the ecclesiastical magisterium; when one of their number falls under the condemnations of the Church the rest of them, to the horror of good Catholics, gather round him, heap public praise upon him, venerate him almost as a martyr to truth. The young, excited and confused by all this glamour of praise and abuse, some of them afraid of being branded as ignorant, others ambitious to be considered learned, and both classes goaded internally by curiosity and pride, often surrender and give themselves up to Modernism.

43. And here we have already some of the artifices employed by Modernists to exploit their wares. What efforts they make to win new recruits! They seize upon chairs in the seminaries and universities, and gradually make of them chairs of pestilence. From these sacred chairs they scatter, though not always openly, the seeds of their doctrines; they proclaim their teachings without disguise in congresses; they introduce them and make them the vogue in social institutions. Under their own names and under pseudonyms they publish numbers of books, newspapers, reviews, and sometimes one and the same writer adopts a variety of pseudonyms to trap the incautious reader into believing in a whole multitude of Modernist writers - in short they leave nothing untried, in action, discourses, writings, as though there were a frenzy of propaganda upon them. And the results of all this? We have to lament at the sight of many young men once full of promise and capable of rendering great services to the Church, now gone astray. And there is another sight that saddens Us too: that of so many other Catholics, who, while they certainly do not go so far as the former, have yet grown into the habit, as though they had been breathing a poisoned atmosphere, of thinking and speaking and writing with a liberty that ill becomes Catholics. They are to be found among the laity, and in the ranks of the clergy, and they are not wanting even in the last place where one might expect to meet them, in religious institutes. If they treat of biblical questions, it is upon Modernist principles; if they write history, it is to search out with curiosity and to publish openly, on the pretext of telling the whole truth and with a species of ill-concealed satisfaction, everything that looks to them like a stain in the history of the Church. Under the sway of certain a priori rules they destroy as far as they can the pious traditions of the people, and bring ridicule on certain relics highly venerable from their antiquity. They are possessed

by the empty desire of being talked about, and they know they would never succeed in this were they to say only what has been always said. It may be that they have persuaded themselves that in all this they are really serving God and the Church - in reality they only offend both, less perhaps by their works themselves than by the spirit in which they write and by the encouragement they are giving to the extravagances of the Modernists.

REMEDIES

44. Against this host of grave errors, and its secret and open advance, Our Predecessor Leo XIII., of happy memory, worked strenuously especially as regards the Bible, both in his words and his acts. But, as we have seen, the Modernists are not easily deterred by such weapons - with an affectation of submission and respect, they proceeded to twist the words of the Pontiff to their own sense, and his acts they described as directed against others than themselves. And the evil has gone on increasing from day to day. We therefore, Venerable Brethren, have determined to adopt at once the most efficacious measures in Our power, and We beg and conjure you to see to it that in this most grave matter nobody will ever be able to say that you have been in the slightest degree wanting in vigilance, zeal or firmness. And what We ask of you and expect of you, We ask and expect also of all other pastors of souls, of all educators and professors of clerics, and in a very special way of the superiors of religious institutions.

I. - The Study of Scholastic Philosophy

45. In the first place, with regard to studies, We will and ordain that scholastic philosophy be made the basis of the

sacred sciences. It goes without saying that if anything is met with among the scholastic doctors which may be regarded as an excess of subtlety, or which is altogether destitute of probability, We have no desire whatever to propose it for the imitation of present generations (Leo XIII. Enc. Aeterni Patris). And let it be clearly understood above all things that the scholastic philosophy We prescribe is that which the Angelic Doctor has bequeathed to us, and We, therefore, declare that all the ordinances of Our Predecessor on this subject continue fully in force, and, as far as may be necessary, We do decree anew, and confirm, and ordain that they be by all strictly observed. In seminaries where they may have been neglected let the Bishops impose them and require their observance, and let this apply also to the Superiors of religious institutions. Further let Professors remember that they cannot set St. Thomas aside, especially in metaphysical questions, without grave detriment.

46. On this philosophical foundation the theological edifice is to be solidly raised. Promote the study of theology, Venerable Brethren, by all means in your power, so that your clerics on leaving the seminaries may admire and love it, and always find their delight in it. For in the vast and varied abundance of studies opening before the mind desirous of truth, everybody knows how the old maxim describes theology as so far in front of all others that every science and art should serve it and be to it as handmaidens(Leo XIII., Lett. ap. In Magna, Dec. 10, 1889). We will add that We deem worthy of praise those who with full respect for tradition, the Holy Fathers, and the ecclesiastical magisterium, undertake, with well-balanced judgment and guided by Catholic principles (which is not always the case), seek to illustrate positive theology by throwing the light of true history upon it. Certainly more attention must be paid to positive theol-

ogy than in the past, but this must be done without detriment to scholastic theology, and those are to be disapproved as of Modernist tendencies who exalt positive theology in such a way as to seem to despise the scholastic.

47. With regard to profane studies suffice it to recall here what Our Predecessor has admirably said: Apply yourselves energetically to the study of natural sciences: the brilliant discoveries and the bold and useful applications of them made in our times which have won such applause by our contemporaries will be an object of perpetual praise for those that come after us (Leo XIII. Alloc., March 7, 1880). But this do without interfering with sacred studies, as Our Predecessor in these most grave words prescribed: If you carefully search for the cause of those errors you will find that it lies in the fact that in these days when the natural sciences absorb so much study, the more severe and lofty studies have been proportionately neglected - some of them have almost passed into oblivion, some of them are pursued in a half-hearted or superficial way, and, sad to say, now that they are fallen from their old estate, they have been dis fig- ured by perverse doctrines and monstrous errors (loco cit.). We ordain, therefore, that the study of natural science in the seminaries be carried on under this law.

II - Practical Application

48. All these prescriptions and those of Our Predecessor are to be borne in mind whenever there is question of choosing directors and professors for seminaries and Catholic Univer- sities. Anybody who in any way is found to be imbued with Modernism is to be excluded without compunction from these offices, and those who already occupy them are to be withdrawn. The same policy is to be adopted towards those

who favour Modernism either by extolling the Modernists or excusing their culpable conduct, by criticizing scholasticism, the Holy Father, or by refusing obedience to ecclesiastical authority in any of its depositaries; and towards those who show a love of novelty in history, archaeology, biblical exegesis, and finally towards those who neglect the sacred sciences or appear to prefer to them the profane. In all this question of studies, Venerable Brethren, you cannot be too watchful or too constant, but most of all in the choice of professors, for as a rule the students are modelled after the pattern of their masters. Strong in the consciousness of your duty, act always prudently but vigorously.

49. Equal diligence and severity are to be used in examining and selecting candidates for Holy Orders. Far, far from the clergy be the love of novelty! God hates the proud and the obstinate. For the future the doctorate of theology and canon law must never be conferred on anybody who has not made the regular course of scholastic philosophy; if conferred it shall be held as null and void. The rules laid down in 1896 by the Sacred Congregation of Bishops and Regulars for the clerics, both secular and regular, of Italy concerning the frequenting of the Universities, We now decree to be extended to all nations. Clerics and priests inscribed in a Catholic Institute or University must not in the future follow in civil Universities those courses for which there are chairs in the Catholic Institutes to which they belong. If this has been permitted anywhere in the past, We ordain that it be not allowed for the future. Let the Bishops who form the Governing Board of such Catholic Institutes or Universities watch with all care that these Our commands be constantly observed.

III. - Episcopal Vigilance Over Publications

50. It is also the duty of the bishops to prevent writings infected with Modernism or favourable to it from being read when they have been published, and to hinder their publication when they have not. No book or paper or periodical of this kind must ever be permitted to seminarists or university students. The injury to them would be equal to that caused by immoral reading - nay, it would be greater for such writings poison Christian life at its very fount. The same decision is to be taken concerning the writings of some Catholics, who, though not badly disposed themselves but ill-instructed in theological studies and imbued with modern philosophy, strive to make this harmonize with the faith, and, as they say, to turn it to the account of the faith. The name and reputation of these authors cause them to be read without suspicion, and they are, therefore, all the more dangerous in preparing the way for Modernism.

51. To give you some more general directions, Venerable Brethren, in a matter of such moment, We bid you do everything in your power to drive out of your dioceses, even by solemn interdict, any pernicious books that may be in circulation there. The Holy See neglects no means to put down writings of this kind, but the number of them has now grown to such an extent that it is impossible to censure them all. Hence it happens that the medicine sometimes arrives too late, for the disease has taken root during the delay. We will, therefore, that the Bishops, putting aside all fear and the prudence of the flesh, despising the outcries of the wicked, gently by all means but constantly, do each his own share of this work, remembering the injunctions of Leo XIII. in the Apostolic Constitution Officiorum: Let the Ordinaries, acting in this also as Delegates of the Apostolic See, exert

themselves to prescribe and to put out of reach of the faithful injurious books or other writings printed or circulated in their dioceses. In this passage the Bishops, it is true, receive a right, but they have also a duty imposed on them. Let no Bishop think that he fulfils this duty by denouncing to us one or two books, while a great many others of the same kind are being published and circulated. Nor are you to be deterred by the fact that a book has obtained the Imprimatur elsewhere, both because this may be merely simulated, and because it may have been granted through carelessness or easiness or excessive confidence in the author as may sometimes happen in religious Orders. Besides, just as the same food does not agree equally with everybody, it may happen that a book harmless in one may, on account of the different circumstances, be hurtful in another. Should a Bishop, therefore, after having taken the advice of prudent persons, deem it right to condemn any of such books in his diocese, We not only give him ample faculty to do so but We impose it upon him as a duty to do so. Of course, it is Our wish that in such action proper regard be used, and sometimes it will suffice to restrict the prohibition to the clergy; but even in such cases it will be obligatory on Catholic booksellers not to put on sale books condemned by the Bishop. And while We are on this subject of booksellers, We wish the Bishops to see to it that they do not, through desire for gain, put on sale unsound books. It is certain that in the catalogues of some of them the books of the Modernists are not unfrequently announced with no small praise. If they refuse obedience let the Bishops have no hesitation in depriving them of the title of Catholic booksellers; so too, and with more reason, if they have the title of Episcopal booksellers, and if they have that of Pontifical, let them be denounced to the Apostolic See. Finally, We remind all of the XXVI. article of the abovementioned Constitution Officiorum: All those who have obtained an apostolic faculty to read and keep forbidden books, are not thereby authorized to read books and periodicals forbidden by the local Ordinaries, unless the apostolic faculty expressly concedes permission to read and keep books condemned by anybody.

IV. - Censorship

52. But it is not enough to hinder the reading and the sale of bad books - it is also necessary to prevent them from being printed. Hence let the Bishops use the utmost severity in granting permission to print. Under the rules of the Constitution Officiorum, many publications require the authorization of the Ordinary, and in some dioceses it has been made the custom to have a suitable number of official censors for the examination of writings. We have the highest praise for this institution, and We not only exhort, but We order that it be extended to all dioceses. In all episcopal Curias, therefore, let censors be appointed for the revision of works intended for publication, and let the censors be chosen from both ranks of the clergy - secular and regular - men of age, knowledge and prudence who will know how to follow the golden mean in their judgments. It shall be their office to examine everything which requires permission for publication according to Articles XLI. and XLII. of the above-mentioned Constitution. The Censor shall give his verdict in writing. If it be favourable, the Bishop will give the permission for publication by the word Imprimatur, which must always be preceded by the Nihil obstat and the name of the Censor. In the Curia of Rome official censors shall be appointed just as elsewhere, and the appointment of them shall appertain to the Master of the Sacred Palaces, after they have been proposed to the Cardinal Vicar and accepted by the Sovereign Pontiff. It will also be the office of the Master of the Sacred

Palaces to select the censor for each writing. Permission for publication will be granted by him as well as by the Cardinal Vicar or his Vicegerent, and this permission, as above prescribed, must always be preceded by the Nihil obstat and the name of the Censor. Only on very rare and exceptional occasions, and on the prudent decision of the bishop, shall it be possible to omit mention of the Censor. The name of the Censor shall never be made known to the authors until he shall have given a favourable decision, so that he may not have to suffer annoyance either while he is engaged in the examination of a writing or in case he should deny his approval. Censors shall never be chosen from the religious orders until the opinion of the Provincial, or in Rome of the General, has been privately obtained, and the Provincial or the General must give a conscientious account of the character, knowledge and orthodoxy of the candidate. We admonish religious superiors of their solemn duty never to allow anything to be published by any of their subjects without permission from themselves and from the Ordinary. Finally We affirm and declare that the title of Censor has no value and can never be adduced to give credit to the private opinions of the person who holds it.

Priests as Editors

53. Having said this much in general, We now ordain in particular a more careful observance of Article XLII. of the above-mentioned Constitution Officiorum. It is forbidden to secular priests, without the previous consent of the Ordinary, to undertake the direction of papers or periodicals. This permission shall be withdrawn from any priest who makes a wrong use of it after having been admonished. With regard to priests who are correspondents or collaborators of periodicals, as it happens not unfrequently that they write mat-

ter infected with Modernism for their papers or periodicals, let the Bishops see to it that this is not permitted to happen, and, should they fail in this duty, let the Bishops make due provision with authority delegated by the Supreme Pontiff. Let there be, as far as this is possible, a special Censor for newspapers and periodicals written by Catholics. It shall be his office to read in due time each number after it has been published, and if he find anything dangerous in it let him order that it be corrected. The Bishop shall have the same right even when the Censor has seen nothing objectionable in a publication.

V. - Congresses

54. We have already mentioned congresses and public gatherings as among the means used by the Modernists to propagate and defend their opinions. In the future Bishops shall not permit Congresses of priests except on very rare occasions. When they do permit them it shall only be on condition that matters appertaining to the Bishops or the Apostolic See be not treated in them, and that no motions or postulates be allowed that would imply a usurpation of sacred authority, and that no mention be made in them of Modernism, presbyterianism, or laicism. At Congresses of this kind, which can only be held after permission in writing has been obtained in due time and for each case, it shall not be lawful for priests of other dioceses to take part without the written permission of their Ordinary. Further no priest must lose sight of the solemn recommendation of Leo XIII.: Let priests hold as sacred the authority of their pastors, let them take it for certain that the sacerdotal ministry, if not exercised under the guidance of the Bishops, can never be either holy, or very fruitful or respectable (Lett. Encyc. Nobilissima Gallorum, 10 Feb., 1884).

55. But of what avail, Venerable Brethren, will be all Our commands and prescriptions if they be not dutifully and firmly carried out? And, in order that this may be done, it has seemed expedient to Us to extend to all dioceses the regulations laid down with great wisdom many years ago by the Bishops of Umbria for theirs.

"In order," they say, "to extirpate the errors already propagated and to prevent their further diffusion, and to remove those teachers of impiety through whom the pernicious effects of such diffusion are being perpetuated, this sacred Assembly, following the example of St. Charles Borromeo, has decided to establish in each of the dioceses a Council consisting of approved members of both branches of the clergy, which shall be charged the task of noting the existence of errors and the devices by which new ones are introduced and propagated, and to inform the Bishop of the whole so that he may take counsel with them as to the best means for nipping the evil in the bud and preventing it spreading for the ruin of souls or, worse still, gaining strength and growth" (Acts of the Congress of the Bishops of Umbria, Nov. 1849, tit 2, art. 6). We decree, therefore, that in every diocese a council of this kind, which We are pleased to name "the Council of Vigilance," be instituted without delay. The priests called to form part in it shall be chosen somewhat after the manner above prescribed for the Censors, and they shall meet every two months on an appointed day under the presidency of the Bishop. They shall be bound to secrecy as to their deliberations and decisions, and their function shall be as follows: They shall watch most carefully for every trace and sign of Modernism both in publications and in teaching, and, to preserve from it the clergy and the young, they shall take all prudent, prompt and efficacious measures. Let them combat novelties of words remembering the admonitions of Leo XIII. (Instruct. S.C. NN. EE. EE., 27 Jan., 1902): It is impossible to approve in Catholic publications of a style inspired by unsound novelty which seems to deride the piety of the faithful and dwells on the introduction of a new order of Christian life, on new directions of the Church, on new aspirations of the modern soul, on a new vocation of the clergy, on a new Christian civilization. Language of this kind is not to be tolerated either in books or from chairs of learning. The Councils must not neglect the books treating of the pious traditions of different places or of sacred relics. Let them not permit such questions to be discussed in periodicals destined to stimulate piety, neither with expressions savouring of mockery or contempt, nor by dogmatic pronouncements, especially when, as is often the case, what is stated as a certainty either does not pass the limits of probability or is merely based on prejudiced opinion. Concerning sacred relics, let this be the rule: When Bishops, who alone are judges in such matters, know for certain the a relic is not genuine, let them remove it at once from the veneration of the faithful; if the authentications of a relic happen to have been lost through civil disturbances, or in any other way, let it not be exposed for public veneration until the Bishop has verified it. The argument of prescription or well-founded presumption is to have weight only when devotion to a relic is commendable by reason of its antiquity, according to the sense of the Decree issued in 1896 by the Congregation of Indulgences and Sacred Relics: Ancient relics are to retain the veneration they have always enjoyed except when in individual instances there are clear arguments that they are false or suppositions. In passing judgment on pious traditions be it always borne in mind that in this matter the Church uses the greatest prudence, and that she does not allow traditions of this kind to be narrated in books except with the utmost caution and with the insertion of the declaration imposed by Urban VIII, and even then she does not guarantee the truth of the fact narrated; she simply does but forbid belief in things for which human arguments are not wanting. On this matter the Sacred Congregation of Rites, thirty years ago, decreed as follows: These apparitions and revelations have neither been approved nor condemned by the Holy See, which has simply allowed that they be believed on purely human faith, on the tradition which they relate, corroborated by testimonies and documents worthy of credence (Decree, May 2, 1877). Anybody who follows this rule has no cause for fear. For the devotion based on any apparition, in as far as it regards the fact itself, that is to say in as far as it is relative, always implies the hypothesis of the truth of the fact; while in as far as it is absolute, it must always be based on the truth, seeing that its object is the persons of the saints who are honoured. The same is true of relics. Finally, We entrust to the Councils of Vigilance the duty of overlooking assiduously and diligently social institutions as well as writings on social questions so that they may harbour no trace of Modernism, but obey the prescriptions of the Roman Pontiffs.

VII - Triennial Returns

56. Lest what We have laid down thus far should fall into oblivion, We will and ordain that the Bishops of all dioceses, a year after the publication of these letters and every three years thenceforward, furnish the Holy See with a diligent and sworn report on all the prescriptions contained in them, and on the doctrines that find currency among the clergy, and especially in the seminaries and other Catholic institutions, and We impose the like obligation on the Generals of Reli-

gious Orders with regard to those under them.

57. This, Venerable Brethren, is what we have thought it our duty to write to you for the salvation of all who believe. The adversaries of the Church will doubtless abuse what we have said to refurbish the old calumny by which we are traduced as the enemy of science and of the progress of humanity. In order to oppose a new answer to such accusations, which the history of the Christian religion refutes by never failing arguments, it is Our intention to establish and develop by every means in our power a special Institute in which, through the co-operation of those Catholics who are most eminent for their learning, the progress of science and other realms of knowledge may be promoted under the guidance and teaching of Catholic truth. God grant that we may happily realize our design with the ready assistance of all those who bear a sincere love for the Church of Christ. But of this we will speak on another occasion.

58. Meanwhile, Venerable Brethren, fully confident in your zeal and work, we beseech for you with our whole heart and soul the abundance of heavenly light, so that in the midst of this great perturbation of men's minds from the insidious invasions of error from every side, you may see clearly what you ought to do and may perform the task with all your strength and courage. May Jesus Christ, the author and finisher of our faith, be with you by His power; and may the Immaculate Virgin, the destroyer of all heresies, be with you by her prayers and aid. And We, as a pledge of Our affection and of divine assistance in adversity, grant most affectionately and with all Our heart to you, your clergy and people the Apostolic Benediction.

Given at St. Peter's, Rome, on the 8th day of September, 1907, the fifth year of our Pontificate.

PIUS X

COMMUNIUM RERUM
ENCYCLICAL OF POPE PIUS X
ON ST. ANSELM OF AOSTA

TO OUR VENERABLE BRETHREN THE PATRIARCHS, PRIMATES, ARCHBISHOPS, BISHOPS, AND OTHER ORDINARIES IN PEACE AND COMMUNION WITH THE APOSTOLIC SEE

Venerable Brethren, Health and the Apostolic Benediction.

Amid the general troubles of the time and the recent disasters at home which afflict Us, there is surely consolation and comfort for Us in that recent display of devotion of the whole Christian people which still continues to be "a spectacle to the world and to angels and to men" (I Cor. iv. 9), and which, if it has now been called forth so generously by the advent of misfortune, has its one true cause in the charity of Our Lord Jesus Christ. For since there is not and there cannot be in the world any charity worthy of the name except through Christ, to Him alone must be attributed all the fruits of it, even in men of lax faith or hostile to religion, who are indebted for whatever vestiges of charity they may possess to the civilization introduced by Christ, which they have not yet succeeded in throwing off entirely and expelling from human society.

2. For this mighty movement of those who would console their Father and help their brethren in their public and private afflictions, words can hardly express Our emotion and Our gratitude. These feelings We have already made known on more than one occasion to individuals, but We cannot delay any longer to give a public expression of Our thanks, first of all, to you, venerable brethren, and through you to all

the faithful entrusted to your care.

3. So, too, We would make public profession of Our gratitude for the many striking demonstrations of affection and reverence which have been offered Us by Our most beloved children in all parts of the world on the occasion of Our sacerdotal jubilee. Most grateful have they been to Us, not so much for Our own sake as for the sake of religion and the Church, as being a profession of fearless faith, and, as it were, a public manifestation of due honor to Christ and His Church, by the respect shown to him whom the Lord has placed over His family. Other fruits of the same kind, too, have greatly rejoiced Us; the celebrations with which dioceses in North America have commemorated the centenary of their foundation, returning everlasting thanks to god for having added so many children to the Catholic Church; the splendid sight presented by the most noble island of Britain in the restored honor paid with such wonderful pomp within its confines to the Blessed Eucharist, in the presence of a dense multitude, and with a crown formed of Our venerable brethren, and of Our own Legate; and in France where the afflicted Church dried her tears to see such brilliant triumphs of the August Sacrament, especially in the town of Lourdes, the fiftieth anniversary of whose origin We have also been rejoiced to witness commemorated with such solemnity.
In these and other facts all must see, and let the enemies of Catholicism be persuaded of it, that the splendor of ceremonial, and the devotion paid to the August Mother of God, and even the filial homage offered to the Supreme Pontiff, are all destined finally for the glory of God, that Christ may be all and in all (Coloss. iii. II), that the Kingdom of God may be established on earth, and eternal salvation gained for men.

4. This triumph of God on earth, both in individuals and in society, is but the return of the erring to God through Christ, and to Christ through the Church, which We announced as the programme of Our Pontificate both in Our first Apostolic Letters "E supremi Apostolatus Cathedra" (Encyclica diei 4 Octobris MDCCCCIII.), and many times since then. To this return We look with confidence, and plans and hopes are all designed to lead to it as to a port in which the storms even of the present life are at rest. And this is why We are grateful for the homage paid to the Church in Our humble person, as being, with God's help, a sign of the return of the Nations to Christ and a closer union with Peter and the Church.

5. This affectionate union, varying in intensity according to time and place, and differing in its mode of expression, seems in the designs of Providence to grow stronger as the times grow more difficult for the cause of sound teaching, of sacred discipline, of the liberty of the Church. We have examples of this in the Saints of other centuries, whom God raised up to resist by their virtue and wisdom the fury of persecution against the Church and the diffusion of iniquity in the world. One of these We wish especially in these Letters to commemorate, now that the eighth centenary of his death is being solemnly celebrated. We mean the Doctor Anselm of Aosta, most vigorous exponent of Catholic truth and defender of the rights of the Church, first as Monk and Abbot in France. and later as Archbishop of Canterbury and Primate in England. It is not inappropriate, We think, after the Jubilee Feasts, celebrated with unwonted splendor, of two other Doctors of Holy Church, Gregory the Great and John Chrysostom, one the light of the Western, the other of the Eastern Church, to fix our gaze on this other star which, if it "differs in brightness" (I. Cor. xv. 41) from them, yet compares well with them in their course, and sheds abroad

a light of doctrine and example not less salutary than theirs. Nay, in some respects it might be said even more salutary, inasmuch as Anselm is nearer to us in time, place, temperament, studies, and there is a closer similarity with our own days in the nature of the conflicts borne by him, in the kind of pastoral activity he displayed, in the method of teaching applied and largely promoted by him, by his disciples, by his writings, all composed "in defense of the Christian religion, for the benefit of souls, and for the guidance of all theologians who were to teach sacred letters according to the scholastic method" (Breviar. Rom., die 21 Aprilis). Thus as in the darkness of the night while some stars are setting others rise to light the world, so the sons succeed to the Fathers to illumine the Church, and among these St. Anselm shone forth as a most brilliant star.

6. In the eyes of the best of his contemporaries Anselm seemed to shine as a luminary of sanctity and learning amid the darkness of the error and iniquity of the age in which he lived. He was in truth a "prince of the faith, an ornament of the Church . . . a glory of the episcopate, a man outranking all the great men" of his time ("Epicedion in obitum Anselmi"), "both learned and good and brilliant in speech, a man of splendid intellect" ("In Epitaphio") whose reputation was such that it has been well written of him that there was no man in the world then "who would say: Anselm is less than I, or like me" ("Epicedion in obitum Anselmi"), and hence esteemed by kings, princes, and supreme pontiffs, as well as by his brethren in religion and by the faithful, nay, "beloved even by his enemies" (Ib.). While he was still Abbot the great and most powerful Pontiff Gregory VII wrote him letters breathing esteem and affection and "recommending the Catholic Church and himself to his prayers" (Breviar. Rom.. die 21 Aprilis): to him also wrote Urban II recognizing "his

distinction in religion and learning" (In libro 2 Epist. S. Anselmi, ep. 32); in many and most affectionate letters Paschal 11 extolled his "reverent devotion, strong faith, his pious and persevering zeal, his authority in religion and knowledge" (In lib. 3 Epist. S. Anselmi, ep. 74 et 42), which easily induced the Pontiff to accede to his requests and made him not hesitate to call him the most learned and devout of the bishops of England.

7. And yet Anselm in his own eyes was but a despicable and unknown good for nothing, a man of no parts, sinful in his life. Nor did this great modesty and most sincere humility detract in the least from his high thinking, whatever may be said to the contrary by men of depraved life and judgment, of whom the Scripture says that "the animal man understandeth not the things of the spirit of God" (I Cor. ii. 14). And more wonderful still, greatness of soul and unconquerable constancy, tried in so many ways by troubles, attacks, exiles, were in him blended with such gentle and pleasing manners that he was able to calm the angry passions of his enemies and win the hearts of those who were enraged against him, so that the very men "to whom his cause was hostile" praised him because he was good ("Epicedion in obitum Anselmi").

8. Thus in him there existed a wonderful harmony between qualities which the world falsely judges to be irreconcilable and contradictory: simplicity and greatness, humility and magnanimity, strength and gentleness, knowledge and piety, so that both in the beginning and throughout the whole course of his religious life "he was singularly esteemed by all as a model of sanctity and doctrine" (Breviar. Rom., die 21 Aprilis).

9. Nor was this double merit of Anselm confined within the walls of his own household or within the limits of the school - it went forth thence as from a military tent into the dust and the glare of the highway. For, as We have already hinted, Anselm fell on difficult days and had to undertake fierce battles in defense of justice and truth. Naturally inclined though he was to a life of contemplation and study, he was obliged to plunge into the most varied and most important occupations even those affecting the government of the Church, and thus to be drawn into the worst turmoil of his agitated age. With his sweet and most gentle temperament he was forced, out of love for sound doctrine and for the sanctity of the Church, to give up a life of peace, the friendship of the great ones of the world, the favors of the powerful, the united affection, which he at first enjoyed, of his very brethren in troubles of all kinds. Thus, finding England full of hatred and dangers, he was forced to oppose a vigorous resistance to kings and princes, usurpers and tyrants over the Church and the people, against weak or unworthy ministers of the sacred office, against the ignorance and vice of the great and small alike; ever a valiant defender of the faith and morals, of the discipline and liberty, and therefore also of the sanctity and doctrine, of the Church of God, and thus truly worthy of that further encomium of Paschal: "Thanks be to God that in you the authority of the Bishop ever prevails, and that, although set in the midst of barbarians, you are not deterred from announcing the truth either by the violence of tyrants," or the favor of the powerful, neither by the flame of fire or the force of arms; and again: "We rejoice because by the grace of God you are neither disturbed by threats nor moved by promises" (In lib. iii. Epist. S. Anselmi, ep. 44 et 74).

10. In view of all this, it is only right, venerable brethren, that We, after a lapse of eight centuries, should rejoice like

Our Predecessor Paschal, and, echoing his words, return thanks, to God. But, at the same time, it is a pleasure for Us to be able to exhort you to fix your eyes on this luminary of doctrine and sanctity, who, rising here in Italy, shone for over thirty years upon France, for more than fifteen years upon England, and finally upon the whole Church, as a tower of strength and beauty.

11. And if Anselm was great "in works and in words," if in his knowledge and his life, in contemplation and activity, in peace and strife, he secured splendid triumphs for the Church and great benefits for society, all this must be ascribed to his close union with Christ and the Church throughout the whole course of his life and ministry.

12. Recalling all these things, venerable brethren, with special interest during the solemn commemoration of the great Doctor, we shall find in them splendid examples for our admiration and imitation; nay, reflection on them will also furnish Us with strength and consolation amid the pressing cares of the government of the Church and of the salvation of souls, helping Us never to fail in our duty of co-operating with all our strength in order that all things may be restored in Christ, that "Christ may be formed" in all souls (Galat. iv. 19), and especially in those which are the hope of the priesthood, of maintaining unswervingly the doctrine of the Church, of defending strenuously the liberty of the Spouse of Christ, the inviolability of her divine rights, and the plenitude of those safeguards which the protection of the Sacred Pontificate requires.

13. For you are aware, venerable brethren, and you have often lamented it with Us, how evil are the days on which we have fallen, and how iniquitous the conditions which

have been forced upon Us. Even in the unspeakable sorrow We felt in the recent public disasters, Our wounds were opened afresh by the shameful charges invented against the clergy of being behindhand in rendering assistance after the calamity, by the obstacles raised to hide the beneficent action of the Church on behalf of the afflicted, by the contempt shown even for her maternal care and forethought. We say nothing of many other things injurious to the Church, devised with treacherous cunning or flagrantly perpetrated in violation of all public right and in contempt of all natural equity and justice. Most grievous, too, is the thought that this has been done in countries in which the stream of civilization has been most abundantly fed by the Church. For what more unnatural sight could be witnessed than that of some of those children whom the Church has nourished and cherished as her first-born, her flower and her strength, in their rage turning their weapons against the very bosom of the Mother that has loved them so much! And there are other countries which give us but little cause for consolation, in which the same war, under a different form, has either broken out already or is being prepared by dark machinations. For there is a movement in those nations which have benefited most from Christian civilization to deprive the Church of her rights, to treat her as though she were not by nature and by right the perfect society that she is, instituted by Christ Himself, the Redeemer of our nature, and to destroy her reign, which, although primarily and directly affecting souls, is not less helpful for their eternal salvation than for the welfare of human society; efforts of all kinds are being made to supplant the kingdom of God by a reign of license under the lying name of liberty. And to bring about by the rule of vices and lusts the triumph of the worst of all slaveries and bring the people headlong to their ruin - "for sin makes peoples wretched" (Prov. xiv. 34) - the cry is ever raised: "We will not have this man reign over us" (Luc. xix. 14). Thus the religious Orders, always the strong shield and the ornament of the Church, and the promotors of the most salutary works of science and civilization among uncivilized and civilized peoples, have been driven out of Catholic countries; thus the works of Christian beneficence have been weakened and circumscribed as far as possible, thus the ministers of religion have been despised and mocked, and, wherever that was possible, reduced to powerlessness and inertia; the paths to knowledge and to the teaching office have been either closed to them or rendered extremely difficult, especially by gradually removing them from the instruction and education of youth; Catholic undertakings of public utility have been thwarted; distinguished laymen who openly profess their Catholic faith have been turned into ridicule, persecuted, kept in the background as belonging to an inferior and outcast class, until the coming of the day, which is being hastened by ever more iniquitous laws, when they are to be utterly ostracized from public affairs. And the authors of this war, cunning and pitiless as it is, boast that they are waging it through love of liberty, civilization, and progress, and, were you to believe them, through a spirit of patriotism - in this lie too resembling their father, who "was a murderer from the beginning, and when he speaketh a lie, he speaketh of his own, for he is a liar" (Ioan. viii. 44), and raging with hate insatiable against God and the human race. Brazen-faced men these, seeking to create confusion by their words, and to lay snares for the ears of the simple. No, it is not patriotism, or zealous care for the people, or any other noble aim, or desire to promote good of any kind, that incites them to this bitter war, but blind hatred which feeds their mad plan to weaken the Church and exclude her from social life, which makes them proclaim her as dead, while they never cease to attack her - nay, after having despoiled

216

her of all liberty, they do not hesitate in their brazen folly to taunt her with her powerlessness to do anything for the benefit of mankind or human government. From the same hate spring the cunning misrepresentations or the utter silence concerning the most manifest services of the Church and the Apostolic See, when they do not make of our services a cause of suspicion which with wily art they insinuate into the ears and the minds of the masses, spying and travestying everything said or done by the Church as though it concealed some impending danger for society, whereas the plain truth is that it is mainly from Christ through the Church that the progress of real liberty and the purest civilization has been derived.

14. Concerning this war from outside, waged by the enemy without, "by which the Church is seen to be assailed on all sides, now in serried and open battle, now by cunning and by wily plots," We have frequently warned your vigilance, venerable brethren, and especially in the Allocution We delivered in the Consistory of December 16, 1907.

15. But with no less severity and sorrow have We been obliged to denounce and to put down another species of war, intestine and domestic, and all the more disastrous the more hidden it is. Waged by unnatural children, nestling in the very bosom of the Church in order to rend it in silence, this war aims more directly at the very root and the soul of the Church. They are trying to corrupt the springs of Christian life and teaching, to scatter the sacred deposit of the faith, to overthrow the foundations of the divine constitution by their contempt for all authority, pontifical as well as episcopal, to put a new form on the Church, new laws, new principles, according to the tenets of monstrous systems, in short to deface all the beauty of the Spouse of Christ for the empty

glamour of a new culture, falsely called science, against which the Apostle frequently puts us on our guard: "Beware lest any man cheat you by philosophy and vain deceit, according to the traditions of men, according to the elements of the world, and not according to Christ (Colos. ii. 8).

16. By this figment of false philosophy and this shallow and fallacious erudition, joined with a most audacious system of criticism, some have been seduced and "become vain in their thoughts" (Rom. i. 1), "having rejected good conscience they have made shipwreck concerning the faith" (I Tim. i. 19), they are being tossed about miserably on the waves of doubt, knowing not themselves at what port they must land; others, wasting both time and study, lose themselves in the investigation of abstruse trifling, and thus grow estranged from the study of divine things and of the real springs of doctrine. This hot-bed of error and perdition (which has come to be known commonly as modernism from its craving for unhealthy novelty) although denounced several times and unmasked by the very excesses of its adepts, continues to be a most grave and deep evil. It lurks like poison in the vitals of modern society, estranged as this is from God and His Church, and it is especially eating its way like a cancer among the young generations which are naturally the most inexperienced and heedless. It is not the result of solid study and true knowledge, for there can be no real conflict between reason and faith (Concil. Vatic., Constit. Dei filius, cap. 4). But it is the result of intellectual pride and of the pestiferous atmosphere that prevails of ignorance or confused knowledge of the things of religion, united with the stupid presumption of speaking about and discussing them. And this deadly infection is further fomented by a spirit of incredulity and of rebellion against God, so that those who are seized by the blind frenzy for novelty consider that they

are all sufficient for themselves, and that they are at liberty to throw off either openly or by subterfuge the entire yoke of divine authority, fashioning for themselves according to their own caprice a vague, naturalistic individual religiosity, borrowing the name and some semblance of Christianity but with none of its life and truth.

17. Now in all this it is not difficult to recognize one of the many forms of the eternal war waged against divine truth, and one that is all the more dangerous from the fact that its weapons are craftily concealed with a covering of ficti-tious piety, ingenuous candor, and earnestness, in the hands of factious men who use them to reconcile things that are absolutely irreconcilable, viz., the extravagances of a fickle human science with divine faith, and the spirit of a frivolous world with the dignity and constancy of the Church.

18. But if you see all this, venerable brethren,. and deplore it bitterly with Us, you are not therefore cast down or with-out all hope. You know of the great conflicts that other times have brought upon the Christian people, very different though they were from our own days. We have but to turn again to the age in which Anselm lived, so full of difficulties as it appears in the annals of the Church. Then indeed was it necessary to fight for the altar and the home, for the sanc-tity of public law, for liberty, civilization, sound doctrine, of all of which the Church alone was the teacher and the defender among the nations, to curb the violence of princes who arrogated to themselves the right of treading upon the most sacred liberties, to eradicate the vices, ignorance, and uncouthness of the people, not yet entirely stripped of their old barbarism and often enough refractory to the educating influence of the Church, to rouse a part of the clergy who had grown lax or lawless in their conduct, inasmuch as not

unfrequently they were selected arbitrarily and according to a perverse system of election by the princes, and controlled by and bound to these in all things.

19. Such was the state of things notably in those countries on whose behalf Anselm especially labored, either by his teaching as master, by his example as religious, or by his assiduous vigilance and many-sided activity as Archbishop and Primate. For his great services were especially accomplished for the provinces of Gaul which a few centuries before had fallen into the hands of the Normans, and by the islands of Britain which only a few centuries before had come to the Church. In both countries the convulsions caused by revolutions within and wars without gave rise to looseness of discipline both among the rulers and their subjects, among the clergy and the people.

20. Abuses like these were bitterly lamented by the great men of the time, such as Lanfranc, Anselm's master and later his predecessor in the see of Canterbury, and still more by the Roman Pontiffs, among whom it will suffice to mention here the courageous Gregory VII, the intrepid champion of justice, unswerving defender of the rights of the Church, vigilant guardian and defender of the sanctity of the clergy.

21. Strong in their example and rivaling them in their zeal, Anselm also lamented the same evils, writing thus to a prince of his people, and one who rejoiced to describe himself as his relation by blood and affection: "You see, my dearest Lord, how the Church of God, our Mother, whom God calls His Fair One and His Beloved Spouse, is trodden underfoot by bad princes, how she is placed in tribulation for their eternal damnation by those to whom she was recommended by God as to protectors who would defend her, with

what presumption they have usurped for their own uses the things that belong to her, the cruelty with which they despise and violate religion and her law. Disdaining obedience to the decrees of the Apostolic See, made for the defense of religion, they surely convict themselves of disobedience to the Apostle Peter whose place he holds, nay, to Christ who recommended His Church to Peter. . . Because they who refuse to be subject to the law of God are surely reputed the enemies of God" (Epist. lib. iii. epist. 65). Thus wrote Anselm, and would that his words had been treasured by the successor and the descendants of that most potent prince, and by the other sovereigns and peoples who were so loved and counseled and served by him.

22. But persecution, exile, spoliation, the trials and toils of hard fighting, far from shaking, only rooted deeper Anselm's love for the Church and the Apostolic See. "I fear no exile, or poverty or torments or death, because, while God strengthens me, for all these things my heart is prepared for the sake of the obedience due to the Apostolic See and the liberty of the Church of Christ, my Mother," (Ib. lib. iii. ep. 73), he wrote to Our Predecessor Paschal amid his greatest difficulties. And if he has recourse to the Chair of Peter for protection and help, the sole reason is: "Lest through me and on account of me the constancy of ecclesiastical devotion and Apostolic authority should ever be in the least degree weakened." And then he gives his reason, which for Us is the badge of pastoral dignity and strength: "I would rather die, and while I live I would rather undergo penury in exile, rather than see the honor of the Church of God dimmed in the slightest degree on my account or through my example" (Ib. Lib. iv. ep. 47).

23. That same honor, liberty, and purity of the Church is ever in his mind; he yearns for it with sighs, prayers, sacrifices; he works for it with all his might both in vigorous resistance and in manly patience; and he defends it by his acts, his writings, his words. He recommends it in language strong and sweet to his brethren in religion; to the bishops, the clergy, and to all the faithful; but with more of severity to those princes who outraged it to the great injury of themselves and their subjects.

24. These noble appeals for sacred liberty have a timely echo in our days on the lips of those "whom the Holy Ghost has placed to rule the Church of God" (Act. xx 28) - timely even though they were to find no hearing by reason of the decay of faith or the perversity of men or the blindness of prejudice. To Us, as you know well, Venerable Brethren, are especially addressed the words of the Lord: "Cry out give yourself no rest, raise your voice like a trumpet" (Isai. lviii. I), and all the more that "the Most High has made His voice heard" (Psalmus xvii. 14), in the trembling of nature and in tremendous calamities: "the voice of the Lord shaking the earth," ringing in our ears a terrible warning and bringing home to us the hard lesson that all but the eternal is vanity, that "we have not here a lasting city, but we seek one that is to come (Hebr. xiii. 14), but, also, a voice not only of justice, but of mercy and of wholesome reminder to the erring nations. In the midst of these public calamities it behooves us to cry aloud and make known the great truths of the faith not only to the people, to the humble, the afflicted, but to the powerful and the rich, to them that decide and govern the policy of nations, to make known to all the great truths which history confirms by its great and disastrous lessons such as that "sin makes the nations miserable" (Prov. xiv. 34), "that a most severe judgment shall be for them that

bear rule" (Sap. vi. 7), with the admonition of Psalm ii.: "And now, ye kings, understand; receive instruction, you that judge the earth. Serve the Lord with fear . . . embrace discipline lest at any time the Lord be angry, and you perish from the just way." More bitter shall be the consequences of these threats when the vices of society are being multiplied, when the sin of rulers and of the people consists especially in the exclusion of God and in rebellion against the Church of Christ: that double social apostasy which is the deplorable fount of anarchy, corruption, and endless misery for the individual and for society.

25. And since silence or indolence on our part, as unfortunately is not unfrequently the case among the good, would incriminate us too, let every one of the sacred Pastors take as said to himself for the defense of his flock, and bring home to others in due season, Anselm's words to the mighty Prince of Flanders: "As you are my Lord and truly beloved by me in God, I pray, conjure, admonish and counsel you, as the guardian of your soul, not to believe that your lofty dignity is diminished if you love and defend the liberty of the Spouse of God and your Mother, the Church, not to think that you abase yourself when you exalt her, not to believe that you weaken yourself when you strengthen her. Look round you and see; the examples are before you; consider the princes that attack and maltreat her, what do they gain by it, what do they attain? It is so clear that there is no need to say it" (Epist., lib. iv. ep. 32). And all this he explains with his usual force and gentleness to the powerful Baldwin, King of Jerusalem: "As your faithful friend, I pray, admonish, and conjure you, and I pray God that you live under God's law and in all things submit your will to the will of God. For it is only when you reign according to the will of God that you reign for your own welfare. Nor permit yourself to believe,

like so many bad kings, that the Church of God has been given to you that you may use her as a servant, but remember that she has been recommended to you as an advocate and defender." In this world God loves nothing more than the liberty of His Church. "They who seek not so much to serve as to rule her, are clearly acting in opposition to God. God wills His Spouse to be free and not a slave. Those who treat her and honor her as sons surely show that they are her sons and the sons of God, while those who lord it over her, as over a subject, make themselves not children but strangers to her, and are therefore excluded from the heritage and the dower promised to her" (Ibid. ep. 8). Thus did he unbosom his heart so full of love for the Church; thus did he show his zeal in defense of her liberty, so necessary in the government of the Christian family and so dear to God, as the same great Doctor concisely affirmed in the energetic words: "In this world God loves nothing more than the liberty of His Church." Nor can We, venerable brethren, make known to you Our feelings better than by repeating that beautiful expression.

26. Equally opportune are other admonitions addressed by the Saint to the powerful. Thus, for example, he wrote to Queen Matilda of England: "If you wish in very deed to return thanks rightly and well and efficaciously to God, take into your consideration that Queen whom He was pleased to select for His Spouse in this world. . . Take her, I say, into your consideration, exalt her, that with her and in her you may be able to please God and reign with her in eternal bliss" (Epist., lib. iii. ep. 57). And especially when you chance to meet with some son who puffed up with earthly greatness lives unmindful of his mother, or hostile or rebellious to her, then remember that: "it is for you to suggest frequently, in season and out of season, these and other ad-

monitions, and to suggest that he show himself not the master but the advocate, not the step-son but the real son of the Church" (Ibid. ep. 59). It behooves Us, too, Us especially, to inculcate that other saying so noble and so paternal of Anselm: "Whenever I hear anything of you displeasing to God and unbecoming to yourselves, and fail to admonish you, I do not fear God nor love you as I ought" (Ibid. Lib. iv. ep. 52). And especially when it comes to Our ears that you treat the churches in your power in a manner unworthy of them and of your own soul, then, We should imitate Anselm by renewing Our prayers, counsels, admonitions "that you think over these things carefully and if your conscience warns you that there is something to be corrected in them that you hasten to make the correction" (Epist., lib. iv. epist. 32). "For nothing is to be neglected that can be corrected, since God demands an account from all not only of the evil they do but also of the correction of evil which they can correct. And the more power men have to make the necessary correction the more vigorously does He require them, according to the power mercifully communicated to them, to think and act rightly . . . And if you cannot do everything all at once, you must not on that account cease your efforts to advance from better to better, because God in His goodness is wont to bring to perfection good intentions and good effort, and to reward them with blessed plenitude" (Ibid. Lib. iii. epist. 142).

27. These and similar admonitions, most wise and holy, given by Anselm even to the lords and kings of the world, may well be repeated by the pastors and princes of the Church, as the natural defenders of truth, justice, and religion in the world. In our times, indeed, the obstacles in the way of doing this have been enormously increased so that there is, in truth, hardly room to stand without difficulty and danger. For

while unbridled license reigns supreme the Church is obstinately fettered, the very name of liberty is mocked, and new devices are constantly being invented to thwart the work of yourselves and your clergy, so that it is no wonder that "you are not able to do everything all at once" for the correction of the erring, the suppression of abuses, the promotion of right ideas and right living, and the mitigation of the evils which weigh on the Church.

28. But there is comfort for us: the Lord liveth and "He will make all things work together unto good to them that love God" (Rom.viii. 28). Even from these evils He will bring good, and above all the obstacles devised by human perversity He will make more splendid the triumph of His work and of His Church. Such is the wonderful design of the Divine Wisdom and such "His unsearchable ways" (Ib. xi. 33) in the present order of Providence - "for my thoughts are not your thoughts, nor my ways your ways, said the Lord" (Isai. Iv. 8) - that the Church of Christ is destined ever to renew in herself the life of her Divine Founder who suffered so much, and in a manner to "fill up what is wanting of the sufferings of Christ" (Coloss. i. 24). Hence her condition as militant on earth divinely constrains her to live in the midst of contentions, troubles, and difficulties, that thus "through many tribulations she may enter into the kingdom of God" (Act. xiv. 21), and at last be united with the Church triumphant in heaven.

29. Anselm's commentary on the passage of St. Matthew: "Jesus constrained His disciples to enter the boat," is directly to the point: "The words in their mystical sense summarize the state of the Church from the coming of Jesus Christ to the end of the world. The ship, then, was buffeted by the waves in the midst of the sea, while Jesus remained on the

summit of the mountain; for ever since the Savior ascended to heaven holy Church has been agitated by great tribulations in the world, buffeted by various storms of persecution, harassed by the divers perversities of the wicked, and in many ways assailed by vice. Because the wind was contrary, because the influence of malign spirits is constantly opposed to her to prevent her from reaching the port of salvation, striving to submerge her under the opposing waves of the world, stirring up against her all possible difficulties" (Hom. iii. 22).

30. They err greatly, therefore, who lose faith during the storm, wishing for themselves and the Church a permanent state of perfect tranquility, universal prosperity, and practical, unanimous and uncontested recognition of her sacred authority. But the error is worse when men deceive themselves with the idea of gaining an ephemeral peace by cloaking the rights and interests of the Church, by sacrificing them to private interests, by minimizing them unjustly, by truckling to the world, "the whole of which is seated in wickedness" (I Ioan. v. 19) on the pretext of reconciling the followers of novelties and bringing them back to the Church, as though any composition were possible between light and darkness, between Christ and Belial. This hallucination is as old as the world, but it is always modern and always present in the world so long as there are soldiers who are timid or treacherous, and at the first onset ready to throw down their arms or open negotiations with the enemy, who is the irreconcilable enemy of God and man.

31. It is for you, therefore, venerable brethren, whom Divine Providence has constituted to be the pastors and leaders of the Christian people, to resist with all your strength this most fatal tendency of modern society to lull itself in a shameful

indolence while war is being waged against religion, seeking a cowardly neutrality made up of weak schemes and compromises to the injury of divine and human rights, to the oblivion of Christ's clear sentence: "He that is not with me is against me" (Matt. xii. 30). Not indeed that it is not well at times to waive our rights as far as may lawfully be done and as the good of souls requires. And certainly this defect can never be charged to you who are spurred on by the charity of Christ. But this is only a reasonable condescension, which can be made without the slightest detriment to duty, and which does not at all affect the eternal principles of truth and justice.

32. Thus we read how it was verified in the cause of Anselm, or rather in the cause of God and the Church, for which Anselm had to undergo such long and bitter conflicts. And when he had settled at last the long contest Our Predecessor Paschal II wrote to him: "We believe that it has been through your charity and through your persistent prayers that the Divine mercy has been persuaded to turn to the people entrusted to your care." And referring to the paternal indulgence shown by the Supreme Pontiff to the guilty, he adds: "As regards the great indulgence We have shown, know that it is the fruit of Our great affection and compassion in order that We might be able to lift up those who were down. For if the one standing erect merely holds out his hand to a fallen man, he will never lift him unless he too bends down a little. Besides, although this act of stooping may seem like the act of falling, it never goes so far as to lose the equilibrium of rectitude" (In lib. iii. Epist. S. Anselmi, ep. 140).

33. In making our own these words of Our most pious Predecessor, written for the consolation of Anselm, We would not hide Our very keen sense of the danger which confronts

the very best among the pastors of the Church of passing the just limit either of indulgence or resistance. How they have realized this danger is easily to be seen in the anxieties, trepidations, and tears of most holy men who have had borne in upon them the terrible responsibility of the government of souls and the greatness of the danger to which they are exposed, but it is to be seen most strikingly in the life of Anselm. When he was torn from the solitude of the studious life of the cloister, to be raised to a lofty dignity in most difficult times, he found himself a prey to the most tormenting solicitude and anxiety, and chief of all the fear that he might not do enough for the salvation of his own soul and the souls of his people, for the honor of God and of His Church. But amid all these anxieties and in the grief he felt at seeing himself abandoned culpably by many, even including his brethren in the episcopate, his one great comfort was his trust in God and in the Apostolic See. Threatened with shipwreck, and while the storm raged round him, he took refuge in the bosom of the Church, his Mother, invoking from the Roman Pontiff pitiful and prompt aid and comfort (Epistol. lib. iii. ep. 37); God, perhaps, permitted that this great man, full of wisdom and sanctity as he was, should suffer such heavy tribulation, in order that he might be a comfort and an example to us in the greatest difficulties and trials of the pastoral ministry, and that the sentence of Paul might be realized in each one of us: "Gladly will I glory in my infirmities that the power of Christ may dwell in me. For which cause I please myself in my infirmities . . . for when I am weak then am I powerful" (2 Cor. xii. 9, 10). Such indeed are the sentiments which Anselm expressed to Urban II.: "Holy Father, I am grieved that I am not what I was, grieved to be a bishop, because by reason of my sins I do not perform the office of a bishop. While I was in a lowly position, I seemed to be doing something; set in a lofty place, burdened by an immense weight, I gain no fruit for myself, and am of no use to anybody. I give way beneath the burden because I am incredibly poor in the strength, virtue, zeal, and knowledge necessary for so great an office. I would fain flee from the insupportable anxiety and leave the burden behind me, but, on the other hand, I fear to offend God. The fear of God obliged me to accept it, the same fear of God constrains me to retain the same burden. Now, since God's will is hidden from me, and I know not what to do, I wander about in sighs, and know not how to put an end to it all" (Epist. Lib. iii. ep. 37).

34. Thus does God bring home even to saintly men their natural weakness, in order the better to make manifest in them the power of strength from above, and, by a humble and real sense of their individual insufficiency, to preserve with greater force their obedience to the authority of the Church. We see it in the case of Anselm and of other contemporaries of his who fought for the liberty and doctrine of the Church under the guidance of the Apostolic See. The fruit of their obedience was victory in the strife, and their example confirmed the Divine sentence that "the obedient man will sing victory" (Prov. xxi. 28). The hope of the same reward shines out for all those who obey Christ in His Vicar in all that concerns the guidance of souls, or the government of the Church, or that is in any way connected with these objects: since "upon the authority of the Holy See depend the directions and the counsels of the sons of the Church" (Epist. Lib. iv. ep. 1).

35. How Anselm excelled in this virtue, with what warmth and fidelity he ever maintained perfect union with the Apostolic See, may be seen in the words he wrote to Pope Paschal: "How earnestly my mind, according to the measure of its power, clings in reverence and obedience to the Apostolic See, is proved by the many and most painful tribulations of

my heart, which are known only to God and myself... From this union I hope in God that there is nothing which could ever separate me. Therefore do I desire, as far as this is possible, to put all my acts at the disposition of this same authority in order that it may direct and when necessary correct them" (Ibid. ep. 5).

36. The same strong constancy is shown in all his actions and writings, and especially in his letters which Our Predecessor Paschal describes as "written with the pen of charity" (In lib. iii. Epist. S. Anselmi, ep. 74). But in his letters to the Pontiff he does not content himself with imploring pitiful aid and comfort; he also promises assiduous prayers, in most tender words of filial affection and unswerving faith, as when, while still Abbot of Bec, he wrote to Urban II: "For your tribulation and that of the Roman Church, which is our tribulation and that of all the true faithful, we never cease praying God assiduously to mitigate your evil days, till the pit be dug for the sinner. And although He seems to delay, we are certain that the Lord will not leave the scepter of sinners over the heritage of the just, that He will never abandon His heritage and that the gates of hell shall not prevail against it" (In libro ii.Epist. S. Anselmi, ep. 33).

37. In this and other similar letters of Anselm We find wonderful comfort not only in the renewal of the memory of a Saint so devoted to the Apostolic See, but because they serve to recall your own letters and your other innumerable proofs of devotion, venerable brethren, in similar conflicts and similar sorrows.

38. Certainly it is a wonderful thing that the union of the Bishops and the faithful with the Roman Pontiff has drawn ever more and more close amid the hurtling of the storms

that have been let loose on Christianity through the ages, and in our own times it has become so unanimous and so warm that its divine character is more apparent than ever before. It is indeed Our greatest consolation, as it is the glory and the invincible bulwark of the Church. But its very force makes it all the more an object of envy to the demon and of hatred to the world, which knows nothing similar to it in earthly societies, and finds no explanation of it in political and human reasoning, seeing that it is the fulfillment of Christ's sublime prayer at the Last Supper.

39. But, venerable brethren, it behooves us to strive by all means to preserve this divine union and render it ever more intimate and cordial, fixing our gaze not on human considerations but on those that are divine, in order that we may be all one thing alone in Christ. By developing this noble effort we shall fulfill ever better our sublime mission which is that of continuing and propagating the work of Christ, and of His Kingdom on earth. This, indeed, is why the Church throughout the ages continues to repeat the loving prayer, which is also the warmest aspiration of Our heart: "Holy Father, keep them in thy name, whom thou hast given me, that they may be one, as we also are" (Ioan. xvii. 11).

40. This effort is necessary not only to oppose the assaults from without of those who fight openly against the liberty and the rights of the Church, but also in order to meet the dangers from within, arising from that second kind of war which We deplored above when We made mention of those misguided persons who are trying by their cunning systems to overthrow from the foundations the very constitution and essence of the Church, to stain the purity of her doctrine, and destroy her entire discipline. For even still there continues to circulate that poison which has been inoculated into many

even among the clergy, and especially the young clergy, who have, as We have said, become infected by the pestilential atmosphere, in their unbridled craving for novelty which is drawing them to the abyss and drowning them.

41. Then again, by a deplorable aberration, the very progress, good in itself, of positive science and material prosperity, gives occasion and pretext for a display of intolerable arrogance towards divinely revealed truth on the part of many weak and intemperate minds. But these should rather remember the many mistakes and the frequent contradictions made by the followers of rash novelties in those questions of a speculative and practical order most vital for man; and realize that human pride is punished by never being able to be coherent with itself and by suffering shipwreck without ever sighting the port of truth. They are not able to profit by their own experience to humble themselves and "to destroy the counsels and every height that exalteth itself against the knowledge of God, and bring into captivity every understanding even unto the obedience of Christ" (2 Cor. x. 4, 5).

42. Nay, their very arrogance has led them into the other extreme, and their philosophy throwing doubt on everything has involved them in darkness: hence the present profession of agnosticism with other absurd doctrines springing from an infinite series of systems in discord with one another and with right reason; so that "they have become vain in their thoughts . . . for professing themselves to be wise they became fools" (Rom. i. 21, 22).

43. But unfortunately their grandiloquent phrases and their promises of a new wisdom, fallen as it were from heaven, and of new methods of thought, have found favor with many young men, as those of the Manicheans found favor with

Augustine, and have returned these aside, more or less un-consciously, from the right road. But concerning such perni-cious masters of an insane knowledge, of their aims, their illusions, their erroneous and disastrous systems, We have spoken at great length in Our Encyclical Letter of September 8, 1907, "Pascendi dominici gregis."

44. Here it is well to note that if the dangers We have men-tioned are more serious and more imminent in our own days, they are not altogether different from those that threatened the doctrine of the Church in the time of St. Anselm, and that we may find in his labors as Doctor almost the same help and comfort for the safeguarding of the truth as we found in his apostolic firmness for the defense of the liberty and rights of the Church.

45. Without entering here in detail into the intellectual state of the clergy and people in that distant age, there was a notable danger in a twofold excess to which the intellects of the time were prone.

46. There was at the time a class of lightminded and vain men, fed on a superficial erudition, who became incredibly puffed up with their undigested culture, and allowed them-selves to be led away by a simulacrum of philosophy and dialectics. In their inane fallacy, which they called by the name of science, "they despised the sacred authority, dared with impious temerity to dispute one or other of the dogmas professed by Catholic faith . . . and in their foolish pride considered anything they could not understand as impos-sible, instead of confessing with humble wisdom that there might be many things beyond the reach of their compre-hension. . . For there are some who immediately they have begun to grow the horns of an overweening knowledge - not

knowing that when a person thinks he knows something, he does not yet know in what manner he should know it - before they have grown spiritual wings through firmness in the faith, are wont to rise presumptuously to the highest questions of the faith. Thus it happens that while against all right rules they endeavor to rise prematurely by their intelligence, their lack of intelligence brings them down to manifold errors" (S. Anselm., De Fide Trinitatis, cap. 2). And of such as these we have many painful examples under our eyes!

47. Others, again, there were of a more timid nature, who in their terror at the many cases of those who had made shipwreck of the faith, and fearing the danger of the science that puffeth up, went so far as to exclude altogether the use of philosophy, if not of all rational discussion of the sacred doctrines.

48. Midway between these two excesses stands the Catholic practice. which. while it abhors the presumption of the first class who "puffed up like bladders with the wind of vanity" (according to the phrase of Gregory XIV in the succeeding age) "went beyond the true limits in their efforts to establish the faith by natural reason adulterating the word of God with the figments of the philosopher" (Gregor. IX, Epist. Tacti dolore cordis ad theologos Parisien, 7 Jul. 1228), so too it condemns the negligence of the second class in their excessive neglect of true investigation, and the absence of all desire in them "to draw profit from the faith for their intelligence" (In lib. ii. Epist. S. Anselmi, ep. 41.), especially when their office requires of them to defend the Catholic faith against the errors that arise on all sides.

49. For this defense, it may well be said that Anselm was raised up by God to point out by his example, his words, and

his writings, the safe road, to unseal for the common good the spring of Christian wisdom and to be the guide and rule of those Catholic teachers who after him taught "the sacred letters by the method of the school" (Breviar. Rom., die 21 Aprilis), and who thus came rightly to be esteemed and celebrated as their precursor.

50. Not, indeed, that the Doctor of Aosta reached all at once the heights of theological and philosophical speculation, or the reputation of the two supreme masters Thomas and Bonaventure. The later fruits of the wisdom of these last did not ripen but with time and the collaboration of many doctors. Anselm himself, with that great modesty so characteristic of the truly wise, and with all his learning and perspicacity, never published any writings except such as were called forth by circumstances, or when compelled thereto by some authority, and in those he did publish he protests that "if there is anything that calls for correction he does not refuse the correction" ("Cur Deus homo," lib. ii. cap. 23), nay, when the question is a debated one, and not connected with the faith, he tells his disciple: "you must not so cling to what we have said as to abide by it obstinately, when others with more weighty arguments succeed in overthrowing ours and establishing opinions against them; should that happen you will not deny at least that what we have said has been of profit for exercise in controversy" ("De Grammatico," cap. 21 sub finem).

51. Yet Anselm accomplished far more than he ever expected or than others expected of him. He secured a position in which his merits were not dimmed by the glory of those that came after him, not even of the great Thomas, even when the latter declined to accept all his conclusions and treated more clearly and accurately questions already treated by him. To

Anselm belongs the distinction of having opened the road to speculation, of removing the doubts of the timid, the dangers of the incautious, and the injuries done by the quarrelsome and the sophistical, "the heretical dialecticians" of his time, as he rightly calls them, in whom reason was the slave of the imagination and of vanity ("De fide Trinitatis" cap. 2).

52. Against these latter he observes that "while all are to be warned to enter with the utmost circumspection upon questions affecting the Sacred Scriptures, these dialecticians of our time are to be completely debarred from the discussion of spiritual questions." And the reason he assigns for this is especially applicable now to those who imitate them under our eyes, repeating their old errors: "For in their souls, reason, which should be the king and the guide of all that is in man, is so mixed up with corporal imaginations that it is impossible to disentangle it from these, nor is itself able to distinguish from them things that it alone and pure should contemplate" (Ibid. cap. 2). Appropriate, too, for our own times are those words of his in which he ridicules those false philosophers, "who because they are not able to understand what they believe dispute the truth of the faith itself, confirmed by the Holy Fathers, just as if bats and owls who see the heaven only by night were to dispute concerning the rays of the sun at noon, against eagles who gaze at the sun unblinkingly" (Ibid.).

53. Hence too he condemns, here or elsewhere, the perverse opinion of those who conceded too much to philosophy by attributing to it the right to invade the domain of theology. In refuting this foolish theory he defines well the confines proper to each, and hints sufficiently clearly at the functions of reason in the things of divinely revealed doctrine: "Our faith," he says, "must be defended by reason against the

impious" (In lib. ii. Epist. S. Anselmi, ep. 41). But how and how far? The question is answered in the words that follow: "It must be shown to them reasonably how unreasonable is their contempt of us" (Ibid.). The chief office, therefore, of philosophy is to show us the reasonableness of our faith and the consequent obligation of believing the divine authority proposing to us the profoundest mysteries, which with all signs of credibility that testify to them, are supremely worthy of being believed. Far different is the proper function of Christian theology, which is based on the fact of divine revelation and renders more solid in the faith those who already profess to enjoy the honor of the name of Christian. "Hence it is altogether clear that no Christian should dispute as to how that is not which the Catholic Church believes with the heart and confesses with the mouth, but even holding beyond all doubt the same faith, loving and living according to it, must seek as far as reason is able, how it is. If he is able to understand let him return thanks, let him not prepare his horns for attack, but bow his head in reverence" ("De fide Trinitatis," cap 2).

54. When, therefore, theologians search and the faithful ask for reasons concerning our faith, it is not for the purpose of founding on them their faith, which has for its foundation the authority of God revealing; yet, as Anselm puts it, "as right order requires that we believe the profundities of the faith before we presume to discuss them with our reason, so it seems to me to be negligence if after we have been confirmed in the faith we do not strive to understand what we believe" ("Cur Deus homo," lib. i. c. 2). And here Anselm means that intelligence of which the Vatican Council speaks (Constit. "Dei filius," cap 4). For, as he shows elsewhere, "although since the time of the Apostles many of our Holy Fathers and Doctors say so many and such great things of

the reason of our faith . . . yet they were not able to say all they might have said had they lived longer; and the reason of the truth is so ample and so deep that it can never be exhausted by mortals; and the Lord does not cease to impart the gifts of grace in his Church, with whom He promises to be until the consummation of the world. And to say nothing of the other texts in which the Sacred Scripture invites us to investigate reason, in the one in which it says that if you do not believe you will not understand, it plainly admonishes us to extend intention to understanding, when it teaches us how we are to advance towards it." Nor is the last reason he alleges to be neglected: "In the midst between faith and vision is the intellectual knowledge which is within our reach in this life, and the more one can advance in this the nearer he approaches to the vision, for which we all yearn" ("De fide Trinitatis," Praefatio).

55. With these and the like principles Anselm laid the foundations of the true principles of philosophical and theological studies which other most learned men, the princes of scholasticism, and chief among them the Doctor of Aquin, followed, developed, illustrated and perfected to the great honor and protection of the Church. If We have insisted so willingly on this distinction of Anselm, it is in order to have a new and much-desired occasion, venerable brethren, to inculcate upon you to see to it that you bring back youth, especially among the clergy, to the most wholesome springs of Christian wisdom, first opened by the Doctor of Aosta and abundantly enriched by Aquinas. On this head remember always the instructions of Our Predecessor Leo XIII, of happy memory (Encyclical "Aeterni Patris," diei 4 Augusti, an. 1879), and those We have Ourself given more than once, and again in the above-mentioned Encyclical "Pascendi dominici gregis." Bitter experience only too clearly proves every

day the loss and the ruin ensuing from the neglect of these studies, or from the pursuit of them without a clear and sure method; while many, before being fitted or prepared, presume to discuss the deepest questions of the faith ("De fide Trinitatis," cap. 2). Deploring this evil with Anselm, We repeat the strong recommendations made by him: "Let no one rashly plunge into the intricate questions of divine things until he has first acquired, with firmness in the faith, gravity of conduct and of wisdom, lest while discussing with uncautious levity amid the manifold twistings of sophistry he fall into the toils of some tenacious error" (Ibid.). And this same incautious levity, when heated, as so often is the case, at the fire of the passions, proves the total ruin of serious studies and of the integrity of doctrine. Because, puffed up with that foolish pride, lamented by Anselm in the heretical dialecticians of his time, they despise the sacred authorities of the Holy Scriptures, and of the Fathers and Doctors, concerning which a more modest genius would be glad to use instead the respectful words of Anselm: "Neither in our own time nor in the future do we ever hope to see their like in the contemplation of the truth" ("De fide Trinitatis," Praefatio.)

56. Nor do they hold in greater account the authority of the Church and of the Supreme Pontiff whenever efforts are made to bring them to a better sense, although at times as far as words go they are lavish of promises of submission as long as they can hope to hide themselves behind these and gain credit and protection. This contempt almost bars the way of all well founded hope of the conversion of the erring; while they refuse obedience to him "to whom Divine Providence as to the Lord and Father of the whole Church in its pilgrimage on earth . . . has entrusted the custody of Christian life and faith and government of His Church; wherefore when anything arises in the Church against the Catholic faith

240

to no other authority but his is it to be rightly referred for correction, and to no other with such certainty as to him has it been shown what answer is to be made to error in order that it may be examined by his prudence" (Ibid. cap. 2). And would to God that these poor wanderers on whose lips one so often hears the fair words of sincerity, conscience, religious experience, the faith that is felt and lived, and so on, learned their lessons from Anselm, understood his holy teachings, imitated his glorious example, and, above all, took deeply to heart those words of his: "First the heart is to be purified by faith, and first the eyes are to be illuminated by the observance of the precepts of the Lord . . . and first with humble obedience to the testimonies of God we must become small to learn wisdom . . . and not only when faith and obedience to the commandments are removed is the mind hindered from ascending to the intelligence of higher truths, but often enough the intelligence that has been given is taken away and faith is overthrown, when right conscience is neglected" ("De Fide Trinitatis," cap. 2).

57. But if the erring continue obstinately to scatter the seeds of dissension and error, to waste the patrimony of the sacred doctrine of the Church, to attack discipline, to heap contempt on venerated customs, "to destroy which is a species of heresy" in the phrase of St. Anselm, and to destroy the constitution of the Church in its very foundations, then all the more strictly must we watch, venerable brethren, and keep away from Our flock, and especially from youth which is the most tender part of it, so deadly a pest. This grace We implore of God with incessant prayers, interposing the most powerful patronage of the august Mother of God and the intercession of the blessed citizens of the Church triumphant, St. Anselm especially, shining light of Christian wisdom, incorrupt guardian and valiant defender of all the sacred

rights of the Church, to whom We would here, in conclusion, address the same words that Our Holy Predecessor, Gregory VII, wrote to him during his lifetime: "Since the sweet odor of your good works has reached Us, We return due thanks for them to God, and We embrace you heartily in the love of Christ, holding it for certain that by your example the Church of God has been greatly benefited, and that by your prayers and those of men like you she may even be liberated from the dangers that hang over her, with the mercy of Christ to succor us" (S. Anselm, "De nuptiis consanguinerorum," cap. 1). "Hence We beg your fraternity to implore God assiduously to relieve the Church and Us who govern it, albeit unworthily, from the pressing assaults of the heretics, and lead these from their errors to the way of truth" (In lib. ii. Epist. S. Anselmi, ep. 31).

58. Supported by this great protection, and trusting in your co-operation, We bestow the Apostolic Benediction with all affection in the Lord, as a pledge of heavenly grace and in testimony of Our goodwill, on all of you, venerable brethren, and on the clergy and people entrusted to each of you.

Given at Rome at St. Peter's on the Feast of St. Anselm, April 21, 1909, in the eighth year of Our Pontificate.
PIUS X

EDITAE SAEPE
ENCYCLICAL OF POPE PIUS X
ON ST. CHARLES BORROMEO

TO THE PATRIARCHS, PRIMATES, ARCHBISHOPS, BISHOPS, AND OTHER ORDINARIES IN PEACE AND COMMUNION WITH THE APOSTOLIC SEE

Venerable Brethren,
Health and the Apostolic Blessing.

1. Sacred Scripture records the divine word saying that men will remember the just man forever, for even though he is dead, he yet speaks. Both in word and deed the Church has for a long time verified the truth of that saying. She is the mother and the nurse of holiness, ever renewed and enlivened by the breath of the Spirit Who dwells in us. She alone conceives, nourishes, and educates the noble family of the just. Like a loving mother, she carefully preserves the memory of and affection for the saints. This remembrance is, as it were, a divine comfort which lifts her eyes above the miseries of this earthly pilgrimage so that she finds in the saints "her joy and her crown." Thus she sees in them the sublime image of her heavenly Spouse. Thus she shows her children in each age the timeliness of the old truth: "For those who love God all things work together unto good, for those who, according to his purpose, are saints through his call." The glorious deeds of the saints, however, do more than afford us comfort. In order that we may imitate and be encouraged by them, one and all the saints echo in their own lives the saying of Saint Paul, "I beg you, be imitators of me, as I am of Christ."

2. For that reason, Venerable Brethren, immediately after Our elevation to the Supreme Pontificate We stated in Our first encyclical that We would labor without ceasing "to restore all things in Christ." We begged everyone to turn their eyes with Us to Jesus, "the apostle and high priest of our confession...the author and finisher of faith." Since the majesty of that Model may be too much for fallen human nature, God mercifully gave Us another model to propose for your imitation, the glorious Virgin Mother of God. While being as close to Christ as human nature permits, she is better suited to the needs of our weak nature. Over and above that, We made use of several other occasions to recall the memory of the saints. We emulated these faithful servants and ministers of God's household (each in his own way enjoying the friendship of God), "who by faith conquered kingdoms, wrought justice, obtained promises." Thus encouraged by their example, we would be "now no longer children, tossed to and fro and carried about by every wind of doctrine devised in the wickedness of men, in craftiness, according to the wiles of error. Rather are we to practice the truth in love, and so grow up in all things in him who is the head, Christ."

3. We have already pointed to how Divine Providence was perfectly realized in the lives of those three great doctors and pastors of the Church, Gregory the Great, John Chrysostom and Anselm of Aosta. Although they were separated by centuries, the Church was beset by many serious dangers in each of their respective ages. In recent years We celebrated all of their solemn centenaries. In a very special way, however, we commemorated Saint Gregory the Great in the encyclical of March 12, 1904, and Saint Anselm in the encyclical of April 21, 1909. In these documents We treated those points of Christian doctrine and morals found in the example and teaching of these saints which We thought were

best suited to our times.

4. As We have already mentioned, We are of the opinion that the shining example of Christ's soldiers has far greater value in the winning and sanctifying of souls than the words of profound treatises. We therefore gladly take this present opportunity to teach some very useful lessons from the consideration of the life of another holy pastor whom God raised up in more recent times and in the midst of trials very similar to those We are experiencing today. We refer to Saint Charles Borromeo, Cardinal of the Holy Roman Church and Archbishop of Milan, whom Paul V, of holy memory, raised to the altar of the saints less than thirty years after his death. The words of Our Predecessor are to the point: "The Lord alone performs great wonders and in recent times He has accomplished marvelous things among Us. In His wonderful dispensation He has set a great light on the Apostolic rock when He singled Charles out of the heart of the Roman Church as the faithful priest and good servant to be a model for the pastors and their flock. He enlightened the whole Church from the light diffused by his holy works. He shone forth before priests and people as innocent as Abel, pure as Enoch, tireless as Jacob, meek as Moses, and zealous as Elias. Surrounded by luxury, he exhibited the austerity of Jerome, the humility of Martin, the pastoral zeal of Gregory, the liberty of Ambrose, and the charity of Paulinus. In a word, he was a man we could see with our eyes and touch with our hands. He trampled earthly things underfoot and lived the life of the spirit. Although the world tried to entice him he lived crucified to the world. He constantly sought after heavenly things, not only because he held the office of an angel but all because even on earth he tried to think and act as an angel."

5. Such are the words of praise Our Predecessor wrote after Charles' death. Now, three centuries after his canonization, "we can rightly rejoice on this day when We solemnly confer, in the name of the Lord, the sacred honors on Charles, Cardinal Priest, thereby crowning his own Spouse with a diadem of every precious stone." We agree with Our Predecessor that the contemplation of the glory (and even more, the example and teaching of the saints) will humiliate the enemy and throw into confusion all those who "glory in their specious errors." Saint Charles is a model for both clergy and people in these days. He was the unwearied advocate and defender of the true Catholic reformation, opposing those innovators whose purpose was not the restoration, but the effacement and destruction of faith and morals. This celebration of the third centenary of his canonization should prove to be not only a consolation and lesson for every Catholic but also a noble incentive for everyone to cooperate wholeheartedly in that work so dear to Our heart of restoring all things in Christ.

6. You know very well, Venerable Brethren, that even when surrounded by tribulation the Church still enjoys some consolation from God. "Christ also loved the Church, and delivered himself up for her, that he might sanctify her...in order that he might present to himself the Church in all her glory, not having spot or wrinkle or any such thing, but that she might be holy and without blemish." When vice runs wild, when persecution hangs heavy, when error is so cunning that it threatens her destruction by snatching many children from her bosom (and plunges them into the whirlpool of sin and impiety) - then, more than ever, the Church is strengthened from above. Whether the wicked will it or not, God makes even error aid in the triumph of Truth whose guardian and defender is the Church. He puts corruption in the service

of sanctity, whose mother and nurse is the Church. Out of persecution He brings a more wondrous "freedom from our enemies." For these reasons, when worldly men think they see the Church buffeted and almost capsized in the raging storm, then she really comes forth fairer, stronger, purer, and brighter with the lustre of distinguished virtues.

7. In such a way God's goodness bears witness to the divinity of the Church. He makes her victorious in that painful battle against the errors and sins that creep into her ranks. Through this victory He verifies the words of Christ: "The gates of hell shall not prevail against it." In her day-to-day living He fulfills the promise, "Behold, I am with you all days, even unto the consummation of the world." Finally, He is the witness of that mysterious power of the other Paraclete (Who Christ promised would come immediately after His ascension into heaven), who continually lavishes His gifts upon her and serves as her defender and consoler in all her sorrows. This is the Spirit Who will "dwell with you forever, the Spirit of truth whom the world cannot receive, because it neither sees him nor knows him...he will dwell with you and be in you." The life and strength of the Church flows forth from this font. As the ecumenical Vatican Council teaches, this divine power sets the Church above every other society by those obvious notes which mark her "as a banner raised up among the nations."

8. In fact, only a miracle of that divine power could preserve the Church, the Mystical Body of Christ, from blemish in the holiness of Her doctrine, law, and end in the midst of the flood of corruption and lapses of her members. Her doctrine, law and end have produced an abundant harvest. The faith and holiness of her children have brought forth the most salutary fruits. Here is another proof of her divine

life: in spite of a great number of pernicious opinions and great variety of errors (as well as the vast army of rebels) the Church remains immutable and constant, "as the pillar and foundation of truth," in professing one identical doctrine, in receiving the same Sacraments, in her divine constitution, government, and morality. This is all the more marvelous when one considers that the Church not only resists evil but even "conquers evil by doing good." She is constantly blessing friends and enemies alike. She is continually striving and ardently desiring to bring about the social and individual Christian restoration which is her particular mission in the world. Moreover, even her enemies benefit from it.

9. This wonderful working of Divine Providence in the Church's program of restoration was seen with the greatest clarity and was given as a consolation for the good especially in the century of Saint Charles Borromeo. In those days passions ran riot and knowledge of the truth was almost completely twisted and confused. A continual battle was being waged against errors. Human society, going from bad to worse, was rushing headlong into the abyss. Then those proud and rebellious men came on the scene who are "enemies of the cross of Christ . . .Their god is the belly...they mind the things of earth." These men were not concerned with correcting morals, but only with denying dogmas. Thus they increased the chaos. They dropped the reins of law, and unbridled licentiousness ran wild. They despised the authoritative guidance of the church and pandered to the whims of the dissolute princes and people. They tried to destroy the Church's doctrine, constitution and discipline. They were similar to those sinners who were warned long ago: "Woe to you that call evil good and good evil." They called this rebellious riot and perversion of faith and morals a reformation, and themselves reformers. In reality, they were corrupt-

248

ers. In undermining the strength of Europe through wars and dissensions, they paved the way for those modern rebellions and apostasy. This modern warfare has united and renewed in one attack the three kinds of attack which have up until now been separated; namely, the bloody conflicts of the first ages, the internal pests of heresies, and finally, in the name of evangelical liberty, the vicious corruption and perversion of discipline such as was unknown, perhaps, even in medieval times. Yet in each of these combats the Church has always emerged victorious.

10. God, however, brought forth real reformers and holy men to arrest the onrushing current, to extinguish the conflagration, and to repair the harm caused by this crowd of seducers. Their many-sided zealous work of reforming discipline was especially consoling to the Church since the tribulation afflicting her was so great. Their work also proves the truth that "God is faithful and . . . with the temptation will also give you a way out ...." In these circumstances God provided a pleasing consolation for the Church in the outstanding zeal and sanctity of Charles Borromeo.

11. God ordained that his ministry would be the effective and special means of checking the rebels' boldness and teaching and inspiring the Church's children. He restrained the former's mad extravagances by the example of his life and labor, and met their empty charges with the most powerful eloquence. He fanned the latter's hopes and kindled their zeal. Even from his youth he cultivated in a remarkable manner all the virtues of the true reformer which others possessed only in varying degrees. These virtues are fortitude, counsel, doctrine, authority, ability, and alacrity. He put them all in the service of Catholic truth against the attacks of error (which is precisely the mission of the Church). He revived

the faith that had either become dormant or almost extinct in many by strengthening it with many wise laws and practices. He restored that discipline which had been overthrown by bringing the morals of clergy and people alike back to the ideals of Christian living. In executing all the duties of a reformer he also fulfilled the functions of the "good and faithful servant." Later he performed the works of the high priest who "pleased God in his days and was found just." He is, therefore, a worthy example for both clergy and laity, rich and poor. He can be numbered among those whose excellence as a bishop and prelate is eulogized by the Apostle Peter when he says that he became "from the heart a pattern to the flock." Even before the age of twenty- three and although elevated to the highest honors and entrusted with very important and difficult ecclesiastical matters, Charles made truly wonderful daily progress in the practice of virtue through the contemplation of divine things. This sacred retirement perfected him, prepared him for later days, and caused him to shine forth as "a spectacle to the world, and angels, and men."

12. Then (again borrowing the words of Our Predecessor, Paul V), the Lord began to work His wonders in Charles. He filled him with a wisdom, justice, and burning zeal for promoting His glory and the Catholic cause. Above all, the Lord filled him with a great concern for restoring the faith in the Church universal according to the decrees of the renowned Council of Trent. That Pontiff himself, as well as all future generations, attributed the success of the Council to Charles, since even before carrying its decrees into action he was its most ardent promoter. In fact, his many vigils, trials, and labors brought its work to its ultimate completion.

13. All these things, however, were only a preparation or

sort of novitiate where he trained his heart in piety, his mind in study, and his body in work (always remaining a modest and humble youth) for that life in which he would be as clay in the hands of God and His Vicar on earth. The innovators of that time despised just that kind of life of preparation. The same folly leads the modern innovators also to spurn it. They fail to see that God's wondrous works are matured in the obscurity and silence of a soul dedicated to obedience and contemplation. They cannot see that just as the hope of the harvest lies in the sowing, so this preparation is the germ of future progress.

14. As We have already hinted, this sanctity and industry prepared under such conditions in due time came to produce a truly marvelous fruit. When Charles, "good laborer that he was left the convenience and splendor of the city for the field (Milan) he was to cultivate, he discharged his duties better and better from day to day. Although the wickedness of the time had caused that field to become overrun with weeds and rank growths, he restored it to its pristine beauty. In time the Milanese Church became an example of ecclesiastical discipline." He effected all these outstanding results in his work of reformation by adopting the rules the Council of Trent had only recently promulgated.

15. The Church knows very well that "the imagination and thought of man's heart are prone to evil." Therefore she wages continual battle against vice and error "in order that the body of sin may be destroyed, that we may no longer be slaves to sin." Since she is her own mistress and is guided by the grace which "is poured forth in our hearts by the Holy Spirit," she is directed in this conflict in thought and action by the Doctor of the Gentiles, who says, "Be renewed in the spirit of your mind...And be not conformed to this world, but

be transformed in the newness of your mind, that you may discern what is the good and acceptable and perfect will of God." The true son of the Church and reformer never thinks he has attained his goal. Rather, with the Apostle, he acknowledges that he is only striving for it: "Forgetting what is behind, I strain forward to what is before, I press on towards the goal, to the prize of God's heavenly call in Christ Jesus."

16. Through our union with Christ in the Church we grow up "in all things in him who is the head, Christ. For from him the whole body...derives its increase to the building up for itself in love...." For that reason Mother Church daily fulfills the mystery of the Divine Will which is "to be dispensed in the fullness of the times: to re-establish all things in Christ."

17. The reformers that Borromeo opposed did not even think of this. They tried to reform faith and discipline according to their own whims. Venerable Brethren, it is no better understood by those whom We must withstand today. These moderns, forever prattling about culture and civilization, are undermining the Church's doctrine, laws, and practices. They are not concerned very much about culture and civilization. By using such high-sounding words they think they can conceal the wickedness of their schemes.

18. All of you know their purpose, subterfuges, and methods. On Our part We have denounced and condemned their scheming. They are proposing a universal apostasy even worse than the one that threatened the age of Charles. It is worse, We say, because it stealthily creeps into the very veins of the Church, hides there, and cunningly pushes erroneous principles to their ultimate conclusions.

19. Both these heresies are fathered by the "enemy" who

"sowed weeds among the wheat" in order to bring about the downfall of mankind. Both revolts go about in the hidden ways of darkness, develop along the same line, and come to an end in the same fatal way. In the past the first apostasy turned where fortune seemed to smile. It set rulers against people or people against rulers only to lead both classes to destruction. Today this modern apostasy stirs up hatred between the poor and the rich until, dissatisfied with their station, they gradually fall into such wretched ways that they must pay the fine imposed on those who, absorbed in worldly, temporal things, forget "the kingdom of God and His justice." As a matter of fact, this present conflict is even more serious than the others. Although the wild innovators of former times generally preserved some fragments of the treasury of revealed doctrine, these moderns act as if they will not rest until they completely destroy it. When the foundations of religion are overthrown, the restraints of civil society are also necessarily shattered. Behold the sad spectacle of our times! Behold the impending danger of the future! However, it is no danger to the Church, for the divine promise leaves no room for doubt. Rather, this revolution threatens the family and nations, especially those who actively stir up or indifferently tolerate this unhealthy atmosphere of irreligion.

20. This impious and foolish war is waged and sometimes supported by those who should be the first to come to Our aid. The errors appear in many forms and the enticements of vice wear different dresses. Both cause many even among our own ranks to be ensnared, seducing them by the appearance of novelty and doctrine, or the illusion that the Church will accept the maxims of the age. Venerable Brethren, you are well aware that we must vigorously resist and repel the enemy's attacks with the very weapons Borromeo used in

his day.

21. Since they attack the very root of faith either by openly denying, hypocritically undermining, or misrepresenting revealed doctrine, we should above all recall the truth Charles often taught. "The primary and most important duty of pastors is to guard everything pertaining to the integral and inviolate maintenance of the Catholic Faith, the faith which the Holy Roman Church professes and teaches, without which it is impossible to please God." Again: "In this matter no diligence can be too great to fulfill the certain demands of our office." We must therefore use sound doctrine to withstand "the leaven of heretical depravity," which if not repressed, will corrupt the whole. That is to say, we must oppose these erroneous opinions now deceitfully being scattered abroad, which, when taken all together, are called Modernism. With Charles we must be mindful "of the supreme zeal and excelling diligence which the bishop must exercise in combating the crime of heresy."

22. We need not mention the Saint's other words (echoing the sanctions and penalties decreed by the Roman Pontiffs) against those prelates who are negligent or remiss in purging the evil heresy out of their dioceses. It is fitting, however, to meditate on the conclusions he draws from these papal decrees. "Above everything else," he says, "the Bishop must be eternally on guard and continually vigilant in preventing the contagious disease of heresy from entering among his flock and removing even the faintest suspicion of it from the fold. If it should happen to enter (the Lord forbid!), he must use every means at his command to expel it immediately. Moreover, he must see to it that those infected or suspected be treated according to the pontifical canons and sanctions."

23. Liberation or immunity from this disease of heresy is possible only when the clergy are properly instructed, since "faith. . . depends on hearing, and hearing on the word of Christ." Today we must heed the words of truth. We see this poison penetrating through all the veins of the State (from sources where it would be the least expected) to such an extent that the causes are the same as those Charles records in the following words: "If those who associate with heretics are not firmly rooted in the Faith there is reason to fear that they will easily be seduced by the heretics into the trap of impiety and false doctrine." Nowadays facility in travel and communication has proven just as advantageous for error as for other things. We are living in a perverse society of unbridled license of passions in which "there is no truth... and there is no knowledge of God," in "all the land made desolate, because there is none that considereth in the heart." For that reason, borrowing the words of Charles, "we have already emphasized the importance of having all the faithful of Christ well instructed in the rudiments of Christian doctrine" and have written a special encyclical letter on that extremely important subject. However, We do not wish to repeat the lamentation Borromeo was moved to utter because of his burning zeal, namely, that "up until now We have received very little success in a matter of such importance." Rather, moved like him "by the enormity and danger of the task," We would once again urge everyone to make Charles his model of zeal so that he will contribute in this work of Christian restoration according to his position and ability. Fathers and employers should recall how the holy Bishop frequently and fervently taught that they should not only afford the opportunity but even consider it their duty to see that their children, servants, and employees study Christian doctrine. Clerics should remember that they must assist the parish priests in the teaching of Christian doctrine. Parish

priests should erect as many schools for this same purpose as the number and needs of the people demand. They should further take care that they have upright teachers, who will be assisted by men and women of good morals according to the manner the holy Archbishop Milan prescribed.

24. Obviously the need of this Christian instruction is accentuated by the decline of our times and morals. It is even more demanded by the existence of those public schools, lacking all religion, where everything holy is ridiculed and scorned. There both teachers' lips and students' ears are inclined to godlessness. We are referring to those schools which are unjustly called neutral or lay. In reality, they are nothing more than the stronghold of the powers of darkness. You have already, Venerable Brethren, fearlessly condemned this new trick of mocking liberty especially in those countries where the rights of religion and the family have been disgracefully ignored and the voice of nature (which demands respect for the faith and innocence of youth) has been stifled. Firmly resolved to spare no effort in remedying this evil caused by those who expect others to obey them (although they refuse to obey the Supreme Master of all things themselves), We have recommended that schools of Christian doctrine be erected in those cities where it is possible. Thanks to your efforts, this work has already made good progress. It is, however, very much to be desired that this work spread even more widely, with many such religious schools established everywhere and teachers of sound doctrine and good morals provided.

25. The preacher (whose duty is closely allied to the teacher of the fundamentals of religion) should also have the same qualities of sound doctrine and good morals. For that reason, when drawing up the statutes of the provincial and diocesan

synods, Charles was most careful to provide preachers full of zeal and holiness to exercise "the ministry of the word." We are convinced that this care is even more urgent in our times when so many men are wavering in the Faith and some vain-glorious men, filled with the spirit of the age, "adulterate the word of God" and deprive the faithful of the food of life.

26. We must spare no pains, Venerable Brethren, in seeing that the flock does not feed on this air of foolish empty-headed men. Rather, it should be nourished with the life-giving food of "the ministers of the word." These can truly say, "On behalf of Christ...we are acting as ambassadors, God, as it were, appealing through us...be reconciled to God...we avoid unscrupulous conduct, we do not corrupt the word of God; but making known the truth, we commend ourselves to every man's conscience in the sight of God..." We are workmen "that cannot be ashamed, rightly handling the word of truth." Those very holy and fruitful rules the Bishop of Milan frequently laid down for his people have a similar value for us. They can best be summarized in these words of Saint Paul: "When you heard and received from us the word of God, you welcomed it not as the word of man, but, as it truly is, the word of God, who works in you who have believed."

27. "The word of God is living and efficient and keener than any two-edged sword." It will not only preserve and defend the faith but also effectively motivate us to do good works since "faith...without works is dead." "For it is not they who hear the Law that are just in the sight of God; but it is they who follow the Law that will be justified."

28. Now in this also we see the immense difference between true and false reform. The advocates of false reform,

imitating the fickleness of the foolish, generally rush into extremes. They either emphasize faith to such an extent that they neglect good works or they canonize nature with the excellence of virtue while overlooking the assistance of faith and divine grace. As a matter of fact, however, merely naturally good acts are only a counterfeit of virtue since they are neither permanent nor sufficient for salvation. The work of this kind of a reformer cannot restore discipline. On the contrary, it ruins faith and morals.

29. On the other hand, the sincere and zealous reformer will; like Charles, avoid extremes and never overstep the bounds of true reform. He will always be united in the closest bonds with the Church and Christ, her Head. There he will find not only strength for his interior life but also the directives he needs in order to carry out his work of healing human society. The function of this divine mission, which has from time immemorial been handed down to the ambassadors of Christ, is to "make disciples of all nations" both the things they are to believe as well as the things they are to do since Christ Himself said, "Observe all that I have commanded you." He is "the way, and the truth, and the life," coming into the world that man "may have life, and have it more abundantly." The fulfillment of these duties, however, far surpasses man's natural powers. The Church alone possesses together with her magisterium the power of governing and sanctifying human society. Through her ministers and servants (each in his own station and office), she confers on mankind suitable and necessary means of salvation.
True reformers understand this very clearly. They do not kill the blossom in saving the root. That is to say, they do not divorce faith from holiness. They rather cultivate both of them, enkindling them with the fire of charity, "which is the bond of perfection." In obedience to the Apostle, they "keep

the deposit." They neither obscure nor dim its light before the nations, but spread far and wide the most saving waters of truth and life welling up from that spring. They combine theory and practice. By the former they are prepared to withstand the "masquerading of error" and by the latter they apply the commandments to moral activity. In such a way they employ all the suitable and necessary means for attaining the end, namely, the wiping out of sin and the perfecting "the saints for a work of ministry, for building up the body of Christ." This is the purpose of every kind of instruction, government, and munificence. In a word, this is the ultimate purpose of every discipline and action of the Church. When the true son of the church sets out to reform himself and others, he fixes his eyes and heart on matters of faith and morals. On just such matters Borromeo based his reformation of ecclesiastical discipline. Thus he often referred to them in his writings, as, for example, when he says, "Following the ancient custom of the holy Fathers and sacred Councils, especially the ecumenical Synod of Trent, we have decreed many regulations on these very matters in our preceding provincial Councils." In the same way, when providing for the suppression of public scandals, he declares that he is following "both the law and sacred sanctions of the sacred canons, and especially the decrees of the Council of Trent."

30. However, he did not stop at that. In order to assure as much as possible that he would never depart from this rule, he customarily concluded the statutes of his provincial Synods with the following words: "We are always prepared to submit everything we have done and decreed in this provincial Synod to the authority and judgment of the Roman Church, the Mother and Mistress of all the churches." The more quickly he advanced in the perfection of the active ministry the more firmly was he rooted in this resolve, not

only when the Chair of Peter was occupied by his uncle, but also during the Pontificates of his successors, Pius V and Gregory XIII. He wielded his influence in having these latter elected; he was tireless in supporting their great endeavors; and he fulfilled in a perfect manner whatever they expected of him.

31. Moreover, he seconded every one of their acts with the practical means needed to realize the end in view, namely, the real reform of sacred discipline. In this respect also he proved that in no wise he resembled those false reformers who concealed their obstinate disobedience under the cloak of zeal. He began "the judgment...with the household of God." He first of all restored discipline among the clergy by making them conform to certain definite laws. With this same end in view he built seminaries, founded a congregation of priests known as the Oblates, unified both the ancient and modern religious families, and convoked Councils. By these and other provisions he assured and developed the work of reform. Then he immediately set a vigorous hand to the work of reforming the morals of the people. He considered the words spoken to the Prophet as addressed to himself; "Lo, I have set thee this day...to root up and to pull down, and to waste and to destroy, and to build and to plant." Good shepherd that he was, he personally set out on wearisome visitation of the churches of the province. Like the Divine Master "he went about doing good and healing." He spared no efforts in suppressing and uprooting the abuses he met everywhere either because of ignorance or neglect of the laws. He checked the rampant perversion of ideas and corruption of morals by founding schools for the children and colleges for youth. After seeing their early beginnings in Rome, he promoted the Marian societies. He founded orphanages for the fatherless, shelters for girls in danger,

widows, mendicants, and men and women made destitute by sickness or old age. He opened institutions to protect the poor against tyrannical masters, usurers, and the enslavement of children. He accomplished all these things by completely ignoring the methods of those who think human society can be restored only by utter destruction, revolution, and noisy slogans. Such persons have forgotten the divine words: "The Lord is not in the earthquake."

32. Here is another difference between true and false reformers which you, Venerable Brethren, have often encountered. The latter "seek their own interests, not those of Jesus Christ." They listen to the deceitful invitation once addressed to the Divine Master, "Manifest thyself to the world." They repeat the ambitious words, "Let us also get us a name" and in their rashness (which We unfortunately have to deplore in these days) "some priests fell in battle, while desiring to do manfully, they went out unadvisedly to fight."

33. On the other hand, the true reformer "seeks not his own glory, but the glory of the one who sent him." Like Christ, his Model, "he will not wrangle, nor cry aloud, neither will anyone hear his voice in the streets...He shall not be sad nor troublesome" but he shall be "meek and humble of heart." For that reason he will please the Lord and bring forth abundant fruit for salvation.

34. They are distinguished one from the other in yet another way. The false reformer "trusteth in man and maketh flesh his arm." The true reformer places his trust in God and seeks His supernatural aid for all his strength and virtue, making his own the Apostle's words: "I can do all things in him who strengthens me."

35. Christ lavishly communicates these aids, among which are especially prayer, sacrifice and the Sacraments, which "become...a fountain of water, springing up into life everlasting." Since the Church has been endowed with them for the salvation of all men, the faithful man will look for them in her. False reformers, however, despise these means. They make the road crooked and, so wrapped up in reforming that they forget God, they are always trying to make these crystal springs so cloudy or arid that the flock of Christ will be deprived of their waters. In this respect the false reformers of former days are even surpassed by their modern followers. These latter, wearing the mask of religiosity, discredit and despise these means of salvation, especially the two Sacraments which cleanse the penitent soul from sin and feed it with celestial food. Let every faithful pastor, therefore, employ the utmost zeal in seeing that the benefits of such great value be held in the highest esteem. Let them never permit these two works of divine love to grow cold in the hearts of men.

36. Borromeo conducted himself in precisely that way. Thus we read in his writings: "Since the fruit of the Sacraments is so abundantly effective, its value can be explained with no little difficulty. They should, therefore, be treated and received with the greatest preparation, deepest reverence, and external pomp and ceremony." His exhortations (which We have also made in Our decree, Tridentina Synodus) to pastors and preachers concerning the ancient practice of frequent Holy Communion is most worthy of notice. "Pastors and preachers," the holy Bishop writes, "should take every possible opportunity to urge the people to cultivate the practice of frequently receiving Holy Communion. In this they are following the example of the early Church, the recommendations of the most authoritative Fathers, the

doctrine of the Roman Catechism (which treats this matter in detail), and, finally the teaching of the Council of Trent. The last mentioned would have the faithful receive Communion in every Mass, not only spiritually but sacramentally." He describes the intention and affection one should have in approaching the Sacred Banquet in the following words: "The people should not only be urged to receive Holy Communion frequently, but also how dangerous and fatal it would be to approach the Sacred Table of Divine Food unworthily." It would seem that our days of wavering faith and coldness need this same fervor in a special way so that frequent reception of Holy Communion will not be accompanied by a decrease in reverence toward this great mystery. On the contrary, by this frequency a man should "prove himself, and so let him eat of that bread and drink of the cup."

37. An abundant stream of grace will flow from these fonts, strengthening and nourishing even natural and human means. By no means will a Christian neglect those useful and comforting things of this life, for these also come from the hands of God, the Author of grace and nature. In seeking and enjoying these material and physical things, however, he will be careful not to make them the end and quasi-beatitude of this life. He will use them rightly and temperately when he subordinates them to the salvation of souls, according to Christ's words: "Seek first the kingdom of God and His justice, and all these things shall be given you besides."

38. This wise evaluation and use of means is not in the least opposed to the happiness of that inferior ordering of means in civil society. On the contrary, the former promotes the latter's welfare - not, of course, by the foolish prattle of quarrelsome reformers, but by acts and heroic efforts, even to the extent of sacrificing property, power, and life itself. We have

many examples of this fortitude during the Church's worst days in the lives of many bishops who, equaling Charles' zeal, put into practice the Divine Master's words: "The good shepherd lays down his life for his sheep." Neither vainglory, party spirit, nor private interest is their motive. They are moved to spend themselves for the common good by that charity "which never fails." This flame of love cannot be seen by the eyes of the world. It so enkindled Borromeo, however, that, after endangering his own life in caring for the victims of the plague, he did not rest with merely warding off present evils but began to provide for the dangers the future might have in store. "It is no more than right that a good and loving father will provide for his children's future as well as their present by setting aside the necessities of life for them. In virtue of our duty of paternal love, we are also prudently providing for the faithful of our province by setting aside those aids for the future which the experience of the plague has taught us are most effective."

39. These same loving plans and considerations can be put into practice, Venerable Brethren, in that Catholic Action We have so often recommended. The leaders of the people are called to engage in this very noble apostolate which includes all the works of mercy which will be prepared and ready to sacrifice all they have and are for the cause. They must bear envy, contradiction, and even the hatred of many who will repay their labors with ingratitude. They must conduct themselves as "good soldiers of Jesus Christ." They must "run with patience to the fight set before us; looking towards the author and finisher of faith, Jesus Christ." Without a doubt, this is a very difficult contest. Nevertheless, even though a total victory will be slow in coming, it is a contest that serves the welfare of civil society in a most worthy manner.

40. In this work we have the splendid example of Saint Charles. From his example each one of us can find much for imitation and consolation. Even though his outstanding virtue, his marvelous activity, his never failing charity commanded much respect, he was nonetheless subject to that law which reads, "All who want to live piously in Christ Jesus will suffer persecution." His austere life, his defense of righteousness and honesty, his protection of law and justice only led to his being hated by rulers and tricked by diplomats and, later, distrusted by the nobility, clergy and people until he was eventually so hated by wicked men that they sought his very life. In spite of his mild and gentle disposition he withstood all these attacks with unflinching courage.

41. He yielded no ground on any matter that would endanger faith and morals. He admitted no claim (even if it was made by a powerful monarch who was always a Catholic) that was either contrary to discipline or burdensome to the faithful. He was always mindful of Christ's words: "Render...to Caesar the things that are Caesar's, and to God the things that are God's." He never forgot the Apostles' declaration: "We must obey God rather than men." Thus he was religion's and society's chief benefactor. In his time civil society was paying the price of almost certain destruction because of its worldly prudence. It was practically shipwrecked in the seditious storms it had stirred up.

42. The Catholics of our days, together with their leaders, the Bishops, will deserve the same praise and gratitude as Charles as long as they are faithful to their duties of good citizenship. They must be as faithful in their loyalty and respect to "wicked rulers" when their commands are just, as they are adamant in resisting their commands when unjust. They must remain as far from the impious rebellion of those

who advocate sedition and revolt as they are from the subservience of those who accept as sacred the obviously wicked laws of perverse men. These last mentioned wicked men uproot everything in the name of a deceitful liberty, and then oppress their subjects with the most abject tyranny.

43. This is precisely what is happening today in the sight of the whole world and in the broad light of modern civilization. Especially is this the case in some countries where "the powers of darkness" seem to have made their headquarters. This domineering tyranny has suppressed all the rights of the Church's children. These rulers' hearts have been closed to all feelings of generosity, courtesy, and faith which their ancestors, who gloried in the name of Christians, manifested for so long a time. It is obvious that everything quickly lapses back into the ancient barbarism of license whenever God and the Church are hated. It would be more correct to say that everything falls under that most cruel yoke from which only the family of Christ and the education it introduced has freed us. Borromeo expressed the same thought in the following words: "It is a certain, well- established fact that no other crime so seriously offends God and provokes His greatest wrath as the vice of heresy. Nothing contributes more to the down fall of provinces and kingdoms than this frightful pest." Although the enemies of the Church completely disagree among themselves in thought and action (which is a sure indication of error), they are nevertheless united in their obstinate attacks against truth and justice. Since the Church is the guardian and defender of both these virtues, they close their ranks in a unified attack against her. Of course, they loudly proclaim (as is the custom) their impartiality and firmly maintain they are only promoting the cause of peace. In reality, however, their soft words and avowed intentions are only the traps they are laying, thus

adding insult to injury, treason to violence. From this it should be evident that a new kind of warfare is now being waged against Christianity. Without a doubt it is far more dangerous than those former conflicts which crowned Borromeo with such glory.

44. His example and teaching will do much to help us wage a valiant battle on behalf of the noble cause which will save the individual and society, faith, religion, and the inviolability of public order. Our combat, it is true, will be spurred on by bitter necessity. At the same time, however, we will be encouraged by the hope that the omnipotent God will hasten the victory for the sake of those who wage so glorious a contest. This hope increases through the fruitfulness of the work of Saint Charles even down to our own times. His work humbles the proud and strengthens us in the holy resolve to restore all things in Christ.

45. We can now conclude, Venerable Brethren, with the same words with which Our Predecessor, Paul V (whom We already mentioned several times), concluded the letter conferring the highest honors on Charles. "In the meantime," he wrote, "it is only right that we return honor, glory, and benediction to Him Who lives for all ages, for He blessed Our fellow servant with every spiritual gift in order to make him holy and spotless in His sight. The Lord gave him to us as a star shining in the darkness of these sins which are Our affliction. Let us beseech the Divine Goodness both in word and deed to let Charles now assist by his patronage the Church he loved so ardently and aided so greatly by his merits and example, thus making peace for us in the day of wrath, through Christ Our Lord."

46. May the fulfillment of our mutual hope be granted

through this prayer. As a token of that fulfillment, Venerable Brethren, from the depth of Our heart We impart to you and the clergy and people committed to your care, the Apostolic Blessing.

Given at Saint Peter's, Rome, on May 26, 1910, in the seventh year of Our Pontificate.

PIUS X

IAMDUDUM
ENCYCLICAL OF POPE PIUS X
ON THE LAW OF SEPARATION IN PORTUGAL

TO OUR VENERABLE BRETHREN, THE PATRIARCHS, PRIMATES, ARCHBISHOPS, BISHOPS, AND THE ORDINARIES OF OTHER PLACES IN PEACE AND COMMUNION WITH THE APOSTOLIC SEE

Venerable Brethren,
Health and Apostolic Benediction.

You are already, We think, well aware, Venerable Brethren, of the incredible series of excesses and crimes which has been enacted in Portugal for the oppression of the Church. For who does not know that, when the Republican form of Government was adopted in that country, there immediately began to be promulgated measures breathing the most implacable hatred of the Catholic religion? We have seen religious communities evicted from their homes, and most of them driven beyond the Portuguese frontiers. We have seen, arising out of an obstinate determination to secularize every civil organization and to leave no trace of religion in the acts of common life, the deletion of the feast days of the Church from the number of public festivals, the abolition of religious oaths, the hasty establishment of the law of divorce and religious instruction banished from the public schools. And then, to pass over in silence other enormities which would take too long to enumerate, the Bishops have been savagely attacked, and two of the most prominent of them, the Bishops of Oporto and Beia, men who are illustrious by the integrity of their lives and by their great services to their country and the Church, have been driven out of their sees and stripped of their honors.

2. Whilst the new rulers of Portugal were affording such numerous and awful examples of the abuse of power, you know with what patience and moderation this Apostolic See has acted towards them. We thought that We ought most carefully to avoid any action that could even have the appearance of hostility to the Republic. For We clung to the hope that its rulers would one day take saner counsels and would at length repair, by some new agreement, the injuries inflicted on the Church. In this, however, We have been altogether disappointed, for they have now crowned their evil work by the promulgation of a vicious and pernicious Decree for the Separation of Church and State. But now the duty imposed upon Us by our Apostolic charge will not allow Us to remain passive and silent when so serious a wound has been inflicted upon the rights and dignity of the Catholic religion. Therefore do We now address you, Venerable Brethren, in this letter and denounce to all Christendom the heinousness of this deed.

3. At the outset, the absurd and monstrous character of the decree of which We speak is plain from the fact that it proclaims and enacts that the Republic shall have no religion, as if men individually and any association or nation did not depend upon Him who is the Maker and Preserver of all things; and then from the fact that it liberates Portugal from the observance of the Catholic religion, that religion, We say, which has ever been that nation's greatest safeguard and glory, and has been professed almost unanimously by its people. So let us take it that it has been their pleasure to sever that close alliance between Church and State, confirmed though it was by the solemn faith of treaties. Once this divorce was effected, it would at least have been logical to pay no further attention to the Church, and to leave her the enjoyment of the common liberty and rights which

belong to every citizen and every respectable community of peoples. Quite otherwise, however, have things fallen out. This decree bears indeed the name of Separation, but it enacts in reality the reduction of the Church to utter want by the spoliation of her property, and to servitude to the State by oppression in all that touches her sacred power and spirit.

4. First, so far as property is concerned, the Portuguese Republic severs itself from the Church in such a way that it leaves her nothing at all from which to provide for the decency of the house of God, the maintenance of the clergy and the exercise of the manifold duties of charity and piety. For by the articles of this decree not only is the Church despoiled of all the property, whether real or movable, which she holds by the strongest of titles, but she is deprived of all power of acquiring anything for the future. It is indeed provided that certain civil bodies shall have the care of exercise of religious worship; but it is astounding to see within what narrow limits permission to receive any offerings for this purpose is circumscribed. Moreover, the obligations under which Catholic citizens have been accustomed to assist or maintain their respective parish priests, these the decree abolishes and suppresses, forbidding anything to be henceforth demanded for this purpose. It allows Catholics to provide for the cost of divine worship by voluntary alms, but it requires that a third of the sum so contributed shall be set apart and employed for works of civil assistance. And to crown all, under this new law, the buildings which may be henceforth acquired or erected for the exercise of religion are, after the lapse of a given term of years, to pass from the rightful owners without any compensation and to become public property.

5. But in those matters with which it is the sacred prerogative of the Church to deal, much more seriously injurious is
this mockery of Separation, which, as We have said, reduces
the Church to shameful servitude.

6. First of all the Hierarchy is set aside as if its existence
were unknown. And if men in holy orders are mentioned, it
is only that they may be prohibited from having anything to
do with the ordering of public worship. This work is entirely
handed over to associations of laymen already established
or to be established as societies of public assistance according to the regulations of the administrative under the power
of the Republic and in no way depending on the authority
of the Church. And if from the actions of the associations
to which this duty is entrusted disputes arise between clerics and lay people or between lay people alone, the decision
is to lie not with the Church but with the Republic, which
claims all power over these bodies. Indeed, so completely do
the rulers of the Portuguese Republic deny any place to the
clergy in the organization of divine worship that they have
definitely laid it down and provided that those who exercise
the ministry of religion may not be coopted as members
of the aforesaid parish associations or be allotted any part
in their administration or direction. Than such a provision
nothing can be imagined more unjust or more intolerable,
for it puts the clergy at the beck of other citizens in the very
matters upon which they are the rightful directors.

7. The way in which the Portuguese law binds and fetters
the liberty of the Church is scarcely credible, so repugnant
is it to the methods of these modern days and to the public
proclamation of all liberty. It is decreed under the heaviest
penalties that the acts of the Bishops shall on no account be
printed and that not even within the walls of the churches

shall there be any announcement made to the people except by leave of the Republic. It is, moreover, forbidden to perform any ceremony outside the precincts of the sacred buildings without permission from the Republic, to go round in procession, to wear sacred vestments or even the cassock. Furthermore, it is forbidden to place any sign which savors of the Catholic religion not only on public monuments, but even on private buildings; but there is no prohibition at all against so exposing what is offensive to Catholics. Similarly, it is unlawful to form associations for the fostering of religion and piety; indeed societies of this sort are placed on a level with the criminal associations which are formed for evil purposes. And whilst on the one hand all citizens are allowed to employ their means according to their pleasure, on the other, Catholics are, against all justice and equity, placed under restrictions like these if they wish to bequeath something for prayers for the dead, or the upkeep of divine worship; and such bequests already made are impiously diverted to other purposes in utter violation of the wills and wishes of the testators. In fine, the Republic - and this is harshest and gravest stroke of all - goes so far as to invade the domain of the authority of the Church, and to make provisions on points which, as they concern the constitution of the priesthood, necessarily claim the special care of the Church. We speak of the formation and training of young ecclesiastics. For not only does the Decree compel ecclesiastical students to pursue their scientific and literary studies which precede theology in the public lycees where, by reason of a spirit of hostility to God and the Church, the integrity of their faith plainly is exposed to the greatest peril; but the Republic even interferes in the domestic life and discipline of the Seminaries, and arrogates the right of appointing the professors, of approving of the textbooks and of regulating the sacred studies of the Clerics. Thus are the old decrees of the

Regalists revived and enforced; but what was grievous arrogance whilst there was concord between Church and State, is it not now, when the State will have nothing to do with Church, repugnant and full of absurdity? And what is to be said of the fact that this law is positively framed to deprave the morals of the clergy and to provoke them to abandon their superiors? For fixed pensions are assigned to those who have been suspended from their functions by the authority of the Bishops, and benefices are given to those priests who in miserable forgetfulness of their duty shall have dared to contract marriage; and what is still more shameful to record, it extends the same benefits to be shared and enjoyed by any children there may be of such a sacrilegious union.

8. Lastly, it is not enough for the Republic, after having despoiled her of her property, to impose an almost slavish yoke upon the Church of Portugal; it even, on the one hand, strives as far as it can, to tear her from the bosom of Catholic unity and from the arms of the Roman Church, and on the other to prevent the Apostolic See from exercising its solicitude and its authority in the religious affairs of Portugal. Thus, in virtue of this Decree, it is not even lawful to publish, without permission publicly given, the commands of the Roman Pontiff. Similarly, a priest who has gained his degrees in sacred science in a college constituted by Papal authority, even though he has made his theological course in his own country, is not permitted to exercise his sacred functions. What the Republic in all this wants is plain; it is to prevent young clerics, who are desirous of improving themselves and finishing in the higher studies, from coming for this purpose to this City, the head of the Catholic world, where certainly more than anywhere else it is a fact of experience that minds are more imbued with the incorrupted truth of Christian teaching and by sincere piety and faith to

the Apostolic See. These, to omit others which are equally pernicious, are the chief points of this wicked Decree.

9. Accordingly, under the admonition of the duty of Our Apostolic office that, in the face of such audacity on the part of the enemies of God, We should most vigilantly protect the dignity and honor of religion and preserve the sacred rights of the Catholic Church, We by our Apostolic authority denounce, condemn, and reject the Law for the Separation of Church and State in the Portuguese Republic. This law despises God and repudiates the Catholic faith; it annuls the treaties solemnly made between Portugal and the Apostolic See, and violates the law of nature and of her property; it oppresses the liberty of the Church, and assails her divine Constitution; it injures and insults the majesty of the Roman Pontificate, the order of Bishops, the Portuguese clergy and people, and so the Catholics of the world. And whilst We strenuously complain that such a law should have been made, sanctioned, and published, We utter a solemn protest against those who have had a part in it as authors or helpers, and, at the same time, We proclaim and denounce as null and void, and to be so regarded, all that the law has enacted against the inviolable rights of the Church.

10. Assuredly, these days of difficulty in which Portugal since the public proclamation of the Republic is so tormented, are to Us a source of great anxiety and sorrow. We are deeply grieved at the sight of so many evils, which are pressing upon a nation so dear to Us; We are torn with anxiety at the apprehension of worse things to come, which certainly threaten it unless the powers that be seriously consider the duty of their position. But in the midst of all this, your eminent virtue, Venerable Brethren, who govern the Church of Portugal, and the earnestness of the clergy which seconds

that virtue, are no small consolation to Us, and afford good hope that with God's help things will one day take a turn for the better. For you all recently showed a sense not of security or of well-being, but of your duty and its dignity, when you openly and fearlessly repudiated this iniquitous Law of Separation; when with one voice you proclaimed that you would rather recover the freedom of your ministry, even at the loss of all your property, than suffer servitude for the sake of paltry pensions; when, in fine, you declared that never, either by promises or by force should your enemies be able to sunder you from your allegiance to the Roman Pontiff Those splendid proofs of faith, constancy, and greatness of mind which you have given in the sight of the whole Church - be assured that they have been a source of joy to all good men, as well as a credit to yourselves and a comfort to Portugal herself in her affliction. Wherefore, continue as you have begun, to defend with all your might the cause of religion with which the very welfare of your common fatherland is bound up; but see to it, first and above all else, that you carefully preserve and strengthen the greatest concord and unity between yourselves, then between yourselves and Christian people, and all of you with this See of Blessed Peter. For, as we have said, the purpose of the authors of this wicked law is not, as they would make out, to separate the Church of Portugal, which they despoil and oppress, from the Republic, but from the Vicar of Christ. If you strive to meet and resist such a design on the part of these men and such a crime with all your might, then certainly you will have done well for the good of Catholic Portugal. Meanwhile, We, for the singular love We bear you, shall be suppliants to Almighty God that He may in His goodness favor your zeal and your efforts. And We beg you, Bishops of the rest of the Catholic world, to fulfill the same duty on behalf of your suffering brethren in Portugal in their time of need.

11. As an earnest of divine gifts and a pledge of Our benevolence, We impart from Our heart to you all, Venerable Brethren, and to your clergy and people the Apostolic Benediction.

Given at St. Peter's, Rome, on the 24th day of May, on the feast of Our Lady Mary, the Help of Christians, in the year 1911, and the eighth of Our Pontificate.
PIUS X

LACRIMABILI STATU
ENCYCLICAL OF POPE PIUS X
ON THE INDIANS OF SOUTH AMERICA

TO THE ARCHBISHOPS AND BISHOPS OF LATIN
AMERICA

Venerable Brethren,
Health and the Apostolic Blessing.

Being greatly moved by the deplorable condition of the
Indians in Lower America, our illustrious predecessor Benedict XIV pleaded their cause, as you are aware, in most
weighty words, in his letter Immensa Pastorum, given on
December 22, 1741; and since we also have to deplore in
many places almost the same things that he then lamented,
we most earnestly recall those letters of his to your memory.
For therein, among other things, Pope Benedict complained
that although the Apostolic See had done much, and for a
long time, to relieve their afflicted fortunes, there were even
the "men of the orthodox faith who, as if they had utterly
forgotten all sense of the charity poured forth in our hearts
by the Holy Ghost, presumed to reduce the wretched Indians, without the light of faith, and even those who had been
washed in the laver of regeneration, to servitude, or to sell
them as slaves to others, or to deprive them of their property,
and to treat them with such inhumanity that they were thus
greatly hindered from embracing the Christian faith, and
most strongly moved to regard it with abhorrence." It is true
that soon afterwards the worst of these indignities - that is
to say, slavery, properly so called - was, by the goodness of
the merciful God, abolished; and to this public abolition of
slavery in Brazil and in other regions the excellent men who
governed those Republics were greatly moved and encour-

aged by the maternal care and insistence of the Church. And we gladly acknowledge that if it had not been for many and great obstacles that stood in the way, their plans would have had far greater success. Nevertheless, though much has thus been done for the Indians, there is much more that still remains to be done. And, indeed, when we consider the crimes and outrages still committed against them, our heart is filled with horror, and we are moved to great compassion for its most unhappy race. For what can be so cruel and so barbarous as to scourge men and brand them with hot iron, often for most trivial causes, often for a mere lust of cruelty; or, having suddenly overthrown them, to slay hundreds or thousands in one unceasing massacre; or to waste villages and districts and slaughter the inhabitants, so that some tribes, as we understand, have become extinct in these last few years?

2. The lust of lucre has done much to make the minds of men so barbarous. But something also is due to the nature of the climate and the situation of these regions. For, as these places are subjected to burning southern sun, which casts a languor into the veins and as it were, destroys the vigor of virtue, and as they are far removed from the habits of religion and the vigilance of the State, and in a measure even from civil society, it easily comes to pass that those who have not already come there with evil morals soon begin to be corrupted, and then, when all bonds of right and duty are broken, they fall away into all hateful vices. Nor in this do they take any pity on the weakness of sex or age, so that we are ashamed to mention the crimes and outrages they commit in seeking out and selling women and children, wherein it may be truly said that they have surpassed the worst examples of pagan iniquity.

3. For our part, indeed, when reports of these things were first brought to us, we hesitated for some time to give credence to such atrocities, since they certainly seemed to be incredible. But after we had been assured by abundant witnesses - to wit, by many of yourselves, Venerable Brethren, by the Delegates of the Apostolic See, by the missioners, and by other men wholly worthy of belief - we can no longer have any doubt as to the truth of these statements.

4. Now, therefore, having pondered long on this matter, so that, as far as lies in our power, we may endeavor to remedy such great evils, with humble and suppliant prayer we beg of God that He may deign in His goodness to show us some opportune way of healing these wounds. For He Himself, Who is the most loving Maker and Redeemer of all mankind, since He has given us this desire of laboring for the saving of the Indians, will also assuredly give us those things that conduce to this end. Meanwhile, it greatly consoles us to know that those who bear rule in these Republics are making every endeavor to remove this outstanding disgrace and this stain from their States; which endeavors, indeed, we cannot sufficiently praise and approve. Since, however, these regions are far from the seats of Government, and are for the most part not readily accessible, these human endeavors of the civil powers, whether from the craft of the criminals, who can speedily cross the frontiers, or through the inactivity or perfidy of the officials, often do little good, and sometimes come to nothing. But if the work of the Church is added to the work of the State, then at length the desired fruit shall be obtained in greater abundance.

5. Wherefore, Venerable Brethren, we call upon you, before all others, to give special care and thought to this cause, which is in every way worthy of your pastoral office and

duty. And leaving the rest to your solicitude and diligence, we particularly urge you to foster and promote all the good works instituted in your dioceses for the benefit of the Indians, and to see that other works likely to contribute to this end may be instituted. In the next place you will diligently admonish your flocks on their most sacred duty of helping religious missions to the natives who first inhabited the American soil. Let them know that they ought to help this work especially in two ways, to wit, by their gifts and by their prayers; and that it is not only their religion, but their country also, that asks this of them. Do you, moreover, take care that wheresoever moral instruction is given, in seminaries, in colleges, in convent schools, and more especially in the churches, Christian charity, which holds all men, without distinction of nation or color, as true brethren, shall be continually preached and commended. And this charity must be made manifest not so much by words as by deeds. Moreover, every opportunity must be taken to show what a great dishonor is done to the Christian name by these base deeds, which we are here denouncing.

6. As for our part, having good reason to hope for the consent and support of the public authorities, we have more especially taken care to extend the field of Apostolic labor in these broad regions, appointing further missionary stations, where the Indians can find safety and succor. For the Catholic Church has ever been a fertile mother of Apostolic men, who, pressed by the charity of Christ, are brought to give their lives for their brethren. And today, when so many abhor the faith or fall away from it, the zeal for spreading the Gospel among the barbarous nations is still strong in the clergy and in religious men and holy virgins; and this zeal grows greater and is spread abroad more widely by the power of the Holy Ghost, who helps the Church, His spouse, accord-

ing to the needs of the time. Wherefore, we think it well to make greater use of those aids which by God's goodness are ready to our hand, in order to deliver the Indians, where their need is greatest from the slavery of Satan and of wicked men. For the rest, since the preachers of the Gospel had watered these regions, not only with their sweat, but sometimes with their blood, we trust that at length a fair harvest of Christian kindness shall spring forth from their great labors and bear abundant fruit. And now, in order that what you shall do for the benefit of the Indians, whether of your own accord or at our exhortation, may be the more efficacious by the help of our Apostolic authority, we, mindful of the example of our aforesaid predecessor, condemn and declare guilty of grave crime whosoever, as he says, "shall dare or presume to reduce the said Indians to slavery, to sell them, to buy them, to exchange or give them, to separate them from their wives and children, to deprive them of goods and chattels, to transport or send them to other places, or in any way whatsoever to rob them of freedom and hold them in slavery; or to give counsel, help, favor, and work on any pretext of color to them that do these things, or to preach or teach that it is lawful, or to co-operate therewith in any way whatever." Accordingly, we will that the power of absolving penitents in the sacramental tribunal from these crimes shall be reserved to ordinaries of the localities.

7. It has seemed well to us, moved by our paternal affection and following the footsteps of your predecessors, among whom we may specially mention Leo XIII, of blessed memory, to write these things to you, Venerable Brethren, on the case of the Indians. But it will be for you to strive according to your strength to give abundant satisfaction to our desires. You will assuredly be helped in this by those who bear rule in these Republics; nor will you want the work and care of

the clergy, especially those devoted to the sacred missions; and, lastly, all good men will be with you, and those who can, with gifts or other offices of charity, will help a cause in which both religion and the dignity of manhood are involved. And, what is the chief thing, the grace of Almighty God will be with you, in token whereof and as a pledge of our goodwill, we most lovingly impart new Apostolic benediction to you, Venerable Brethren, and to your flocks.

Given at Rome, at St. Peter's, on the 7th of June, 1912, in the ninth year of our Pontificate.

PIUS X

SINGULARI QUADAM
ENCYCLICAL OF POPE PIUS X
ON LABOR ORGANIZATIONS

TO OUR BELOVED SON, GEORGE KOPP,
CARDINAL PRIEST OF THE HOLY ROMAN CHURCH,
BISHOPS OF BRESLAU, AND TO THE OTHER
ARCHBISHOPS AND BISHOPS OF GERMANY

Beloved Son and Venerable Brethren, Health and the Apostolic Blessing.

We are moved by particularly affectionate and benevolent sentiments toward the Catholics of Germany, who are most loyally and obediently devoted to the Apostolic See and accustomed to battle generously and courageously on behalf of the Church. We therefore feel compelled, Venerable Brethren, to devote Our full strength and attention to the discussion of that issue which has arisen among them about workingmen's associations. Concerning this problem several of you, as well as qualified and respected representatives of both viewpoints, have already informed Us repeatedly during the past few years. Conscious of Our Apostolic Office, We have studied this problem most diligently. We fully realize that Our sacred duty is to labor unceasingly that Our beloved sons may preserve the Catholic teaching unadulterated and unimpaired, in no way allowing their Faith to be endangered. If they are not in time urged to be on guard, they would obviously, gradually and inadvertently, fall into the danger of being satisfied with a vague and indefinite form of the Christian religion which has lately been designated as intercredal. This amounts to nothing more than an empty recommendation of a generalized Christianity. Obviously, nothing is more contrary to the teachings of Jesus Christ.

Moreover, since Our most ardent desire is the promotion and fortification of concord among Catholics, We constantly try to remove all those occasions of quarrels which dissipate the strength of men of good will and are advantageous only for the enemies of religion. Finally, We desire and intend that the faithful live with their non-Catholic fellow citizens in that peace without which neither the order of human society nor the welfare of the State can endure.

If, however, as We have already said, the existence of this question was known to Us, We nevertheless thought it wise to obtain each of your opinions, Venerable Brethren, before announcing Our decision. You have answered Our questions with that conscientiousness and diligence which the seriousness of the question demands.

2. Accordingly, We first of all declare that all Catholics have a sacred and inviolable duty, both in private and public life, to obey and firmly adhere to and fearlessly profess the principles of Christian truth enunciated by the teaching office of the Catholic Church. In particular We mean those principles which Our Predecessor has most wisely laid down in the encyclical letter Rerum Novarum. We know that the Bishops of Prussia followed these most faithfully in their deliberations at the Fulda Congress of 1900. You yourselves have summarized the fundamental ideas of these principles in your communications regarding this question.

3. These are fundamental principles: No matter what the Christian does, even in the realm of temporal goods, he cannot ignore the supernatural good. Rather, according to the dictates of Christian philosophy, he must order all things to the ultimate end, namely, the Highest Good. All his actions, insofar as they are morally either good or bad (that is to say,

whether they agree or disagree with the natural and divine law), are subject to the judgment and judicial office of the Church. All who glory in the name of Christian, either individually or collectively, if they wish to remain true to their vocation, may not foster enmities and dissensions between the classes of civil society. On the contrary, they must promote mutual concord and charity. The social question and its associated controversies, such as the nature and duration of labor, the wages to be paid, and workingmen's strikes, are not simply economic in character. Therefore they cannot be numbered among those which can be settled apart from ecclesiastical authority. "The precise opposite is the truth. It is first of all moral and religious, and for that reason its solution is to be expected mainly from the moral law and the pronouncements of religion."

4. Now, concerning workingmen's associations, even though their purpose is to obtain earthly advantages for their members, nonetheless those associations are to be most approved and considered as most useful for the genuine and permanent advantage of their members which are established chiefly on the foundation of the Catholic religion and openly follow the directives of the Church. We have repeated this declaration on several previous occasions in answer to question from various countries. Consequently, such so-called confessional Catholic associations must certainly be established and promoted in every way in Catholic regions as well as in all other districts where it can be presumed that they can sufficiently assist the various needs of their members. However, when there is a question about associations which directly or indirectly touch upon the sphere of religion and morality, it would not be permitted to foster and spread mixed organizations, that is, associations composed of Catholics and non-Catholics, in the areas just mentioned. Over and above other

matters, in such organizations there are or certainly can be for our people serious dangers to the integrity of their faith and the due obedience to the commandments and precepts of the Catholic Church. Venerable Brethren, you yourselves have also openly called attention to this question in several of your answers which We have read.

5. We therefore lavish praise upon each and every one of the strictly Catholic workingmen's associations existing in Germany. We wish them every success in all their endeavors on behalf of the laboring people, hoping they will enjoy a constant increase. However, in saying this We do not deny that Catholics, in their efforts to improve the workers' living conditions, more equitable distribution of wages, and other justified advantages, have a right, provided they exercise due caution, to collaborate with nonCatholics for the common good. For such a purpose, however, We would rather see Catholic and non-Catholic associations unite their forces through that new and timely institution known as the cartel.

6. Not a few of you, Venerable Brethren, have asked Us whether it is permissible to tolerate the so-called Christian Trade Unions that now exist in your dioceses, since, on the one hand, they have a considerably larger number of members than the purely Catholic associations and, on the other hand, if permission were denied serious disadvantages would result. In view of the particular circumstances of Catholic affairs in Germany, We believe that We should grant this petition. Furthermore, We declare that such mixed associations as now exist within your dioceses can be tolerated and Catholics may be permitted to join them, as long as such toleration does not cease to be appropriate or permissible by reason of new and changed conditions. Necessary precautions, however, must be adopted in order to avoid the

dangers which, as has already been mentioned, follow upon such associations.

The following are the most important of these precautions: In the first place, provision should be made that Catholic workers who are members of the trade unions must also belong to those Catholic associations which are known as Arbeitervereine. In the event that they must make some sacrifice for this cause, even in a monetary way, We are convinced that they will readily do so for the sake of safeguarding the integrity of their Faith. As has been happily demonstrated, the Catholic workingmen's associations, aided by the clergy and by its leadership and alert direction, are able to achieve very much toward preserving the truths of religion and the purity of morals among their members, and nourish the religious spirit through frequent practices of piety. Therefore, the leaders of such associations, clearly recognizing the needs of the age, are undoubtedly prepared to instruct the workers about their duties in justice and charity, especially regarding all those commandments and precepts in which an accurate knowledge is needed or useful in order to enable them to take an active part in their trade unions according to the principles of Catholic doctrine.

7. Furthermore, if Catholics are to be permitted to join the trade unions, these associations must avoid everything that is not in accord, either in principle or practice, with the teachings and commandments of the Church or the proper ecclesiastical authorities. Similarly, everything is to be avoided in their literature or public utterances or actions which in the above view would incur censure.

The Bishops, therefore, should consider it their sacred duty to observe carefully the conduct of all these associations and to watch diligently that the Catholic members do not suffer any harm as a result of their participation. The Catholic members themselves, however, should never permit the unions, whether for the sake of material interests of their members or the union cause as such, to proclaim or support teachings or to engage in activities which would conflict in any way with the directives proclaimed by the supreme teaching authority of the Church, especially those mentioned above. Therefore, as often as problems arise concerning matters of justice or charity, the Bishops should take the greatest care to see that the faithful do not overlook Catholic moral teaching and do not depart from it even a finger's breadth.

8. We are convinced, Venerable Brethren, that you will diligently take care to see that all these directives of Ours are conscientiously and exactly fulfilled, carefully and constantly reporting to Us concerning this very serious problem. Since We have taken this matter under Our jurisdiction and, after hearing the views of the Bishops, since the decision rests with Us, We hereby command all Catholics of good will to desist from all disputes among themselves concerning this matter. We are confident that with fraternal charity and perfect obedience they will completely and gladly carry out Our command. If any further difficulty arises among them, they should seek its solution in the following manner: Let them first turn to their Bishops for counsel, and then submit the matter to the Apostolic See for its decision.

There is one more point to consider, and it was already implied in what has been said. On the one hand, no one could accuse of bad faith and, under such a pretext, bear ill will toward those who, while firmly defending the teachings and rights of the Church, nonetheless for good reasons have joined or wish to join mixed labor associations in those places where, under certain safeguards, ecclesiastical authority has permitted them in view of local conditions. On the other hand, it would likewise be most reprehensible to oppose or attack the purely Catholic associations (this type of association must, on the contrary, be supported and promoted in every possible manner), and to demand that the so-called intercredal associations be introduced and force their establishment on the grounds that all Catholic associations in every diocese ought to be set up along one and the same pattern.

9. While expressing Our desire that Catholic Germany may make great progress in religion and civil life, and in order that this wish may be happily fulfilled, We beseech for the beloved German people the special help of Almighty God and the protection of the Virgin Mother of God, the Queen of Peace. As a pledge of the divine graces and also as sign of Our particular love, We impart, most lovingly, to you, Beloved Son and Venerable Brethren, to your clergy and people, the Apostolic Blessing.

Given at Saint Peter's, Rome, on September 24, 1912, the tenth year of Our Pontificate.
PIUS X